Women in the Indian Diaspora

Amba Pande

Editor

Women in the Indian Diaspora

Historical Narratives and Contemporary Challenges

 Springer

Editor
Amba Pande
Centre for Indo-Pacific Studies,
  School of International Studies
Jawaharlal Nehru University
New Delhi, Delhi
India

ISBN 978-981-10-5950-6   ISBN 978-981-10-5951-3   (eBook)
https://doi.org/10.1007/978-981-10-5951-3

Library of Congress Control Number: 2017947840

Printed on acid-free paper

This Springer imprint is published by Springer Nature
The registered company is Springer Nature Singapore Pte Ltd.
The registered company address is: 152 Beach Road, #21-01/04 Gateway East, Singapore 189721, Singapore

Preface

Patterns of migration and settlement among Indian women are as diverse as that of the overall Indian diaspora. They have shared space with men in most of the groups and streams of people moving beyond Indian borders. However, the initial theoretical and empirical models either omitted or undermined their experiences under homogenised perceptions. As a result, women's voices, experiences and their critical role in the success story of the Indian diaspora remain to be unnoticed and unmapped. Feminist epistemological interventions in diaspora and migration studies made gender fundamental to the critical understanding of migration and settlement processes and the ongoing course of identity formation in a foreign setting. However, the centrality of gender still revolved around the 'victimhood' or 'passive agents' paradigm, particularly with regard to women from the Third World. The feminist and subaltern scholarship did take note of this stereotypical representation and started articulating the voice of the 'other' woman in the receiving societies. The increasing feminisation of international migration from and among the developing societies further made the incorporation of the sociocultural moorings of the women from these societies an imperative. As the diasporas are embedded in both host and homelands simultaneously, the natural corollary is that factors from both the host land and the homeland—including gender relations and gender hierarchies—have an impact on diasporic women. Feminist inquiries suggest that migration and diasporic conditions, on the one hand, can be liberating, bringing more egalitarianism in the family and opening avenues for women to strengthen their agency and create new opportunities for themselves. However, on the other hand, it is also sometimes evident that gender hierarchy gets reinforced and becomes more rigid and traditional than in the homeland. Although standing 'in-between' the two worlds—with complex realities of unequal power dynamics of the homeland and stereotypical spaces of the host land—Indian women tend to experience conflicting subjectivities of freedom and subjugation, yet they do find a freedom for self-exploration and deliberation to conceive new identities and move beyond the fixed definitions of femininity.

This volume is an attempt to capture the processes of migration and settlement of women in the Indian diaspora during the colonial as well as contemporary period and map their struggles, challenges and agency. The principal aim motivating the present volume is to look beyond the stereotypical representation of Indian women as the 'victim', the 'passive agents' or mere 'custodians of Indian culture', and bring into focus the agency and space women have shown in redefining roles and transforming the lives of their own and those of their families in process of migration and settlement. I am not a scholar of gender studies but during my work on Indian diaspora and transnational migration I came across various issues related to women and developed an understanding of their problems, challenges and their agency in addressing and redressing the complex issues faced by them; structuring and restructuring the cultural formats of patriarchy and gender relations; managing the emerging conflicts over what is to be transmitted to the following generations, and how social history is to be interpreted; renegotiating their domestic roles and embracing new professional and educational successes; and adjusting with the institutional structures of the host state. The essays included in the volume discuss women in the Indian diaspora from a multidisciplinary perspective eschewing the essentialising tendencies and acknowledging the intersectionality of the gender with race, class, religion, national and several other categories. Overall, this volume resists the portrayal of women in the Indian diaspora only as victims by emphasising their agency. Such an effort will privilege women's experiences and perspectives by raising consciousness and developing a deeper understanding about their issues in academia and among policymakers.

New Delhi, India   Amba Pande

Acknowledgements

I wish to thank various people for their contribution in the completion of this project. First and foremost I would like to thank Centre for Diaspora Studies, MS University, Kanyakumari, Tamil Nadu for encouraging me to conceive and proceed with this project. I would also like to express my appreciation to Centre for African Studies, School of International Studies, Jawaharlal Nehru University (JNU) and the Organisation for Diaspora initiative (ODI) for helping me organise an international conference on women in the Indian diaspora in 2014 which was sponsored by National Commission for Women, New Delhi, India. This volume is a vastly updated and edited outcome of selected papers from the conference. My sincere thanks goes also to the Global Research Forum on Diaspora and Transnationalism (GRFDT) for their constant encouragement and advice.

This project would have been impossible without the support and expert advice of my fellow scholars and colleagues in diaspora studies. I am particularly grateful to Prof. Samual Asir Raj (M.S. University), Prof. Ajay Dubey (JNU), Prof. Irudaya Rajan (CDS, Trivandrum), Prof. Bhaswati Sarkar (JNU), Prof. Arvinder Ansari (Jamia Milia Islamia), Prof. Malakar (JNU), Dr. Kavita Sharma (South Asia University), Dr. JM Moosa (JNU) and Dr. Nadaraja Mannikkam. My special thanks also to Dr. Sadanand Sahoo (Indira Gandhi National Open University), Dr. Mahalingam (Jamia Milia Islamia) and several other friends and colleagues for their constant support and encouragement.

I wish to acknowledge the help given by Mr. Sunil Varan Arya in the editing and formatting of this book. A retired civil servant, Mr. Arya, has used his time most productively, in the process also helping in the completion of this project. I would also like to thank my publisher Springer and Ms. Shinjini Chatterjee and Ms. Priya Vyas for taking this project forward.

In the end, I would like to thank my fellow practitioners of Bharat Soka Gakkai who have been the source of constant support and encouragement. I also extend my sincere and heartfelt gratitude to my family: my parents, my husband Shailendra and especially my children Aarsh and Ishita for their useful critique and advice and for pushing me to do better.

Contents

Editor and Contributors

About the Editor

Amba Pande is associated with the School of International Studies, Jawaharlal Nehru University. Dr. Pande received her Ph.D. from Centre for Southeast Asia and South West Pacific Studies, School of International Studies, JNU, New Delhi. Her research interests include the Indian diaspora, and international migration. She has been a visiting faculty/scholar at the University of Amsterdam (the Netherlands), University of South Pacific (Fiji) and Otego University (New Zealand). She has done major projects on the Indian diaspora with University Grants Commission (UGC) and Indian Council of Social Science Research (ICSSR). Dr. Pande is a prolific writer and has many publications to her credit in national and international journals. She has been invited to give independent lectures, present papers, be a discussant and chair in a number of national and international seminars and conferences. She is currently working on a book manuscript on Fiji Indians and diasporic identities.

Contributors

Amrit Kaur Basra is Associate Professor in Delhi College of Arts and Commerce, University of Delhi. She has held several positions in University of Delhi including Deputy, Dean (Foreign Students), Fellow and Academic Secretary in Institute of Lifelong Learning in 2012–2017. She was Professor Tatya Tope Chair set up by the Ministry of Culture, Government of India. Her areas of research are Sikhism and interfaith, communalism and communal riots in Colonial Punjab, history of Canada and the historiography and print culture and built heritage. She has published 35 articles in books/journals/textbooks/e-journals. Her two books, namely *Communal Riots in the Punjab 1923–1928* and *Press and Politics in the Punjab 1860–1905* have been published in 2015. She has edited two e-books and co-edited one book on *Gender & Diversity, India, Canada and Beyond* (2015). She has been a recipient of many awards. She wrote the script of the film *Nanakshah Faqir* which was released worldwide in 2015. The film has been awarded the Nargis Dutt Award for best film on national integration at the 63rd National Film Awards, 2015.

Mahua Bhattacharya is Associate Professor of Japanese and Asian Studies and has taught at Elizabethtown College since 2001. In the past she has held joint appointments with the departments of Modern Languages and Sociology and Anthropology. A native of India, she has taught Japanese in one of the premier institutions of India, Jawaharlal Nehru University in New Delhi for 13 years where she also got her undergraduate and graduate degrees in Japanese Language and Japanese Studies. Before coming to Elizabethtown College, she was a Visiting Fellow at University of Chicago and taught Japanese at DePaul University in Chicago and Millersville University in Pennsylvania. She has also served as the Director of the Women and Gender Studies program in the College and is part of the Asian Studies program there. Her research interests include postcolonial theory, women's studies, popular culture, language ideology, and second language acquisition.

Nabanita Chakraborty is Assistant Professor of English at Hansraj College, University of Delhi. She has been a recipient of Charles Wallace Fellowship of the British Council in 2012–2013. Her Ph.D. on "Rhetoric of Love and Politics of Power: Speeches and Writings of Queen Elizabeth I" is from the University of Delhi. Besides her specialisation in Early-Modern English Studies, she has varied interests. She has also presented many papers in various national and international conferences and has many publications to her credit on diaspora studies.

Bernard D'Sami served as an Associate Professor in History and former Head of the Department of History at Loyola College, Chennai. Currently he is a Senior Fellow at LISSTAR (Loyola Institute of Social Science Training and Research) Loyola College (Autonomous), Chennai and also a guest faculty at the Indian Institute of Technology Madras. He is a Salzburg Fellow (1994) and Olaf Palme North-South Fellow to the Stockholm Institute of Education (2002). He is a media commentator and a columnist.

Binod Khadria is Professor of Economics and Education at Jawaharlal Nehru University. He is also the Director of International Migration and Diaspora Studies (IMDS) Project. Presently, he holds the prestigious Indian Council for Cultural Relations (ICCR) Chair of Contemporary Indian Studies at Rutgers University, USA.

Kate Kirk is Assistant Professor at University College Utrecht in the Netherlands and a research fellow at the VU University Amsterdam, Department of Social and Cultural Anthropology. She holds a Ph.D. in Political Science from Queens University Belfast. Her research concerns the relationship between migration and integration policies in the Netherlands and migrant experiences in the country.

Ann Lobo is presently working with the University of Reading, UK. Dr. Lobo obtained a Master's Degree from the University of London, Institute of Education in 1988 and a Ph.D. from the University of London in 1994. She became a Fellow of the Trinity College of London in 1965. She obtained a B.Ed.(Hons) in 1984 from the University of Reading. She is a writer and has written a number of articles about Anglo-Indians.

Radica Mahase is Senior Lecturer in History at the College of Science, Technology and Applied Arts of Trinidad and Tobago. She completed a Ph.D. in History at the University of the West Indies, St. Augustine, Trinidad and a MA in Modern Indian History at Jawaharlal Nehru University, Delhi. She was a Visiting Commonwealth Scholar at the Centre for the History of Science, Technology and Medicine, University of Manchester. For the past 15 years, she has been researching and writing on Indian indentureship, Indian women and Indian diaspora as well as the history of the Caribbean/Trinidad and Tobago.

Sandhya Rao Mehta is presently in the Department of English Language and Literature, Sultan Qaboos University, Oman. Her research interests include literature of the Indian diaspora and women of the diaspora. She is the editor of an anthology *Exploring Gender in the Literature of the Indian Diaspora* and co-editor of *Language Studies: Stretching the Boundaries*, both published by Cambridge Scholars Publishing. She has published widely on the Indian diaspora, particularly in the Arabian Gulf.

Gopalan Ravindran has worked in Japan, Malaysia and India. Currently, he is Professor and Head in Department of Journalism and Communication, University of Madras. He is interested in the areas of diasporic cultures, film cultures, digital cultures, cross-cultural communication and critical political economy of communication. In the domain of diasporic cultures, he has a special interest in working on Malaysia and South Africa.

Movindri Reddy is Associate Professor in the Department of Diplomacy and World Affairs at Occidental College in Los Angeles. Dr. Reddy received her Ph.D. from Cambridge University and held postdoctoral fellowship positions at Yale, Princeton and the University of Chicago. She recently published *Social Movements and the Indian Diaspora*, a book based on her intellectual interests in diasporas, national and transnational identities, and social movements. She is currently working on a book manuscript about resistance and revolutions in Southern Africa.

Sheetal Sharma is Assistant Professor at the Centre for European Studies, JNU. Her research interests include social and cultural issues in contemporary Europe and India and their historical roots, multiculturalism and diversity, methodology of social sciences, diaspora, gender and empowerment of women. Dr. Sharma avidly follows methodological and theoretical trends in the social sciences and international relations. She writes regularly on socially relevant issues in India and Europe for journals and magazines of national and international repute. She is also interested in and writes on issues relevant to education in India particularly higher education. She has completed Video Lecture Series in Sociology for CIET, NCERT's project NROER (National Repository for Educational Resources and Training, these lectures can be accessed on NROER website). She has also been invited as a discussant on number of programs on radio and TV. She has presented papers in a number of national and international seminars and conferences.

Kathinka Sinha-Kerkhoff is Professor at the Asian Development Research Institute (ADRI) at Patna in India and a Senior Research Fellow (ICSSR, New Delhi). She also is a honourable research fellow at the IISH, Amsterdam and holds a Ph.D. from the University of Amsterdam (UvA) in the Netherlands. She has widely published among others on the Indian diaspora in Suriname and on return migration to India.

Archana Tewari is Associate Professor in the Department of Western History, University of Lucknow, Lucknow. Her doctoral thesis was on Indian indentured labour in Trinidad, awarded in 2003. The history of Indian indentured labour in the Caribbeans has always fascinated her and she contributed a number of research paper on the various aspects of indentured labour like literature, issues relating to women of Indian origin, etc.

Narender Thakur is Assistant Professor of Economics at Bhim Rao Ambedkar College, University of Delhi. Presently, he is a postdoctoral fellow of the Indian Council for Social Science Research (ICSSR), at Zakir Husain Centre for Educational Studies, School of Social Sciences, Jawaharlal Nehru University. His areas of interest are economics of education and migration, and econometrics.

Shinder S. Thandi is currently Visiting Professor in Global Studies at UC Santa Barbara, USA teaching courses in Sikh Diaspora, Global Diasporas and Global Development. He is founder–editor of the *Journal of Sikh and Punjab Studies*, published since 1994. He has published widely on Indian and Punjabi migration and on different dimensions of Sikh diaspora and homeland relations. He is co-author of (with Michael Fisher and Shompa Lahiri) *A South Asian History of Britain: Four Centuries of Peoples from the Indian Sub-Continent*, (Greenwood Press, 2007). He also co-edited two books: *People on the Move: Punjabi Colonial and Post-Colonial Migration* (edited with Ian Talbot, OUP, 2004) and *Punjabi Identity in a Global Context* (edited with Pritam Singh, OUP, 1999).

Chapter 1
Women in Indian Diaspora: Redefining Self Between Dislocation and Relocation

Amba Pande

The initial theoretical and empirical models of the migration discourse either omitted any specific reference to women migrants or downplayed their experiences generally presuming that it would same as those of the men. The experiences of Indian women were also subsumed under homogenised perceptions and meta-narratives of the processes of migration and settlement of the Indian Diaspora. An upsurge in the feminist scholarship on Migration Studies definitely brought the dimension of gender to the forefront, but unfortunately issues related to women's identity and women's agency remain marginalised with very limited systematic research being undertaken. In reality, the conditions propelling the migration of women, their experiences during the process of migration and the subsequent efforts at adaptation and settlement have always been different; rather they have been unique and very specific to them. As highly skilled women professionals, they successfully balance domestic life with professional life. Similarly, semiskilled and skilled women migrants risk the hostilities of a new environment and struggle to improve the conditions of their families back home and at the same time enhance their own career prospects. Women married into diaspora families attempt to recreate home and culture in a foreign setting often ridden with politics of race. As the indentured labourers, women faced the tyranny of the plantation life as well as exploitation by their own men yet rapidly adapting and liberating themselves through education and economic opportunities.

Indian women usually migrate within the patriarchal framework and cultural considerations, and are supposed to preserve it as the 'bearers of Indian tradition,' yet the process of migration and economic self-dependency give them an opportunity to assert independence, and redefine roles and perceptions of the self. While many of the problems, women in the Indian Diaspora face, arise out of patriarchal

A. Pande (✉)
Centre for Indo-Pacific Studies, School of International Studies,
Jawaharlal Nehru University, New Delhi, India
e-mail: ambapande@gmail.com

© Springer Nature Singapore Pte Ltd. 2018
A. Pande (ed.), *Women in the Indian Diaspora*,
https://doi.org/10.1007/978-981-10-5951-3_1

structures besides foreign settings, one can find innumerable instances of their struggles and triumphs over adversities and hostile situations. Standing 'in-between' the two worlds, with complex realities of unequal power dynamics of the homeland and stereotypical spaces of the hostland, women tend to experience conflicting subjectivities of freedom and subjugation. The space of the 'hyphen' often gives them a freedom for self-exploration and deliberation to conceive new identities and move beyond the fixed definitions of femininity. This volume is an attempt to capture the process of migration and settlement of women in the Indian Diaspora during the colonial as well as contemporary period. The essays map the struggles, challenges and agency of the immigrant women in their ongoing process of the reproduction of identity and culture in a foreign setting.

Migration and Diaspora: Theoretical Understandings

Migration is a perpetual phenomenon that human beings have undertaken but in the last century or so, it has grown exponentially and is a much more marked, analysed and theorised phenomenon that has received attention from numerous disciplines and cross-disciplinary studies. Closely related to the process of migration is the term diaspora which is in a sense more specific (because it concerns only with International migration and permanent or long term settlements) but in another sense it is more inclusive (because it also includes second- and third-generation migrants) (Tigau et al. 2017, 183). There has been a significant shift in the understanding of the term diaspora over the years, as Jewish and Armenian paradigms marked by exile, loss and victimhood have given way to vibrant communities who maintain multiple ties with their homelands while at the same time also getting incorporated into the countries that receive them (Pande 2017, 27).

In my conceptualization of Indian Diasporas (EPW 2013, 59–65) I have tried to draw four basic characteristics or core elements that can be treated as the starting point for the understanding of the diasporas

1. Cross-border Migration/Dispersion and Settlement which implies voluntary or involuntary cross border movement leading to permanent or long-term settlement;
2. Hostland Participation which signifies not only residence but participation in the socio-economic and political processes of receiving country;
3. Homeland Consciousness which can also be termed as 'continuity' or 'manifestation' of 'roots';
4. Creation and Recreation of a Multi-locational 'Self' or Identity which involves recreating an identity that draws from both home and hostlands, and which is hybrid and distinct in itself.

In a nutshell, diasporas are specific types of transnational communities marked by migrations, by continuity and rupture, by hybridity and by dual or even a multiple belongingness which, manifest through economic, political and social interaction with home and the hostland simultaneously (see Pande 2013; Pande 2017). Rather than being wedged into either home or hostland the diasporas are embedded in both the cultures and in the process negotiate and create new hybridised cultures and identities that intersect nations, races, class and gender (see Bhabha 1994; Sheffer 1986; Schiller et al. 1995; Clifford 1994; Safran 1991; Cohen 1997). In the present world, diasporas are seen as 'vibrant communities', much 'in demand' as they seek to participate in the developmental process of both home and the hostland.

Indian Diaspora with all its heterogeneities can be considered as a representative case of diasporic formation. A broad definition of Indian Diaspora has been given in the Report of the Singhvi Committee or the High Level Committee on Indian Diaspora constituted by Government of India: 'Indian diaspora is a generic term used for addressing people who have migrated from the territories that are currently within the borders of the Republic of India' (High Level Committee 2001). As far as the classification of Indian Diaspora is concerned, as mentioned earlier it is a diverse group. This diversity is not only a representation of the plurality of Indian society (in terms of region, religion, language, caste, creed, etc.) and heterogeneity in the phases and patterns of migration over a long period of time, but also emerges out of the variations of the more than hundred countries where Indians are now settled (see Pande 2013). While the government of India's definition has only three categories for the diaspora, namely: Non-Resident Indians (NRIs),[1] People of Indian Origin (PIOs)[2] and Overseas Indian Citizens (OICs)[3] researchers and academicians/scholars have identified classifications on the basis of history, nature and pattern of migration. I have presented these in Fig. 1.1.

At the first level, I divide the Indian Diaspora into two parts: the 'Old Diaspora' that emerged from the colonial migrations and the 'New Diaspora' that emerged from the post-colonial migrations. The 'Old Diaspora' can be further divided broadly, into another two subdivisions—first group includes 'Indentured' labourers and migrants under similar systems and the convicts; the second category comprises of 'Free Migrants' like traders, professionals and employees of the British Government. On the other hand, 'New Diaspora' may be broadly divided into different categories of people who migrate to western countries—first highly skilled/skilled, and small-time traders and retailers; second, to semiskilled/unskilled labourers to the West and to Southeast Asia; third student migrants; and finally political diaspora. Most of the Indian Diaspora groups have achieved astounding success contributing significantly in their respective adopted countries in economic political, academic and social spheres. They have also made considerable contribution to the development of the homeland giving pride or winning accolades for India and its people (see Pande 2014).

---

[1]NRIs are Indian citizens and hold Indian passport. MOIA records their number as 10037761.

[2]PIOs are no longer Indian citizens and number around 11872114.

[3]OIC is a partial citizenship given to PIOs. Till 2014 around 1203613 OCI cards were issued by Government of India.

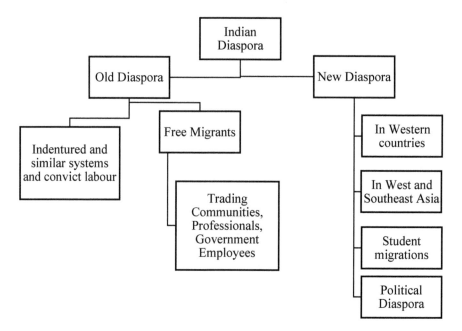

Fig. 1.1 Classifications on the basis of history, nature and pattern of migration

Women in the Diaspora Discourse

A major thrust of scholarship on Migration Studies has focussed on patterns of migration and settlement and economic contribution of the migrants but has failed to specify the unique experiences of women who have always been part of the migration process voluntarily or involuntarily. Overall women either remained as passive agents, or their experiences were overlooked under homogenised perceptions. As a result till the 1960s and early 1970s the term 'migrants' largely stood for male migrants and their families that included their wives and children (Boyd and Grieco 2003). Ever since the rise of feminist scholarship, the scholarly discourse on migration has shifted decisively towards gender sensitive discourse bringing women from the margins to the centre. A review of the literature on migration reveals that although feminist empiricism did not necessarily include 'migrant women' in its ambit, it had an impressive and effective impact on Migration Studies. Migration theories were reinvented to incorporate and privilege the issues and experiences of women under the feminist influence.

However this shift was not sudden and can be divided into three phases (see Nawyn 2010; Pessar and Mahler 2001; Altamirano 1997; Helen Ralson 1988; Rayaprol 1997; Boyd and Grieco 2003; Hondagneu-Sotelo 2000; McDowell 1993). The first phase that started from late 60s to early 70s, 'added women' in the migration research in terms of a binary of male versus female. As the field evolved into the mid- and late-1980s—towards what has been termed as the 'Feminist Standpoint

Theory'—the gender became the core analytical category. This was radical feminist perspective that not only emphasised the difference but also tried to establish the superiority over the equality of the gendered analysis. Further during the 1990s, the centrality of gender as an analytical category in relation to other critical categories was questioned under the so called 'Post-rational Feminism'. For these scholars the issue of 'gender' was not the basic criteria of difference but other differences such as poverty, class, ethnicity, race, etc. hold equal if not more importance. In other words the scholarship became aware that the enthusiasm towards correcting the 'invisibility' of migrant/diaspora women ought not to overlook other analytical categories like race, class, language, caste and history of migration, etc.

In the recent, feminist epistemology and knowledge production consider gender an essential variable that impacts women and produces differential outcomes for them at every stage of migration—i.e. during the pre-migration stage, then through the process (of migration); and finally in the course of settlement (see Boyd and Grieco 2003; United Nations, 28). Gender is understood to be a constitutive element of society that permeates through micro- and macro-level processes, and institutions and creates complex layers of identity formations which ultimately become fundamental for understanding of economic, social and demographic realities. In this regard the inter-sectionality of gender with other social and cultural constructs like race/ethnicity/class and nationality comes out to be a powerful factor in the analysis of women's migration and their role afterwards (see Madonald 2007; Hom 1999; Shepporson 1966).

Within this framework one of the important variables of differences and fields of inquiry is the context of the 'Third World' and that of Asia where gender relations and hierarchies within the family, the society and the access to resources are markedly different from those in the western societies (see McDowell 1993; Di Stifano 1990). For decades after its emergence, feminist scholarship remained predominantly ethnocentric in its approach, tilting heavily and visibly towards perspectives and experiences of the West or of America (see Alund 1991; Mohanty 1991, 2003). The immigrant women from the third world in Western societies were stereotypically typified as oppressed and dominated by repressive patriarchical traditions. The concept of welfare of the immigrant women from the third world countries revolved around 'modernising' or 'liberating' them according to the Western paradigms. These ethnocentric and neo-colonialist theories and concepts were in many cases not even relevant from the perspective of the third world societies whose cultural formats were different and produced different readings of women's position and experiences. The research, analysis and policy options for the women from the third world remained deficient because of two reasons: first, gender as a category remained a marginalised subfield in diaspora studies[4]; and second, nearly all the research which focussed on women treated women from

---

[4]As a matter of fact the term 'diaspora' itself is said to be phallocentric and conveys a male act of dispersal and assert 'male procreation and patrilinear descent' (see Gopinath 2005, 5–6; Kosnick 2010, 123).

Asian countries in a stereotypical 'victimhood' paradigm projecting them as docile victims with little, if any, say in matters concerning them.

Although a bit late, the feminist discourse in the third world did take note of this oversight and started articulating the voice of the 'other' woman and also challenging her stereotypical representation (see Hugo 1999; Zlotnik 1995). The increasing feminization of International migration[5] from and among the developing societies further made the empirical and theoretical incorporation of the sociocultural understanding of other societies an imperative. As the diasporas are embedded in both host and homelands, the natural corollary is that factors from both the hostland and the homeland—including gender relations and gender hierarchies—impact the diasporic women. As diaspora studies developed over time, the androcentricism and western paradigms were further challenged. The narratives shifted to analysing how gender shapes both the material experience of migration and the ways in which diaspora is conceived and represented in gendered terms (see Emma Parker). Such efforts require a deeper understanding of how women cope with changes due to migration, their adjustment patterns and strategies, how their status in society and relationships with family members and spouses change with migration. It is important to raise several questions in this context: does migration affect women's authority within the family; does it influence power relations and decision making in the family and alter patriarchal structures? How do these women create a niche for themselves through personal growth, social networks and economic participation in the host country; as well as flaunt their multicultural identities? Most importantly, how do women adapt to the host country as well as maintain links with their country of origin negotiating and recreating new identities? Many studies have continued to assess several such questions. According to Reinhart (as quoted in Rayaprol 1997, 38) feminist ethnography mainly aims at three goals; (1) to document the activities and the lives of the women; (2) to understand and present women's experience from their own point of view; (3) to represent women's behaviours as an expression of their particular social context.

Indian Women in Diaspora

Women have been part of almost all the groups of people moving out of Indian borders which today constitute the Indian Diaspora. However as discussed before, their experiences have largely been subsumed under male-centric homogenised perceptions and meta-narratives. As a result their voices, experiences and their

[5]Recent migration statistics by the United Nations (27) Population Division estimates that as of 2000, overall 49% of all international migrants were women or girls, and in the developed regions it is 51%. Although the majority of women migrate as dependent family members they also migrate in several other forms such as professionals moving on their own, conflict-induced migrants, as labour force, illegal, temporary, permanent, forced, and trafficked migrants. All these factors have a significant bearing on the role, the behaviour and identity formation of migrant women.

critical role in the success story of the Indian Diaspora remain unnoticed and unmapped. Women in India are deeply embedded in the sociocultural moorings and belief systems that are ingrained in historical antecedents and mythical/religious narratives. Patriarchy, power hierarchies and gendered perceptions are the fundamentals of these narratives. Although Indian culture in reality is immensely diverse and heterogeneous with no uniform template, the patriarchal social order tends to dominate the overarching frame. The paradox is that, within this framework, women have been considered important agents in sustaining Indian culture and tradition, functioning as nodal points in the patriarchal family structure. Notwithstanding a subservient position in a culture riddled with patriarchy, women have been the bearers of tradition and the transmitters of culture to the next generation. Women in India have also shown and enjoyed a kind of power/ agency/space/and rights, at times drawing from the very sources that provide the patriarchal order and at times creating it through their own sources. The example of Sita[6] in 'Ram Charit Manas'[7] conveys an appropriate illustration of this paradoxical representation. Sita is presented as the ideal woman with ultimate grace and character, who moves from her father's home to her husband's home, goes to 'banbaas' (in exile) with her husband, resists the overtures of the richest and the most powerful king 'Ravana' and so remains loyal to her husband, goes to the extent of undergoing the 'agni pariksha' (trial by fire) to prove her fidelity; and yet she accepts her fate when she is abandoned by her husband. Nevertheless, within this patriarchal framework also she is the centre of Rama's life. He never remarries. His life, his yagna (Sacrificial ritual) is incomplete without her. Sita also has the space to argue and reason with her husband and with her brother-in-law and make them accept her decision but of course—without ever crossing the limits set by the patriarchal order. Sita's character has been an important metaphor presented to Indian women—often selectively to impose the patriarchal power structure on them. This paradigm has also constantly undergone change and there has been a visible decline in women's position in India over the past few millennia. Women have faced extreme forms of exploitative practices such as 'sati' (widow immolation), 'Purda' (veil), dowry, female infanticide and deprivation in terms of education, upward mobility and other activities in the public arena over these years. Nevertheless, in the present context with education, modernization, economic independence and state intervention, Indian women have not only improved their position in the society but have also challenged—often successfully—the patriarchal order in several ways.

The same conditions are carried through in the process of migration. In the context of a country as diverse as India, what women carry as cultural baggage is an extremely heterogeneous, complex, fluid and dynamic set of values and practices that are rooted in centuries old civilizational consciousness. Women of all classes,

---

[6]Lord Rama's wife who is also considered as the incarnation of the "Shakti' or the female power.
[7]It is the epic poem composed by sixteenth-century Indian Bhakti poet Goswami Tulsidas. It narrates the life and deeds of lord Rama and represents the popular faith of Indian people.

castes, religions and social backgrounds have migrated from India. It is important here to understand how the notion of culture and tradition plays out in a diasporic setting. As we understand it, culture is not a static collection of customs, beliefs and practices, rather it is a dynamic process which continually gets reshaped and reconstructed by various factors and influences. In a diasporic setting the heterogeneity of the Indian culture further increases as several other factors and aspects of diversity are added to it. The 'continuity' with Indian cultural trends or manifestation of 'roots' is an important component of the diasporic identity and—in the case of Indians—is very well pronounced and marked. But at the same time association with new cultures and local conditions bring about significant ruptures and leads to the evolution of hybrid cultures with their own sociocultural distinctiveness (see Pande 2017, 33–34). These factors result in significant diversities and differences within the Indian Diaspora. The normative 'Indianness' too differs in the context of different groups based on the period during which the migration took place—for example the Indentured diaspora and the new diaspora and even within these groups. What they are bound by is a sense of 'belonging' to an ancient civilizational worldview that represents 'Indianness'. This sense of belongingness leads to Indian cultures being sustained even after centuries of separation and integration with the cultures of the receiving countries. Thus the Indian culture in a diasporic setting is under constant making and remaking while women as carriers of Indian culture play an important role in this process of both continuity and rupture. Their role in the inheritance of the 'Indianness' is as important as their role in integration in the host societies.

Feminist inquiries suggest that migration and diasporic conditions also affect women's authority and power relations within the family and alter patriarchal structures according to the changing socio-economic contexts of home and host countries. But such changes do not show a linear pattern and are unevenly expressed. On the one hand, migration can be liberating and bring about more egalitarianism in the family, and can open avenues for women to strengthen their agency, to negotiate many critical matters, to create new opportunities for themselves and even recreate alternative cultural practices (see Hondagneu-Sotelo 2000; Buijs 1993; Levitt et al. 2007). However, on the other hand, it is also sometimes evident that gender hierarchy gets reinforced and becomes more rigid and traditional than in the homeland. The idea of losing control over women, in a perceived insecure, hostile or immoral (as liberal societies are often seen) receiving society, results in situations like physical abuse, honour killings and other cruelties (see Kang 2003; Kurien 1999; Judge 1992, 1994). Moreover, issues like marital disputes, lack of adjustment in the changed environment; dowry demands; nostalgia; insecurity; get perpetuated. The dual belongingness between the host and the homelands is also at times more disadvantageous because home state intervention on welfare issues becomes a complex and difficult proposition. The Feminist and Civil Rights movements in various countries have not necessarily made the issues of migrant women rights as part of their agenda. Still there has been an overall positive impact of these movements on migrant women.

These conditions can be witnessed in almost all sections of women in the Indian Diaspora. For example, in the case of Indentured women who faced exploitation by colonial authorities and plantation management as well as by their male counterparts because of the imbalance in the sex ratio of the labourers. It gave rise to suspicion and insecurity and consequently led to physical assault and other exploitation for women. Moreover the widely held view over the years (even during the campaign against the system of indenture in the early twentieth century) projected these women as morally lax, reckless individuals, which made them a target of malicious accusations (see Lal 1985; Reddock 1985; Niranjana 2006). This trend was strongly contested by later women scholars and also scholars of subaltern studies like Peter Emmer. They highlighted that migration through the system of indenture and the capacity of the indentured women to adapt, and respond to the rapidly evolving socio-economic conditions through education and economic opportunities had given them an opportunity to escape the exploitative situation in India, and also renegotiate gender roles and patriarchal structures.

A similar situation has been witnessed by the unskilled and semiskilled women migrating to Gulf countries in response to the gender-specific demand for labour. Although, in the present, the socio-economic conditions have undergone major change in terms of values, norms, stereotypes and gendered hierarchies, several of these factors have taken new forms of exploitation instead of getting annihilated. The so-called 'Gulf Wives' migrate according to the aspirations and parameters of their families, leaving behind the husband and children, with the consequential resultant experience of loneliness and emotional crisis in the new environment. Such a wife is deprived of a family life while, on the other hand, her children are deprived of proper maternal care (see Appadurai 2011; UNESCAP 2003). Yet the new generation is definitely more self-confident. Independent migrant females often find an outlet to their agency and thus experience empowerment in the process of migration as they contribute: directly to the economic development of their families, children and relatives and in turn, also to their countries of origin and destination. Women in India are also part of the highly skilled diaspora. Global economic opportunities and freedom for movement have provided these women space and empowerment. However they remain largely bound by the Indian family norms in the roles of wives and of mothers, at times even reproducing power relations in the family. Very often they are said to be carrying the burden of the 'respectable background' of Indian families and become the, so-called, 'symbolic capital of cultural superiority' (see Radhakrishnan 2011; Talukdar 2012). Yet, it cannot be denied that they do taste a new liberalism in a diasporic setting and exercise their agency for upward professional mobility. They are able to find—often —not one, but several wider scopes for social interaction, and opportunities to create new ties, new bonds—in the hostland—while still retaining their cultural roots of India.

It is clearly evident that in spite of many difficulties and constraints, the process of migration and the resultant diasporic conditions, still do offer women—new opportunities and financial independence in addition to the improved status within their homes and communities. Their encounters and contacts with other cultures also empower women by enabling them to become aware of their own repressive conditions, and exposing them to liberating notions of womanhood in different nations. In this process of widening of vision, they also become active in taking up larger issues of women's liberation and gender equality and become catalysts of social change. Participating actively in 'transnational spaces' Indian women have also, now punctured into the male dominated transnational diaspora organizations. We see many contradictions as women encounter and negotiate with multiple conflicting situations from the public and the private spheres of both the homeland and the hostlands, in the process, shifting their perspectives from traditional to contemporary (see Thadani 1984; Pessar and Mahler 2003). It is a complex play, as the nostalgia and the sense of identity makes them adhere to, maybe cling to, Indian traditions and culture on the one hand but on the other diasporic spaces also provides them agency to flirt with new cultures and opportunities.

The twentieth-century scholarship on Diaspora Studies was slow and partial to take note of these perspectives, explore women's agency and the way they create their space in the diasporic conditions. The dominant thread in the discourses on Indian women diaspora was about women's role as agents and custodians of Indian culture, thus restricting them to subservient positions in society. The intention behind highlighting women's agency in this volume is not to undermine women's victimization in diasporic conditions but at the same time not to eulogise or enter into the politics of victimhood. Rather, I aspire to explore women's agency and the inventive tactics they develop to transform the lives of their own and those of their families holding on to tradition with one hand while also grasping change with the other.

This volume aims to bring into focus a range of less discussed, newly emergent or already recognised issues related to women in the Indian Diaspora. The essays included in the volume discuss women in the Indian Diaspora from a multidisciplinary perspective involving social, economic, cultural and political aspects. Overall this volume resists the portrayal of women in Indian Diaspora only as victims by emphasizing their agency. Such an effort will privilege women's experiences and perspectives by raising consciousness and developing a deeper understanding about their issues in academia and among policy makers.

References

Altamirano, Aha Tollefsen. 1997. Feminist Theories and Migration Research-Making Sense in the Data Feast. *Refuge* 16 (4).

Alund, Aleksandra. 1991. The Power of Definitions: Immigrant Women and Problem Ideologies. In *Paradoxes of Multiculturalism: Essays on Swedish Society*, ed. Aleksandra Alund, and Carl-Ulrik Schierup. Aldershot; Brookfield, USA: Avesbury.

Appadurai, Arjun. 2011. *Disjuncture and Difference in the Global Cultural Economy*. http://www.worldhistory.pitt.edu/DissWorkshop2011/documents/Appadurai.pdf.

Bhabha, Homi. 1994. *The Location of Culture*. London: Routledge.

Boyd, Monica, Elizabeth Grieco. 2003. *Women and Migration: Incorporating Gender into International Migration Theory*. Migration Policy Institute. http://www.migrationpolicy.org/article/women-and-migration-incorporating-gender-international-migration-theory.

Buijs, Gina (ed.). 1993. *Migrant Women: Crossing Boundaries and Changing Identities*. Oxford: Berg Publishers Limited.

Clifford, James. 1994. Diasporas. *Cultural Anthropology* 9 (3): 302–338.

Cohen, Robin. 1997. *Global Diasporas: An Introduction*. London: UCL Press.

Di Stefano, Christine. 1990. Dilemmas of Difference: Feminism, Modernity and Postmodernism. In *Feminism/Postmodemism*, ed. Linda Nicholson. London: Routledge.

Gopinath, Gayatri. 2005. *Impossible Desires: Queer Diasporas and South Asian Public Cultures*. Durham: Duke University Press.

Hom, Sharon K. 1999. *Chinese Women Traversing Diaspora: Memoirs, Essays, and Poetry*. Routledge.

Hugo, G. 1999. *Gender and Migrations in Asian Countries*. Liege: International Union for the Scientific Study of Population.

Judge, Paramjit. 1992. Patterns of Migration and Intra-family Conflicts among Punjabis in India. *Guru Nanak Journal of Sociology* 13 (2): 97–113.

Judge, Paramjit. 1994. *Punjabis in Canada: A Study of Formation of an Ethnic Community*. Delhi: Chanakya Publications.

Kang, Neelu. 2003. Family Abuse against Punjabi Women in Canada. In *Development, Gender and Diaspora*, ed. Paramjit Judge, S.L. Sharma, Satish K. Sharma, and Gurpreet Bal, 275–96. Jaipur: Rawat.

Kosnick, Kira. 2010. Sexuality and Migration Studies: The Invisible, the Oxymoronic and Heteronormative Othering. In Framing Intersectionality. Debates on a Multi-faceted Concept in Gender Studies, ed. H. Lutz, M.T.H. Vivar, L. Supik. Farnham: Ashgate, pp. 121–135.

Kurien, Prema. 1999. Gendered Ethnicity: Creating a Hindu Ethnic Identity in the United States. *American Behavioral Scientist* 42 (4): 648–670.

Lal, Brij V. 1985. Kunti's Cry: Indentured Women on Fiji Plantations. *The Indian Economic and Social History Review* 22 (1): 55–71.

Levitt, Peggy, and B. Nadya Jaworsky. 2007. Transnational Migration Studies: Past Developments and Future Trends. The *Annual Review of Sociology* 33: 129–56. http://soc.annualreviews.org.

Macdonald, Catriona M.M. 2007. Imagining the Scottish Diaspora: Emigration and Transnational Literature in the Late Modern Period. *Edinberg University Press Journals* 5 (1): 12–42.

McDowell, Linda. 1993. Space, Place and Gender Relations: Part 11. Identity, Difference, Feminist Geometries and Geographies. *Progress in Human Geography* 17 (3): 305–318.

Mohanty, Chandra Talpade. 1991. Cartographies of Struggle: Third World Women and the Politics of Feminism. In *Third World Women and the Politics of Feminism*, ed. C.T. Mohanty, A. Russo, and L. Torres. Bloomington, IN: University of Indiana Press.

Mohanty, Chandra Talpade. 2003. *Feminism without Borders: Decolonizing Theory*. Practicing Solidarity: Duke University Press.

Nawyn, Stephanie J. 2010. Gender and Migration: Integrating Feminist Theory into Migration Studies. *Sociology Compass* 4 (9): 749–765.

Pande, Amba. 2013. Conceptualising Indian Diaspora: Diversities within a Common Identity. *Economic & Political Weekly* 48 (49): 59–65.

Pande, Amba. 2014. Diaspora and Development: Theoretical Perspectives. In *India Migration Report, 2014*, ed. Irudaya Rajan, 36–46. Routledge.

Pande, Amba. 2017. Diaspora: Identities, Spaces and Practices. In *Through the Diasporic Lens, 2017*, ed. Nandini Sen, 27–37. Authors Press.

Pessar, Patricia R., and Sarah J. Mahler. 2001. Gender and Transnational Migration. Paper presented at the Conference on Transnational Migration: Comparative Perspectives, Princeton University, June 30–July 1. http://www:transcomm.ox.ac.uk/working%25%20papers/Wptc-01-20%25%20Pessar.doc.pdf.

Pierrette, Hondagneu-Sotelo. 2000. Feminism and Migration. *Annals of the American Academy of Political and Social Science* 571: 107–120.

Radhakrishnan, Smitha. 2011. *Appropriately Indian: Gender and Culture in a New Transnational Class*. NC: Duke University Press.

Ralson, Helen. 1988. Arranged, 'Semi Arranged' and 'Love' Marriages Among South Asian Immigrant Women in the Diaspora and their Non-migrant Sisters in India and Fiji: A Comparative Study. *International Journal of Sociology of the Family* 27 (2): 43–68.

Rayaprol, Aparna. 1997. *Negotiating Identities: Women in the Indian Diaspora*, Cambridge.

Report of the High Level Committee on India Diaspora. 2002. Government of India. http://indiandiaspora.nic.in.

Reddock, Rhoda E. 1985. *Latin American Perspectives*, vol. 12, No. 1, Latin America's Colonial History (winter): 63–80.

Safran, William. 1991. Diasporas in Modern Societies: Myths of Homeland and Return. *Diaspora* 1 (1): 83–99.

Schiller, Nina Glick, Linda Basch, and Cristina Szanton Blanc. 1995. Immigrant to Transmigrant: Theorizing Transnational Migration. *Anthropological Quarterly*. 68 (1): 48–63.

Sheffer, G. 1986. A New Field of Study: Modern Diasporas in International Politics. In *Modern Diasporas in International Politics*, ed. G. Sheffer. London: Croom Helm. Retrieved October 2010. http://books.google.co.in/books.

Shepporson, George. 1966. The African Diaspora—Or the African Abroad. *African Forum* 1 (2): 76–93.

Talukdar, Jaita. 2012. Appropriately Indian: Gender and Culture in a New Transnational Class (Review Article). *American Journal of Sociology* 117 (5): 1527–1528.

Tejaswini, Niranjana. 2006. *Mobilizing India: Women, Music and Migration Between India and Trinidad*. North Carolina: Duke University Press.

Thadani, Veena N., and Michael P. Todaro. 1984. Female Migration: A Conceptual Framework. In *Women in the Cities of Asia: Migration and Urban Adaptation*, ed. James T. Fawcett, Siew-Ean Khoo, and Peter C. Smith. Boulder, CO: Westview Press.

Tigau, Camelia, Amba Pande, and Yan Yuan. 2017. Diaspora Policies and Co-development: A Comparison between India China and Mexico. *Migration Letters* 14 (2): 181–195.

UN (UNITED NATIONS). 2003. *Women and International Migration Division for the Advancement of Women*. Department of Economic and Social Affairs, United Nations. http://www.un.org/en/development/desa/population/migration/events/coordination/3/docs/P01_DAW.pdf.

Zlotnik, Hania. 1995. The South-to-North Migration of women. *International Migration Review* xxix (1): 229–254.

Part I
The Context of Theory and Identity

Chapter 2
Centring Gendered Narratives of the Indian Diaspora

Sandhya Rao Mehta

Coupled with the assumption that diaspora etymologically associates geographical movement with male agency, this study examines the multiple ways in which gender has hitherto remained marginal to the narratives of a diaspora. Studies on the Indian Diaspora have often shown that women have not, traditionally, been active agents, and that the decision of moving is often a male one. This privileges the male narrative at the expense of numerous, undocumented narratives of women who have travelled, forcibly or otherwise, to different parts of the world over the course of the last three centuries. This study investigates existing scholarship on gender and diaspora, focussing on the lacunae of studies on socially disadvantaged women outside the first world. Tracing the rise in diaspora studies over the last three decades, it underlines the manifold ways in which research on the diaspora has been determined by class, thus often rendering invisible a number of women, who add to the national economy by working in the Middle East, and focusing, only briefly, on them as victims of exploitation—as suggested by the mainstream media and government officials. This study calls for a more dynamic approach to the migration of women within the Indian context as it is incorporated into the framework of diaspora studies, centring the various layers of the gendered migrant experience and then moving on—beyond the binaries of the narratives of the victims.

S.R. Mehta (✉)
Department of English Language and Literature, Sultan Qaboos University,
Muscat, Oman
e-mail: sandhyamehta4@gmail.com

Introduction

Dear Kumari,

I, of course, do not know if Kumari was really your name,

It became a custom in the Gulf to change the name of the servant upon arrival,

The mama says to you, "Your name is Maryam/Fatima/Kumari/Chandra,"

Even before she gives you your cotton apron,

The same apron that the previous Kumari used

before she ran away.... (Kareem 2016)

Mona Kareem's address to the South Asian domestic worker in Saudi Arabia reflects on one of the most iconic pictures of diasporic exploitation—that of the migrant woman working in the domestic confines of a conservative family. While pointing towards a significant phenomenon in migration in the Global South, this picture focuses on a single aspect of the migrant experience, undercutting the layered, complex exigencies of migration and diaspora among women. Long swept under the rubrics of general diaspora studies, the role of gender in the process of migration and subsequent settlement have only recently become central to scholarship, despite the fact that women have always been essential to the process of migration. Often seen as being passively accompanying male relations, the central role played by women has only recently been recognised for its economic, social and cultural potential. This 'feminisation of migration' (Piper 2008, 4), however, largely addresses the contexts of migration to the West, most often from developing countries in Asia and Africa. Such studies privilege notions of belonging, negotiating domestic roles and re-defining changing diasporic identities as diaspora intersects with gender, race and class in new geographical spaces. While imperative to diaspora studies, this work reflects on a very specific experience of diaspora while ignoring other, numerically substantial experiences of migration within the Global South where gendered labour is primarily perceived to be service-oriented, including nursing, palliative care and domestic work. When such areas are discussed, they are most often viewed through the prism of exploitation and victimization, thereby denying agency and choice to the woman migrant and her narratives. Such women have often been spoken for, most often by privileged scholarship, which marginalises their contributions to the economy, the family and themselves. This article attempts to centre gendered narratives of the South by exploring the multiple ways in which agency is sought and established by those women who leave families to work in foreign lands, almost always leaving their own families in the hands of the larger family and community. Such migratory patterns tend to be long-standing and often replicate conditions of diaspora in terms of negotiation of power and self. While focusing on the 'everyday life' (Hannam et al. 2006, 3) of Indian migrant women workers, this paper focuses on a hitherto marginalised narrative of expatriate experience, while suggesting that diaspora scholarship establish a wider framework which could contest largely victim narratives, and centre the complex and heterogeneous experience of gendered diaspora. While acknowledging that diaspora, as a literary and sociological term, remains distinct from migration this paper uses the terms interchangeably as the two have gradually coalesced to situate themselves as significant facets of transnationalism.

Migration as Diaspora

As the scholarship of diaspora expanded following Tölölyan's famous definition of the diaspora as 'the exemplary communities of the transnational moment' (1991, 4) many critics began to note the very messy turn that it was taking, away from the very specific focus on the Jewish and the Armenian experience (Bauböck and Faist 2010). Tölölyan pointed to its expanding possibilities of this term by suggesting that '[t]he term that once described Jewish, Greek, and Armenian dispersion now shares meanings with a larger semantic domain that includes words like immigrant, expatriate, refugee, guest worker, exile community, overseas community, ethnic community' (4–5). In 2012, Tölölyan responded to the assertion that the term had gone rogue by accepting various different categories: 'Such crowding is not merely additive, but transformative. As Ferdinand de Saussure pointed out in 1916, no term has its meaning independently, but rather acquires it in its relationship to, and nuanced difference from, related others' (4). Shuval (2002) too suggests that 'the term diaspora has acquired a broad semantic domain. It now encompasses a motley array of groups such as political refugees, alien residents, guest workers, immigrants, expellees, ethnic and racial minorities, and overseas communities. It is used increasingly by displaced persons who feel, maintain, invent or revive a connection with a prior home' (41). Temporary migration has only recently been considered a significant part of diaspora studies, primarily because it fulfils the criteria established by early studies on the diaspora involving a notion of home, the return to which remains an essential desire as well as a common sense of community across the globe. Further, global concerns of transnationalism have ensured that migration is no longer associated with service workers who are inevitably economically weaker, but have now begun to include technocrats and workers in multinational companies who travel and stay in different countries on short tenures.

Gendering the Diaspora

Taking cue from Gopinath's (2005) observation of the etymological underpinning of diaspora a male act of dispersal and procreation in a new land and Kosnick's (2010) suggestion that such androcentric images assert 'male procreation and patrilinear descent' (123), scholarship on diaspora has focussed on the multiple ways in which gender has remained marginal to predominant work on the diaspora.

This is primarily because the state has historically privileged male immigration while women have accompanied them under family joining rules. As Jain (2009) suggests, in the United States, H1B and H4 visas empower the male complete control over their family as the dependent (usually the wife) cannot work. This is, historically, supported by such Acts as the British Nationality Act of 1948 through which migration to Britain was primarily male as they came with work permits for specific jobs. This is still primarily relevant in the family joining programmes of various countries where the family is defined as a husband requesting immigration for his wife and children (Kosnick 2010). Women's migration was thus historically seen to be a part of the larger movement of families (Pessar 1999; Thadani and Todaro 1984; Weinberg 1992). As Pessar (1999) suggests, men were seen more prone to take risks, with women 'portrayed as guardians of community tradition and stability' (578). In all this, the domestic roles of women and the hegemonic roles of men as providers of the family remained unchanged. With the change in global capitalist contexts, migration came to be more feminised, in so far as women came to be seen to offer radicalised and gendered services in specific industries, particularly as caregivers. The reduction of welfare facilities in various western countries allowed for large-scale emigration of women, albeit in ways that replicated their traditional roles. Thus, even when women were recognised as an important section of the migrating group, it was often in positions which duplicated the existing patriarchal hierarchies (Hagan 1998; Piper 2008). The repercussions of these large-scale migrations—particularly from the Global South to the North, at various micro- and macro-levels of the individual and the community, and the effect of such migrations on the migrant, the home left behind by women—remain rich areas of research. Yet, such works primarily focused on the binary of migration, being either emancipatory or limiting for women, pre-empting more complex intersection with race, class and colour.

As Pessar and Mahler (1999) demonstrate, early attempts to correct the gender bias in migration studies resulted in a plethora of work which almost eliminated the focus on male migration, thereby missing out the point of including gender in migration studies: '[b]oth omissions are objectionable, and both missed the more important theoretical innovation of treating gender less as a variable and more as a central concept for studying migration' (814). Pessar and Mahler's later establishment of a framework called 'gendered geographies of power' (818) allowed for the study of social agency by examining the various ways in which women negotiate within multiple diasporic contexts and complex relationships by examining the individual as well the social, hierarchical contexts within which transnational migration was experienced. While admitting to gender as a central differential, such an approach allows for a problematic study of the way in which gender is 'imagined and lived' (818). Nicola Piper's work similarly incorporated the recognition that gender remained an important consideration in migration studies, particularly the recognition that migrants 'leave *and enter* gendered and stratified societies' (Piper; italics author's). This has far reaching implications for the study of gendered diasporas' impact, not only on the individual's relationship with the host community but of further impact upon return, thus addressing concerns that migration cannot be seen to be a homogenous single journey. Piper's study suggests that increased prosperity in the developed world coupled with the reduction of availability of jobs for males in the country of origin as well as increased visibility of women's work as seen through increased remittances, all contribute to the centring of gender in migration and diaspora studies. This is particularly valuable when research is located in specific contexts, which could aid in the development of a body of work privileging gendered narratives and agency. Piper's work on Mexican and Guatemalan women in North America as well as other case studies of South–South migration, particularly in South-East Asia, point to the multifarious ways in which migration takes place in the global context. It is a project that continues to be relevant in South Asia which is one of the largest exporters of human capital in the world.

Women in the Indian Diaspora

Poet Meena Alexander's poignant articulation of the diasporic experience, 'I am, a woman cracked by multiple migrations, uprooted so many times she can connect nothing with nothing' (1993, 3) evokes the sense of loss, nostalgia and memory that has become characteristic of the Indian Diaspora, the largest diasporic group in the world. In fact, (World Bank 2015a, b) remittance data for 2015 shows that India is now the largest recipient of remittances from overseas at $69 billion, having taken over from China which received $64 billion. This comes from the more than 16 million Indians who are accounted to live overseas, according to the statistics of 2015 of the (United Nations 2016). These groups have been richly investigated from diverse perspectives including the historical roles played by early Sikhs in the United States, the politics of identity among Indians in the United Kingdom as well as the multiple journeys of Gujarati Indians settled in Uganda and subsequently England. The historical diaspora of the indentured labour began to gain cognizance in recent years, particularly with the rise of biographies seeking to find voices for those whose journeys along the Indian Ocean remained silent for a long time. Studies such as those of Vijay Mishra's *The Literature of the Indian Diaspora: Theorizing the Diasporic Imaginary* (2007) and Gauitra Bahadur's *Coolie Woman: Story of Indenture* (2013) and Mehta's *Exploring Gender in the Literature of the Indian Diaspora* (2015) established a framework within which to investigate the establishment of the Indian Diaspora in the eighteenth and nineteenth centuries in Surinam, Fiji and the Caribbean. The role of women in such communities has only now begun to be investigated with such works as Bahadur's, which examine homemaking and language retention strategies of indentured women. Scholarship revolving around Indian women, particularly those socially advantaged (and had thus come under the category of Skilled Worker visas) in the West, has become more popular in the last two decades, with focus, not only on gender as a variable in the migration process, but with specific regional, linguistic and religious studies. This has been largely facilitated with the growth and popularity of Indian writing in

English, including those of Bharati Mukherjee and Jhumpa Lahiri in the United States and Meena Syal and Kiran Desai in the United Kingdom. Collections such as the *Indivisible: An Anthology of Contemporary South Asian American Poetry* (Banerjee et al. 2010) as well as online journals such as *Desilit* and *Jaggery* attempt to bring together the experiences of Indian women as people of colour, problematized by race, ethnicity and dress. Thus Naidu (2008), Puwar and Raghuram (2003) explore how Indian women negotiate identities through the maze of public spaces while Rayaprol (1998) examines the role that women play in sustaining culture and community through their involvement in Indian temples. In the private sphere, women negotiate between traditional roles as homemakers and mothers, while facing other more public forms of struggle such as wage inequality, the lack of flexible working hours and paid leave. In this context George (2005), Hussain (2005) all suggest that women seek to recreate their roles of adapting, creating memories and establishing of a home culture through material and non-material forms of belonging, by creating transnational identities and by ensuring continuity with the homeland. In this sense, women's migration lacks agency as it is framed within the larger contexts of family expectations, usually as established by patriarchal assumptions. As Al-Ali (2010) suggests, 'The control of women's bodies and sexualities is key in the context of constructions of ethnic and national communities, especially when in flux' (120). While problematizing gender within diaspora studies, such a framework fails to reflect on the multiple strategies adopted to make creative spaces within which autonomy and agency is articulated.

An important consideration within scholarship revolving around gender in the Indian Diaspora is its preoccupation with class. Two major trends have thus emerged. On the one hand, transnational capitalist forces have allowed for a focus on the rapidly rising class of technocrats in the Western hemisphere, negotiating diaspora through strategies of religion, language as well as cultural tropes such as dress and culinary reinventions. On the other, emerging scholarship on indentured communities along the Indian Ocean and the Caribbean have investigated historical diasporas (the first wave) and their sporadic links with the homeland, primarily owing to the recognition accorded to them by the Indian State. Such research has successfully created an Indian Diaspora, which is both historically rooted and contemporary at the same time. However, a significant area which this scholarship continues to ignore is one of the most populated as well as economically significant regions for the Indian Diaspora—the GCC (Gulf Cooperation States) which is populated by more than 6 million Indians (40% of the total number of overseas Indians), of whom, more than 10% (600,000) consist of documented women (Ozaki 2012). Existing studies show that most of these women are domestic workers with low literacy levels and many of them actually work in the Gulf without valid documentation, making it difficult for them to access organizational help (Kohli 2014; Rajan and Joseph 2015). Including the narratives of women working in the GCC countries into the scholarship of the Indian Diaspora is essential, not only because they have been hitherto marginalised and remain outside the boundaries of established literature, but because their narratives are an example of how migration studies can help to problematize everyday lives by investigating its intersection with social structure, personal, familial and professional lives. Methodologies to ground such research within the Gulf, enabling conceptualizing of such gendered diasporas is presently minimal and requires sustained focus.

Indian Women in the Arabian Gulf

Scholarship on the Indian Diaspora in the Gulf has only recently developed, although most of the work revolves around remittances and the condition of the migrants, the latter owing largely to its focus by the Western media. Very little literature (Vora 2013; Gardner 2010; Deffner 2014; Mehta and Onley 2015) is available regarding the social, cultural and personal lives of the Indian Diaspora perhaps because it lives in geographical proximity to the homeland. Research on women migrants have shown that women migrate as caregivers (nursing and old age homes), as teachers, or as domestic help. Kohli (2014), Shah (2013), Potnuru and Sam (2015), Percot (2015), among others, have brought out the rise in the number of women going to the Gulf as domestic help as well as nurses. While the exact number of women who work as domestic workers cannot be completely ascertained, Ozaki's (2012) report summarises the context of women in the Gulf:

> Overall, women constitute approximately 15% of the total migrant workers from South Asia: 6.5% in Bangladesh; and approximately 10% in India and Nepal. In Sri Lanka, women constituted 52% of the total migration outflow in 2009. The majority of women migrant workers from South Asia are involved in domestic work followed by manufacturing. A small portion of them also work as nurses. Most of them are illiterate or only with the elementary level of education (4).

Few studies (Percot 2015; Potnuru and Sam 2015) have focused on specific areas in which women have been involved in the Gulf. Percot's study of nurses from Kerala reflects on the liberatory possibilities of migration for conservative girls for whom migration to the Gulf is often a stepping-stone to the West. Potnuru and Sam's research investigates the changing trends among women migrants in the various countries of the Gulf, suggesting that Saudi Arabia, Kuwait and the United Arab Emirates retain the largest pool of Indian domestic workers. More recently, the India Migration Report has released a special issue on gender and migration, including a study by Rajan and Joseph (2015), which examines the conditions of women domestic workers in Saudi Arabia. This study reflects on the empowering nature of migrant work in that women are seen to make an effective difference to their communities and families back home through their remittances: 'Migrant women workers play an important role as drivers of development both at home and at the destination and should not be obscured from analysis' (10). This is in direct contradiction to Sahoo and Goud's (2015) work in Telangana which suggests that women did not benefit considerably through their migration as much of their remittances went into paying off recruitment agents and travel expenses. Jain and Oommen (2016) also suggest that migration to the Gulf remains problematic for women as '[t]he South Asian countries, except Sri Lanka, have approached women's migration within the framework of patriarchy with restrictive policies and irrational conditions' (29). Such policies include the Indian government's age restriction whereby women below 30 are not allowed to work in the Gulf countries, making illegal migration more rampant. Rajan suggests that, rather than having the State impose regulations which deny agency to women who may want to work abroad, more facilities need to be set up to provide recourse to domestic workers by giving them access to more information and help via NGOs and embassies in the concerned countries. Jain (2009, 17) similarly asks if the 'flexibilities' of the Indian government go beyond the patriarchal protection of women, from exploitative marriages to 'recognition of women's agency in shaping everyday processes'.

The limited fieldwork available about Indian women domestic workers has thus focused upon them as voiceless victims of a patriarchal State before and after migration. On the one hand, migrant women who leave India as domestic workers to the Gulf are viewed by the Indian government as potential victims of exploitation, but on the other, the remittances which are sent home by these women, however modest, represent a large contribution to the immediate community, which often sees a direct improvement in developmental indicators such as education, health care and mortality. Remittances thus achieve more than what the State actually does, in providing for welfare of the individual and the community. This is corroborated by reports of the United Nations (2016), which maintain that migrant women workers typically invested their remittances in 'schools, wells, hospitals and local development' (Clarke 2013, 5). It is thus imperative for studies on gendered migration to the Gulf States to investigate the multiple conditions of migration, both from the origin and destination perspectives, in order to voice individual as well as collective experiences of domestic workers and its impact on the individuals, their families and their communities. An example of how complex such a narrative can be is illustrated by a closer study at the way in which domestic workers operate in the GCC countries, most notably through the use of the *Kafala*.

The *Kafala* system of sponsorship entails a citizen of the countries in the GCC to sponsor a worker for individual/domestic use or for a company, which they may have registered. Such individuals are thus tied to their sponsor for the entire duration of their stay. Sponsorships are usually for a period of 2 years after which the contract can be renewed if so desired, by both, the employer and the employee. This much-maligned system is often termed modern day slavery as it ties the workers to a particular person at whose mercy they remain. Women workers are often brought as domestic help and thus find accommodation inside the home of the sponsor or their relatives. This, as Rajan and Joseph (2015) note, limits their access to the outside help and even makes documentation difficult as they are consigned to private spaces. Kohli (2014) also adds that women domestic workers—do not come under the purview of the labour laws of the local governments as they—are considered to be part of the local family. While the *Kafala* system of employment in the Gulf is rightly seen to be demeaning, restrictive and actually illegal in other parts of the world, many migrants have been able to find ways to surmount such obstacles and work on their own. This is largely because the local employer does not require all the workers who they may have sponsored. For a certain amount of monthly payment (ranging from $50 to $100), they allow these workers to find work independent of the sponsor. This 'free visa' is a system which is as common as it is illegal, for it benefits the migrant woman as well as the sponsor. Having paid their sponsor, women are free to work as part-time help in several houses instead of just one, thus earning more per household. Working in this way enables them to decide on their working hours as well as ensuring leisure hours. Women in such cases tend to share accommodation with other women from their states in India, thus sharing the chore of cooking and entertainment options such as watching television programmes in their languages (Mehta and Onley 2015). In addition to domestic work, women with such visas are beauticians in saloons, cleaners and nannies in nursery schools and secretaries in small companies. They send as much money as they can at the beginning of the month to the caretakers of their children, often keeping just enough for their own rent, groceries and phone cards.

Such 'free visas' are rampantly used throughout the Gulf countries in spite of their being of an illegal nature. The way in which women make use of this legal loophole in sponsorship regulations provides an insight into a critical, subversive strategy adopted by migrant women in the Gulf to seek advancement in their employment as well as to evade exploitation. Such strategies empower them to make decisions pertaining to, not only where and how long they will work, but in what way they disburse their incomes as they are often in touch with their family back home, notably their children. Within a system, which is rigged entirely against the migrant domestic worker, the 'free visa' offers possibilities of agency within the larger framework of strict employment regulations. It also affirms the heterogeneity of the migrant experience of women, particularly those not privileged by class, thus asserting their agency even amidst seemingly impossible contexts.

Conclusion

Pessar and Mahler's (1999) conceptualization of the 'geographies of power', with regard to gender in migration studies, points to multiple ways in which the notion of gender could be researched beyond the binaries of victimhood and empowerment. Their categories of 'geographic scales', 'social locations' and 'power geometries' point to the intersectional relationship between gender, social hierarchies and social locations (7). Drawing upon (Massey 1994), they suggest that people exert power over these forces and processes as well as being affected by them. Such a conceptual framework, imperative in the investigation of the situation, role and responsibilities of Indian women in the diaspora, remains still in its nascent stages. The way in which gender intersects with social hierarchies through the very act of migration, the negotiations with existing models of patriarchy, and the subversive strategies adapted to in order to negotiate within and through such contexts, remains an important aspect of the exploration of gendered diasporic spaces. As evidenced from an exploration of women domestic workers in the GCC countries,

homogeneous narratives of victimhood and exploitation, while being relevant to the
study of migration and diaspora, must include wider discussions of agency, choice
and empowerment. The multiple levels in which women negotiate their roles as
migrants requires scholarship which represents the complex nuances of real lives,
not the oft repeated syllogisms of patriarchal protection.

Acknowledgments This paper is part of a research project funded by the Humanities Research
Centre, Sultan Qaboos University, Oman. The author would like to thank Dr. Rahma
Al-Mahrooqi, Director of the Centre, for her support of this project.

References

Al-Ali, Nadje. 2010. Diasporas and Gender. In *Diasporas: Concepts, Intersections, Identities*, ed.
    Kim Knott and Sean McLoughlin, 118–122. London & New York: Zed Books.
Alexander, Meena. 1993. *Fault Lines*. New York: Feminist Press.
Bahadur, Gauitra. 2013. *Coolie Woman: The Odyssey of Indenture*. Chicago: University of
    Chicago Press.
Banerjee, Neelanjana, Summi Kaipa, and Pireeni Sundaralingam. 2010. *Indivisible: An Anthology
    of Contemporary South Asian American Poetry*. Fayetteville: Arkansas University Press.
Bauböck, Rainer, and Thomas Faist (eds.). 2010. *Diaspora and Transnationalism: Concepts,
    Theories and Methods*. Amsterdam: Amsterdam University Press.
Clarke, Roberta. 2013. Foreword. *Contribution of Migrant Domestic Workers to Sustainable
    Development*. http://asiapacific.unwomen.org/~/media/7148BD87A4F7412D8CBD104821462
    76F.ashx. Accessed February 12, 2016.
Deffner, Veronika. 2014. The Indian Diaspora in Oman. In *India Migration Report 2014:
    Diaspora and Development*, ed. S. Irudaya Rajan, 181–92. New Delhi: Routledge.
Gardner, Andrew M. 2010. *City of Strangers: Gulf Migration and the Indian Community in
    Bahrain*. Ithaca: Cornell Press.
George, Sheba M. 2005. *When Women Come First: Gender and Class in Transnational
    Migration*. Berkeley, CA: University of California Press.
Gopinath, Gayatri. 2005. *Impossible Desires: Queer Diasporas and South Asian Public Cultures*.
    London: Duke University Press.
Hagan, Jacqueline Maria. 1998. Social Networks, Gender, and Immigrant Incorporation: Change.
    Journal of American Ethnic History 63 (1): 25–46.
Hannam, Kevin, Mimi Sheller, and John Urry. 2006. Editorial: Mobilities, Immobilities and
    Moorings. *Mobilities* 1 (1): 1–22.
Hussain, Yasmin. 2005. *Writing Diaspora: South Asian Women, Culture, and Ethnicity*.
    Burlington, VT: Ashgate Publishing Company.
Jain, Prakash C., and Ginu Zachariah Oommen. 2016. *Migration to Gulf Countries: History,
    Policies, Development*. London: Routledge.
Jain, Shobhita. 2009. Transmigrant Women's Agency in Global Processes: India and Its Diaspora.
    Anthropologist 4: 15–25.
Kareem, Mona. 2016. Manifesto Against the Woman. *Jadaliyya*. http://www.jadaliyya.com/pages/
    index/23548/manifesto-against-the-woman. Retrieved February 23, 2016.
Kohli, Neha. 2014. Indian Migrants in the Gulf Countries: Developments in the Gulf Region. In
    *Developments in the Gulf Region: Prospects and Challenges for India in the Next Two
    Decades*, ed. Rumel Dahiya, 115–147. New Delhi: Institute for Defence Studies and Analysis.

Kosnick, Kira. 2010. Diasporas and Sexuality. In *Diasporas: Concepts, Intersections, Identities*, ed. Kim Knott, and Seán McLoughlin, 123–127. London: Zed Books.

Massey, Doreen. 1994. *Space, Place and Gender*. Minneapolis: University of Minnesota Press.

Mehta, Sandhya Rao (ed.). 2015. *Exploring Gender in the Literature of the Indian Diaspora*. Newcastle: Cambridge Scholars Publishing.

Mehta, Sandhya Rao, and James Onley. 2015. The Hindu Community in Muscat: Creating Homes in the Diaspora. *Journal of Arabian Studies* 5 (2): 156–183.

Mishra, Vijay. 2007. *The Literature of the Indian Diaspora: Theorizing the Diasporic Imaginary*. New York: Routledge.

Naidu, Sam. 2008. Introduction: Women Writers of the South Asian Diaspora. In *Tracing an Indian Diaspora: Contexts, Memories, Representations*, ed. Parvati Raghuram, Ajaya Sahoo, Brij Maharaj, and Dave Sangha, 368–391. New Delhi: Sage Publications.

Ozaki, Mayumi. 2012. Worker Migration and Remittances in South Asia. *South Asia Working Paper Series*. http://www.adb.org/sites/default/files/publication/29852/worker-migration-remittances-south-asia.pdf.

Percot, M. 2015. Malayali Nurses in the Gulf Countries: Migration as a Factor of Women Empowerment. In *Diaspora, Development and Distress*, ed. by Ajaya Kumar Sahoo, 87–98. New Delhi: Rawat Publications.

Pessar, Patricia. R. 1999. Engendering Migration Studies: The Case of New Immigrants to the United States. *American Behavioral Scientist* 42: 577–600.

Pessar, Patricia. R., and Sarah J. Mahler. 1999. Transnational Migration: Bringing Gender. *The International Migration Review* 37 (3): 812–846.

Piper, Nicola. 2008. International Migration and Gendered Axes of Stratitification. In *New Perspectives on Gender and Migration*, ed. Nicola Piper, 1–18. London: Routledge.

Potnuru, Basant Kumar, and Vishishta Sam. 2015. International Migration of Women from India to the Gulf: The Case of Domestic Workers. In *Diaspora, Development and Distress*, ed. by Ajaya Kumar Sahoo, 68–86. New Delhi: Rawat Publications.

Puwar, Nirmal, and Parvati Raghuram (eds.). 2003. *South Asian Women in the Diaspora*. New York: Berg.

Rajan, S.Irudaya, and Jolin Joseph. 2015. Migrant Women at the Discourse Policy Nexus: Indian Domestic Workers in Saudi Arabia. In *India Migration Report 2015: Gender and Migration*, ed. Irudaya S. Rajan, 9–25. London: Routledge.

Rayaprol, Aparna. 1998. *Negotiating Identities: Women in the Indian Diaspora*. Delhi: Oxford University Press.

Sahoo, Ajaya Kumar, and Trilok Chandan Goud. 2015. Development and Distress: A Study of Gulf returnees. In *Diaspora, Development and Distress*, ed. by Ajaya Kumar Sahoo, 201–215. New Delhi: Rawat Publications.

Shah, N. 2013. Labour Migration from Asian to GCC Countries: Trends, Patterns and Policies. *Middle East Law and Governance* 5 (20/5): 36–70.

Shuval, Judith. T. 2002. Diaspora Migration: Definitional Ambiguities and a Theoretical Paradigm. *International Migration* 38 (5): 41–56.

Thadani, Veena N., and Michael P. Todaro. 1984. Female Migration: A Conceptual Framework. In *Women in Cities of Asia: Migration and Urban Adaptation*, ed. J.T. Fawcett, S.E. Khoo, and P. C. Smith, 36–59. Boulder, CO: Westview Press.

Tölölyan, Khaching. 1991. In Lieu of a Preface. *Diaspora* 1 (1): 3–7.

Tölölyan, Khaching. 2012. *Diaspora Studies Past, Present and Promise*. Paper presented at the Oxford Diasporas Programme, June 2011.

United Nations. 2016. *244 Million International Migrants Living Abroad Worldwide, New UN Statistics Reveal*. http://www.un.org/sustainabledevelopment/blog/2016/01/244-million-international-migrants-living-abroad-worldwide-new-un-statistics-reveal/.

Vora, Neha. 2013. *Impossible Citizens: Dubai's Indian Diaspora*. New York: Duke University Press.

Weinberg, Sydney Stahl. 1992. The Treatment of Women in Immigration History: A Call for Resources and Constraints. *American Sociological Review* 63 (1): 55–67.

World Bank. 2015a. Data. http://data.worldbank.org/indicator/BX.TRF.PWKR.CD.DT.

World Bank. 2015b. http://www.worldbank.org/en/news/press-release/2015/12/18/international-migrants-and-remittances-continue-to-grow-as-people-search-for-better-opportunities-new-report-finds.

Chapter 3
The Rhetoric of Deliberation and the Space of the Hyphen: Identity Politics of the Indian Women Diaspora in the Fictions of Jhumpa Lahiri

Nabanita Chakraborty

Theorising Gendered Hyphenated Spaces

In linguistic studies, a hyphen is used to conjoin two words to form a compound term where each word receives equal stress. The absence of a hyphen in a compound word might carry a different signification and accent than the hyphenated term.[1] The same logic applies in the case of the hyphenated or diasporic identities where an individual might either nurture a hybrid and multicultural identity or retain the unique cultural values and heritage of both the homeland and the host land. The political connotation of the hyphen in relation to an ethnic sociocultural identity underlines the divided loyalties towards the nation of origin and the nation of adoption where both cultures have imprinted indelible marks upon the self. R. Radhakrishnan in his introduction to *Diasporic Mediations* defines the diasporic location as 'the space of the hyphen that tries to coordinate, within an evolving relationship, the identity politics of one's place of origin with that of one's present home' (1996, xiii). But Vijay Mishra warns that the politics of the hyphen is itself hyphenated since the classification makes the people 'empoweringly-disempowered' (2007, 184). Does the hyphenated status of an individual threaten to destabilise a fluid multicultural identity? Does this act of straddling both worlds create a perpetual sense of dislocation? Is the hyphenated experience of women different from that of men? My paper attempts to answer these questions by engaging in a close textual analysis of Lahiri's novels, *The Namesake* (2004) and *The Lowland* (2013).

---

[1]For instance 're-creation' means to create again while 'recreation' means entertainment or relaxation.

N. Chakraborty (✉)
Department of English, Hansraj College, University of Delhi, New Delhi, India
e-mail: cnita.in@gmail.com

© Springer Nature Singapore Pte Ltd. 2018
A. Pande (ed.), *Women in the Indian Diaspora*,
https://doi.org/10.1007/978-981-10-5951-3_3

Scholars have agreed that the predicament of the Indian middle-class woman diaspora is unique since it is rooted in the idea of having no home of her own while moving from her father's to her husband's domain. She migrates not of her own volition but to accompany her newly wedded husband after marriage. As Sandhya Rao Mehta points out, while the choice of moving out of the country lies with the man, 'the onus of retaining memories of home, of recreating them within new contexts and ultimately acting as cultural harbingers of homeland culture, remain vividly feminine' (2015, 1). Yet the immigrant woman is often seen as an individual 'without an anchor, without horizon, colourless, stateless, rootless'[2] (Fanon 1967, 176). My intervention to this debate is to enquire if this uncertainty of 'belonging' and 'not belonging'; of being 'without an anchor' can provide a sense of liberation for the woman who is trapped in the unjust social structures of a patriarchal society. It is not to deny the fact that migrant women feel alienated in the new land at the beginning. But very often they transcend their geopolitical, cultural and linguistic boundaries to embark on another journey of self-exploration and self-conception.[3] My paper argues that the hyphen metaphorically signifies an in-between space occupied by a woman migrant, a space of memory, deliberation and articulation. In other words, a hyphen is the site of confluence between the subjective memories and the desires of the woman.

Language and Power

My intention is to employ rhetoric as a methodological tool of enquiry into the issues of gender, identity politics and agency in the cited novels of Jhumpa Lahiri. Rhetoric is not simply used to establish, perpetuate and validate the double bind of the woman diaspora; rather rhetoric is a tool for deliberation and purposive action. Thus I wish to trace the rhetorical agency of Lahiri's women subjects and their journey from self-exploration to determination. It is to be underscored that the experience of each woman as a migrant is different from that of another, though she may share certain cultural memories with the other women immigrants. Thus an ethnic homogenization of Bengali-American women is not possible. Language, for the immigrant woman, can be an essential means of access to power. Who can better express this than Jhumpa Lahiri, a hyphenated identity herself, a female writer who needs to possess language to empower herself? Lahiri has recently published her semi-autobiographical text written in a foreign language, Italian, translated by Ann Goldstein, titled *In Other Words*. The book is a provocative self-exploration of the author to conquer another language, to seek a new voice and

---

[2]Fanon uses these words in a colonial context.

[3]I do not include the victims of forced migration or refugees of war and state-orchestrated violence in my analysis since I limit my paper to Jhumpa Lahiri's Bengali middle-class diaspora in search of better lives.

struggle to create and interpret the world afresh. In this book, Italian is the medium, the subject matter and more importantly 'the mask, the filter, the outlet, the means' (Lahiri 2015, 197). Lahiri admits that she is used to a linguistic exile:

> My mother tongue, Bengali, is foreign in America. When you live in a country where your own language is considered foreign, you can feel a continuous sense of estrangement. You speak a secret, unknown language, lacking any correspondence to the environment. An absence that creates a distance within you. (Lahiri 2015, 22)

Yet, as a second-generation immigrant, Lahiri can speak but cannot read or write Bengali. Thus her mother tongue is equally foreign to her as is Italian. The author's attempt to resort to a third foreign language can be seen almost as a 'third space of enunciation'[4] to explore her multicultural identity and celebrate her limitless self.

This brings me to enquire into the relationship of power with rhetoric. Language can express degrees of authority as evident in an individual's variation of intonation, accent, vocabulary and form. While language can be an instrument of coercion, intimidation or abuse[5]; it can also be an intermediary between motivation and purposive action.[6] My conceptualization of rhetoric is not limited to speech acts but to language which is implicated in power structures. It is important to register that deliberative oratory and purposive action have always been associated with a democratic state where people have the option to choose and decide the best course of action.[7] Thus deliberative discourse delineates the power to argue, to persuade, to negotiate and to break free from the stereotypical constraints of passive womanhood.

Woman Diaspora in *The Namesake*

Indian middle-class women are considered to be the custodians of cultural specificity since they are less assimilated, both culturally and linguistically, into the wider society. Jhumpa Lahiri in her narratives traces the vacillation of the Bengali women migrants who have to migrate after marriage into an alien land and are hence driven by both anxiety and desire to appropriate the culture of the 'other'. Lahiri in her interview admits 'It bothered me growing up, the feeling that there was

---

[4]Bhabha (2004) conceptualises a postcolonial identity through language as the 'third space of enunciation' in *Location of Culture*.

[5]Bourdieu (1991) provides an excellent study of interrelationship between language and power in his book *Language and Symbolic Power*.

[6]Kenneth Burke's *Rhetoric of Motives* accentuates this point.

[7]Oratory as an art of speaking, since the time of Plato and Aristotle in ancient Greece, has been acknowledged as an essential practical art in a democratic society, an art that empowered citizens 'to deliberate among themselves'.

no single place to which I fully belong' (2016). In her first novel, *The Namesake*, Ashima who has migrated to Massachusetts with her newly wedded husband soon ventures to reformulate her identity in the process of communication with the ethnic diaspora. For Ashima, cultural identity seems to be a collective, shared history among individuals affiliated by race or ethnicity that is stable. It is therefore important for her to retain the Bengali custom of honouring the decision of the elders in naming her child. It is equally important for her to associate with other Bengali immigrants in her neighbourhood and invite them for special occasions at home like Gogol's rice ceremony:

> As the baby grows, so, too, does their circle of Bengali acquaintances...they all come from Calcutta, and for this reason alone they are friends...the husbands are teachers, researchers, doctors, engineers. The wives, homesick and bewildered, turn to Ashima for recipes and advice...they sit in circles on the floor, singing songs by Nazrul and Tagore ... They argue riotously over the films of Ritwik Ghatak versus those of Satyajit Ray. The CPIM versus the Congress party. North Calcutta versus South. (Lahiri 2004, 38)

It is to be noted that the cultural and political affiliations of these individuals are also based upon their shared collective memory of the lost homeland. While the men have willingly migrated in search of better prospects, the wives have been offered limited choice. They are able to recreate an imaginary homeland[8] through the rhetorical process of persuasion, argument and identification. Notice the phrase 'argue riotously' which underlines the rhetorical agency of these women to debate and deliberate within a closed social circle. Kenneth Burke has proposed a 'new rhetoric' in the postmodern age the key term of which is identification. According to Burke this identification is neither complete deliberation nor unconscious appeal, but 'lies midway between aimless utterance and speech directly purposive'.[9] So while differences may exist among members of the group, these are hidden in the process of identification with a shared culture. The women nurture their sociability by constructing a collective sense of culture and history. Yet, this social and cultural affinity with other female members of the community does not allow Ashima to assert her individuality, to articulate her needs or to become liberated from the social roles of a wife and of a mother. She realises that her name signifies a limitlessness which she desires: 'True to the meaning of her name, she will be without borders, without a home of her own, a resident everywhere and nowhere' (Lahiri 2004, 276).

---

[8]Imaginary Homeland uses this term to discuss how racism manifests a crisis of culture in the country of adoption.

[9]Kenneth Burke has an extensive study of identification as a trope of new rhetoric in the postmodern age.

Memory: Individual and Cultural

Stuart Hall underlines two different perspectives to the notion of 'cultural identity'. The first position defines 'cultural identity' in terms of a shared culture, a shared history and ancestry which form a collective 'one true self'. This shared identity provides people with stable, unchanging and continuous frames of reference and meaning. The second view recognises that despite some points of similarity, there are also critical points of deep and significant differences which 'constitute "what we really are", or rather—since history has intervened—"what we have become"' (1993, 94). Cultural identities are subject to the continuous 'play' of history, culture and power. Ashima and the other women construct a collective memory in shaping their lives in this new land. In this context, we require to chart out the differences between individual memory (the act of memory as a subjective process) and cultural memory (memory as a product of interaction among members of the diaspora community). The nostalgic memory of the pristine past is a constructed narrative of every diaspora. Stuart Hall rightly argues that the reconstruction of the past is complexly mediated and transformed 'by memory, fantasy, narrative and myth' (1993, 226). This shared national culture restricts any social exchange with the other mainstream American community. This is the failure of the 'third space of enunciation' as Homi K. Bhabha explains in *The Location of Culture*:

> The non-synchronous temporality of global and national cultures opens up a cultural space – a third space – where the negotiation of incommensurable differences creates a tension peculiar to borderline existences...hybrid hyphenisations emphasize the incommensurable elements as the basis of cultural identities. (Bhabha 2004, 218)

It is crucial to recognise that Ashima does not articulate any subjective personal memory of her childhood days. Her own memory is subsumed in the collective memory of the other immigrants. There is no oral history or testimony which she can share with her children who grow up to repudiate their cultural ethnicity, being forced to undertake compulsory visits to their country of origin. Ashima's future plans also are subsumed by the plans of her family. Thus it seems that lack of her rhetorical memory limits her agency in the new country. Ashima's experiences during her pregnancy, her distaste for food, the heavy and dizzy sensations and the swollen feet, are experiences of any pregnant woman across borders. However, Ashima's distress caused by the idea of motherhood in a foreign land, isolated from her family, is distinctive of a diasporic woman. Moreover, even after years of staying abroad, the feeling of alienation and distress is hard to overcome.

> For being a foreigner, Ashima is beginning to realize, is a sort of lifelong pregnancy – a perpetual wait, a constant burden, a continuous feeling out of sorts. It is an ongoing responsibility, a parenthesis in what has once been ordinary life, only to discover that the previous life has vanished, replaced by something more complicated and demanding. (Lahiri 2004, 49)

Ashima is bound by her domestic chores of cooking, childbearing and rearing within the domestic space of her American household. Her domestic space is circumscribed to her house at Pemberton Road, the neighbourhood market and the shared homogenous space of immigrant Bengali community. But when Ashima visits Calcutta, she acquires a different identity of Monu (her petname by which her relatives know her). She is neither responsible for any household chores there nor is she confined to her domestic space.

> For eight months she does not set foot in a kitchen. She wanders freely around a city in which Gogol, in spite of his many visits, has no sense of direction. (Lahiri 2004, 83)

It takes more than two decades for Ashima to become independent in America. She has always considered herself as a foreigner in America, unable to call the house at Pemberton Road as her home. She becomes more liberated and exercises her rhetorical agency when her son and daughter grow up and settle elsewhere. She starts working at a public library and decides to stay back at home alone, when her husband takes up a 9-month research project outside Cleveland. She makes American friends at the library, spends time by herself (without having to worry about familial responsibilities), stops sitting down for elaborate meals and drives the car. Yet, she is caught in the rhetoric of ambivalence, tied both to her ethnic identity and her American lifestyle. The hyphen in her status is the space of conflict, ambivalence and negotiation.[10]

Woman Diaspora in *The Lowland*

The Lowland, Lahiri's latest novel has a young widow, Gauri, who migrates to America after she marries Subhash, the brother of her ex-husband. Lahiri scripts a unique diasporic experience for Gauri although she almost shares the same subject position as Ashima—a middle-class Bengali woman migrating to America after her marriage. Yet, Gauri's experiences are different since she has been a witness to the state-orchestrated violence inflicted upon her first husband. Udayan was killed by the police for his involvement in a radical student movement in 1970s Bengal known as the Naxalbari uprising. Gauri was living the life of a lonely pregnant widow in her in-law's house and a prime suspect for the police as the wife of a dead Naxalite. The decision to marry Subhash after her husband Udayan's death and thus escape from the forsaken and dreary life of a widow in a Bengali household was not taken by Gauri willfully. Subhash saves her from this turmoil, marries her against his parents' wishes and takes her away to Rhode Island where he teaches at the university. Gauri agrees to marry Subhash, Udayan's twin brother since he

---

[10]In the film adaptation of the novel by Mira Nair, the powerful metaphors of suitcases, bridges and airports express the dual identity of the immigrants and their continuous state of transition between the land of origin and the land of adoption.

resembles her dead husband. Though she feels grateful towards Subhash for offering her an escape route from the drudgery of widowhood, she fails to love him.

> She'd wanted to leave Tollygunge. To forget everything her life had been. And he had handed her the possibility. In the back of her mind she told herself she could come one day to love him, out of gratitude if nothing else. (Lahiri 2013, 127)

Gauri's migration is supposed to liberate her from the traumatic memories of the state manoeuvered violence perpetrated against her husband. Yet, the rest of her life as an immigrant in America is spent in the act of remembering her time spent with her first husband, Udayan. Her borderline existence as a widow, her complicity in the student revolution, her guilt (of escaping death while her husband was killed) added to her political and cultural dislocation pushes her to transgress further from the stereotypical role of passive femininity.

Rhetorical Agency and Memory

I wish to focus on the act of remembering as a rhetorical process, we need to register not simply the facts which are remembered but enquire into the process of remembrance (how), the agency (by whom), the purpose (why) and its effect on the audience. In other words, reclaiming memory is a rhetorical process since it involves issues of agency, truth claims and relations of power.[11] Gauri consciously deletes the memory of the night of brutal killing of Udayan but chooses to remember the happy times spent with him. Her function of selecting, constructing and revising memory has given her agency to deliberate and engage in internal rhetoric or self-persuasion. She constantly participates in an internal dialogue with conflicting voices of the rhetorical self. Unlike Ashima of *The Namesake*, Gauri does not wish to interact with the other Indian diaspora. Her personal memory of the political uprising in Bengal and of Udayan's role in it does not match with the harmonious nostalgic, collective memories of the other Indians. The conversation of Subhash and Gauri on their way back home from the first social gathering makes it clear:

> The women seemed friendly. Who were they?
>
> I don't remember the names, she said.
>
> The enthusiasm she'd mustered in the company of others had been discarded. She seemed tired, perhaps annoyed. He wondered if she had not really enjoyed herself, if she she'd only been pretending. Still he persisted.
>
> Should we invite a few of them to our place, sometime?
>
> It's up to you.
>
> They might be helpful, after the baby comes.

---

[11]The idea is borrowed from the Ph.D. dissertation of Tammie M. Kennedy titled *Reclaiming Memoria for Writing Pedagogies*.

I don't need their advice.

I meant as companions.

I don't want to spend my time with them.

Why not, Gauri?

I have nothing in common with them, she said. (Lahiri 2013, 140)

It is interesting to see how the experiences of the two Bengali women migrating to America after their marriage have almost nothing in common. The archetypal notion of categorising all Indian women diaspora into one bracket seems grossly erroneous. While Ashima's world is restricted to Ashok and her Bengali neighbours in Massachusetts (for a larger part of her life), Gauri lives a life alienated from Subhash and his Indian friends in Rhode Island. Gauri's memory is personal and resistant to public articulation. She does not need to construct her diasporic identity by sharing the same cultural values of the community. Yet, Gauri's personal memory also provides the lens to view the political landscape of the Naxalite movement of 1970s Bengal. So her memory constructs a survivor's testimony of the political narrative of a momentous event in the pages of Indian history. Can her personal, traumatic and selective memory with radical breaks, gaps and repetitions be trusted as an authentic narrative of the past? History with its objective accuracy has been criticised by postmodernists for a singular version of the past. Many scholars have thus relied on oral testimonies and subjective impressions of refugees, war victims and survivors of calamities since memory seems to offer a more cautious and qualified lens to view the past. Yet, the appeal to memory in determining the events of the past is as problematic as historical authenticity.

Gauri's personal memory is traumatic and unique, thus not to be shared with others. Her memory makes her feel alienated from the other expatriates. Her location in the margins of her own ethnic community provides an impetus to assimilate with the Americans. Gauri starts to attend Philosophy lectures at the University, interacts with American classmates and professors, discards her ethnic clothing and adopts western wear within a few months of her migration. Her clothing is a shield, a mask, a refuge from her cultural alienation. She wants to erase her identity as an erstwhile widow of Udayan, a wife of Subhash and a mother of Bela. In the beginning, she escapes for a few minutes leaving 5-year-old Bela alone in the house. These few minutes away from home, away from her duties as a mother, give her a space to pause, to reflect and to deliberate on her life.

The five minutes doubled to ten, sometimes a bit more. Fifteen minutes to be alone, to clear her head. It was time to run across the quadrangle to the library to return a book, a simple errand she could have done at any time but that she was determined to accomplish at that moment. Time to go to the post office and send a letter, requesting an application for one of the doctoral programs Otto Weiss had suggested she look into. Time to speculate that, without Bela or Subhash, her life might be a different thing..... So it began in the afternoons. Not every afternoon but often enough, too often. Disoriented by the sense of freedom, devouring the sensation as a beggar devours food. (Lahiri 2013, 174)

Later, she escapes from the responsibilities of a family life forever. Gauri's transgression from the role of a dutiful wife and caring mother to a solitary, self-absorbed academician results in a symbolic and literal exclusion of her 'home'. Her rhetorical agency goads her to negotiate, deliberate, plan ahead and plunge into action. She feels alienated from her husband and daughter and ultimately decides to take up a job and shift to a new locale, California. She neither consults Subhash about her plan, nor informs him before leaving the house. She asserts her multicultural identity, travelling across America without any boundaries, without any moorings and juggles multiple temporary lovers. Once she even indulges in a sexual relationship with a female research student to explore her sexual orientation. A new spatial parameter outside home permits her to transgress moral and sexual codes set by the patriarchal middle-class society. The hyphen in her status sanctions Gauri the space for self-conception and rhetorical agency. But she cannot erase her ethnic identity:

> And yet she remained, in spite of her western clothes, her western academic interests, a woman who spoke English with a foreign accent, whose physical appearance and complexion were unchangeable and against the backdrop of most of America, still unconventional. She continued to introduce herself by an unusual name, the first given by her parents, the last by the two brothers she had wed. (Lahiri 2013, 236)

Gauri is not able to erase the old memories of her past life with Udayan either. A material artefact like a wooden table ordered in America floods her mind with unbidden memories. The visual image and aroma of the teak reminds her of the furniture at her home in Tollygunge—'the wardrobe and dressing table, the bed with slim posts on which she and Udayan had created Bela' (Lahiri 2013, 242). The table thus works as a vehicle of memory but interestingly it strategically freezes the memory to a particular moment of passion—the memory of lovemaking with Udayan on the bed. Unlike Ashima in *The Namesake*, Gauri never travels back to her native land. Yet Gauri's life is a constant negotiation between her memories, her desire and her motivated impending action.

Second-Generation Women Diaspora

Lahiri, a second-generation diaspora herself, is able to identify with the conflicting desires and anxieties of American born children of diaspora parents. The author also speaks of attempting to strike a balance between pleasing her parents and her American peers to meet both their expectations. For the female expatriate, rhetoric is a negotiated space of enunciation as she refuses to be restricted within a stable, homogeneous, ethnic sociocultural identity. As second-generation diaspora, Moushumi, Ashima's daughter-in-law, in *The Namesake* seeks to repudiate her Bengali identity and seeks inclusion in an American way of living. Moushumi promises herself never to marry a Bengali man as desired by her parents but agrees to marry Gogol after he has changed his name to Nikhil or (Americanized) Nick.

Similarly, she attains expertise in a third foreign language, French, to celebrate her multicultural identity. In another instance, she is compelled to wear a sari on her wedding day since the wedding ceremony was organised by her parents according to the Bengali custom. However, on the day of her reception, Gogol changes into a suit while she changes into a red Banarasi gown with spaghetti straps. She wears the gown in spite of her mother's protests and happily bares her slim bronze shoulders for the rest of the evening having purposely left the shawl behind. When she was just 5 years old, Moushumi was asked by her relatives in India if she planned to get married in a red sari or a white gown. Her red Banarasi gown is a tool of empowerment, a device to break away from traditional homogenous cultures and power structures. She self-fashions herself as a global citizen and resists any attempt to ghettoise her identity in America.

In *The Lowland* we come across a second-generation diaspora Bela, who is brought up by her stepfather and uncle Subhash singlehandedly since the time her mother Gauri left the house. Bela's inclusion within the American society is not a repudiation of her own culture but rather an urge to fill the void in her life left by her absent mother. She becomes an extrovert, embraces the western lifestyle, gets involved in social activities and spends time working in a farm.

> She wore denim coveralls, heavy soiled boots, a cotton kerchief tied over her hair. She woke at four in the morning. A man's undershirt with the sleeves pushed up to her shoulders, dark strips of leather knotted around her wrist in place of bangles. Each time there was something new to take in. A tattoo that was like an open cuff above her ankle. A bleached section of her hair. A silver hoop in her nose. (Lahiri 2013, 222)

She refuses to travel with her father to Calcutta when her grandmother expires. Her agency in negotiating life on her own terms does not seem to create a tension with her hybrid bohemian identity. Yet she seems to reject the feminine self in order to disclaim the mother figure. Bela is informed about her real father Udayan, Gauri's first husband, when she herself is about to become a single parent to her unborn child. But Bela's failure to relate to her ethnic background is caused by her inability to identify or remember her real parents Gauri and Udayan. Thus the primordial link with her homeland has been snapped when she loses the memory of her parents.

Conclusion

Jhumpa Lahiri challenges any homogenous, singular representation of the women diaspora. The novelist traces the trajectory of their lives from physical, material displacement and alienation to a celebration of multicultural, fluid identity politics. In *The Namesake*, the first-generation woman suffers from a double consciousness as she tries to coordinate between her ethnic culture and the borrowed culture. The second-generation woman, as a beneficiary of an American system of education and economic growth, has the rhetorical agency to deliberate, exercise choice and move towards a purposive action. In *The Lowland*, a woman located in the margins of her society gets assimilated within the mainstream American culture, but is still haunted by her memories. Her multiple locations across geographical, cultural and psychic boundaries enable her to move beyond any fixed definition of femininity. The daughter of such a woman born in a foreign land rejects her mother and her mother's history, language and ethnicity and instead adopts a hybrid bohemian culture. It is certain that the experiences of the women diaspora who migrate under obligation or compulsion are definitely different from the experiences of the male migrants. Lahiri, however, shows that women are not simply custodians of culture and memory. They are complex subjects struggling with the desires of the future and trauma of the past and often get estranged from their home, their language and even from their own selves. Kristeva refuses to define a 'woman': a woman is 'that which cannot be represented, that which is not spoken, that which remains outside naming and ideologies' (Kristeva 1974, 21). Kristeva attempts to subvert the phallocentric symbolic order which defines a woman as marginal. The polyphonic narratives of *The Namesake* and *The Lowland* similarly articulate the dissenting voice of the 'other', that is, the multicultural woman, who challenges her stereotypical representation in a globalised world still dominated by patriarchy.

References

Bhabha, Homi K. 2004. *The Location of Culture*. London and New York: Routledge.
Bourdieu, Pierre. 1991. *Language and Symbolic Power. Translated by Gino Raymond and Matthew Adamson*. Cambridge: Harvard University Press.
Fanon, Frantz. 1967. *The Wretched of the Earth. Translated by Constance Farrington*. Harmondsworth: Penguin.
Hall, Stuart. 1993. Cultural Identity and Diaspora, Colonial Discourse and Post-colonial Theory: A Reader. Edited by Patrick Williams and Laura Chrisman. New York: Harvester Wheatsheaf.
Kristeva, Julia. Autumn, 1974. "La Femme." Tel Quel 59.
Lahiri, J. 2004. *The Namesake*. New Delhi: Harper Collins Publishers.
Lahiri, J. 2013. *The Lowland*. India: Random House.
Lahiri, J. 2015. *In Other Words. Translated from the Italian by Anne Goldstein*. Penguin Group: Hamish Hamilton.
Lahiri, Jhumpa. 2016. Jhumpa Lahiri on her Debut Novel: An Interview with the Author. http://hinduism.about.com/library/weekly/extra/bl-jhumpainterview.htm#. Accessed 31 Mar.
Mehta, Sandhya Rao. 2015. Exploring Gender in the Literature of the Indian Diaspora. UK: Cambridge Scholars Publishing.
Mishra, Vijay. 2007. *The Literature of the Indian Diaspora: Theorizing the Diasporic Imaginary*. London: Taylor & Francis Group.
Radhakrishnan, R. 1996. *Diasporic Mediations: Between Home and Location*. Minneapolis: University of Minnesota Press.

Chapter 4
Freedom or Subjugation: Interpreting the Subjectivity of Women in Indian Diaspora Communities

Sheetal Sharma

Introduction

For ages people have been moving—from one place to another. As humanity settled and cultures evolved, different communities came in contact with each other for a variety of purposes. Gradually the movement of people started getting defined technically as migration, along with associated concepts/terms such as legal or illegal migration, displacement, exodus, seasonal, temporary, permanent, emigration, immigration and so on. Migration necessarily entails the movement of individuals, of groups or of communities, from one place to another in search of better living conditions, of sources of livelihood, safety, freedom, protection or of seeking refuge, or saving life from natural disasters. People who move in search of work, safety and better opportunities to different locations are cultural beings with a set of sociocultural characteristics that are diverse in nature and are a product of the history of their respective societies. Throughout history, people have settled in different areas and locations—near or far—across continents and regions. These settlers have come to be known as diaspora communities. These groups of people or migrants collectively form what is known as a diaspora.[1] Brubaker (2005, 1–9) refers to

---

[1] 'Diaspora' originally referred to major historical migrations, such as the scattering of the Jews from Israel. Although the term refers to the physical dispersal of Jews throughout the world, it also carries religious, philosophical, political, and eschatological connotations, in as much as Jews perceive a special relationship between the land of Israel and themselves. The term 'diaspora' comes from the Greek, which means scattered or dispersed. Some other instances include the colonial expansion of the Greeks, the removal through slavery of millions of Africans, and the exile of Armenians following massacres by the Turks in the early twentieth century (http://oxforddictionaries.com/definition/english/diaspora and http://www.britannica.com/EBchecked/topic/161756/Diaspora).

S. Sharma (✉)
Centre for European Studies, School of International Studies,
Jawaharlal Nehru University, New Delhi 110067, India
e-mail: sheetal88@gmail.com; sheetal@mail.jnu.ac.in

© Springer Nature Singapore Pte Ltd. 2018
A. Pande (ed.), *Women in the Indian Diaspora*,
https://doi.org/10.1007/978-981-10-5951-3_4

'diaspora' as: '...group[s] of people dispersed from their home country for socio-economic and other reasons. It refers to particular cultural and ethnic communities spread [out] in different parts of the world, who continue to maintain links with their homeland, follow their religion, speak [the] native language, and retain a sense of belongingness... [in] identi[fying] ... [with] their native culture and community'.

The diaspora community has diverse sociocultural influences both on the areas to which they move—or the destination, and the areas from which they have moved out of—the origin. They profoundly affect the sociocultural fabric of society—both at the destination and at the origin.

The phenomenon of migration and settlement of diaspora communities in any given area is multidimensional in nature. The subject can be analysed from both, the quantitative perspective and the qualitative perspective. When analysed from the quantitative perspective, studies on diaspora and migration tend to take into account aspects related to numbers and the profiles of the members of this diaspora community (age, skill, category, education, last residence, etc.); the (re)distribution of population due to migration over time and space; patterns of migration or migratory flows like rural to urban, urban to rural, urban to urban and rural to rural; settlement patterns of diaspora groups; the duration of the migration (temporary, long term, seasonal); reasons for the initial migration including any push and pull factors; and also an understanding of objectives, intended causes and consequences of migration.

On the other hand, the qualitative aspects of the process of migration and the consequent settlement of diaspora communities concern themselves on the one hand with the structural and institutional changes produced by the migratory flows, and on the other with the diaspora and their relationships with the process of the sociocultural transformation of the host society. The qualitative dimension also includes the interaction between the cultures of the destination and host society. It is interesting to study this interaction from a sociological perspective. At times, the integration of the diaspora community in the host country is smooth and harmonious. However at times, it may pose challenges for both the host society and the incomers as is the case in the contemporary times. Although different social, cultural and emotional issues have always been interwoven with the movement of people across borders and the establishment of diaspora communities, but in recent decades these issues have become sources of friction between the host country and the set of people coming from other areas. The sociocultural differences and distinctiveness of migrants and diaspora communities, their integration and acceptance in host societies, their religious affiliations, their distinct identities, their exclusion or marginalisation and the phenomena of xenophobia and racism are some of the emerging challenges that national governments are commonly facing (Sharma 2013).

Yet another important qualitative dimension includes analysing the process of migration and diaspora communities from a feminist perspective. Scholars call the current era—'The Age of Migration', because five phenomena characterise the nature of migration in contemporary times: its *globalisation* (there are a greater number of countries affected by migratory movements); its *acceleration* (reflected in an increased volume of migrants); its *differentiation* (migrants moving to a single country belong to a variety of ethnicities and groups); its *politicisation* (domestic policies, bilateral and regional relations and national security policies of States are being increasingly affected by concerns about the risks of international migration and vice-versa); and its *feminisation.*[2] The feminist framework of analysis attempts to study the subjective state of mind of women in diaspora communities and/or lived experiences of migrant women. Analysing from a qualitative perspective the feminist perspective attempts to explore the experiences of women in everyday life far away from their homeland. Women who at times are working, and in most cases accompanying their spouses tend to experience the shift in a different manner. While dealing with the everyday reality in a strange land how they negotiate and manage to hold on to the traditional way of life that they had been socialised into since childhood. Caught between the two extremes of freedom and liberty to choose and lead life according to their own choices on the one hand and the pain of physical and cultural distanciation from the home country on the other, how women belonging to the diaspora community at times find themselves caught between the opposites and challenging environments.

Women in Diaspora

In the last two decades owing to globalisation and international streams of migrations running across the globe, migration as a phenomenon and its dimensions are being studied and researched thoroughly. A vast amount of literature exists on migration, the diaspora communities and their experiences. However, there is paucity of research on the experiences of migrant women in general and about Indian women in particular. Migrants, both males and females, experience massive social, cultural and psychological transformation in the host country. They confront a new culture, discard some traditional practices, learn to adapt to new circumstances and in the process evolve different mechanisms to cope with the new way of life and adopt distinct ways of life over time. Gender and its associated aspects have rarely been paid attention to while conducting studies on migration, and the associated processes of cultural change and adaptation. The diaspora communities and migrant groups are often treated as gender neutral, or in homogeneous terms, and the gender-specific experiences and dimensions of migration are ignored. Women have remained almost invisible in studies related to diaspora and migration in India. Although there are statistics pertaining to their numbers and as a percentage among the total population; however the socioeconomic contributions,

---

[2]Castles and Miller (1998).

psychological experiences, the strategies to cope with change in the new cultural setup, etc., have not been taken into account adequately or studied in detail. During the 1970 and early 1980s there was an inherent assumption in the diaspora studies that migration is an androcentric phenomenon and so women were either not recognised or were just seen as accompanying men as spouses or other dependents, like daughters, mothers sisters, etc. Buijs (1993) observed that until the mid-1970s, women were invisible in the study of diaspora communities. Their experiences were understudied despite the fact that women constitute almost half of the percentage of diaspora and of the total migrants at an international level. Though they have been a part of the families that have migrated, the focus remained mostly on the males and there was a silence on the presence of women. But:

> the past decades have seen an increase in women autonomous migration as the main economic providers or – breadwinners for their families. Men and women show differences in their migratory behaviours, face different opportunities and have to cope with different risks and challenges, such as vulnerability to human rights abuses, exploitation, discrimination and specific health risks. Therefore, it is becoming increasingly obvious that migration is not a – gender-neutral phenomenon. From the very moment they decide to migrate, women's experience as migrants differs from that of men.[3]

In recent years, a few attempts have been made by scholars to study the 'lived experiences' of women in diaspora communities. Migration or a change of place leads to a sudden disconnect from the homeland. The change of place or dislocation carries with it narratives of separation, issues of identity, quest of belongingness, anxiety of confronting the new and the unfamiliar, the struggle for establishment, the need for strategy to cope with the strange and stability. It also involves the quest of finding meaningfulness of the purpose, and desire to connect what is lost and what is found. Most of the literature dealing with psychological aspects of migration tends to subsume the experiences of women as similar to men and does not require special investigation. The lived experiences of women who migrate from their homelands either alone or with their husband or families are very rich and varied. There are several dimensions of this experience. The movement involves change in established economic, cultural, social and familial dynamics. Yet another important issue pertaining to women is whether this shift or displacement brings about any change in the status of women as well. For example, do they think that their experiences of migration to the other country, say developed western society, dilute Indian patriarchal structures to any degree and enhance women's autonomy or do they perpetuate dependency and the further subjugation of women?

---

[3]Caritas Paper page 2.

Women in Indian Diaspora and Their Everyday Experiences

After India gained independence, a new phase of migration began from India to the western countries primarily as a consequence of rising pressure on limited resources. An expanding population and shrinking resources acted as a push factor for people from the middle class, especially young professionals and semi-skilled workers, to go abroad for better prospects. Many of these immigrants were semi-skilled and had low educational or professional qualification. Hailing mostly from rural areas, they knew little or no English. A large number of immigrants were those who had lost their homes, property and jobs during the partition of India in 1947. Many anthropological studies have been done on these migrant groups present all over the world. Owing to its colonial connections a special focus has always been on the Indian community or the Indian migrants in the UK. These studies establish that the social life and emotional bonding of the people from South Asia during these years centred around members of their own community. Women appeared in these studies in a very limited manner but nevertheless one can identify specific phases in the literature about the life and experiences of women in the diaspora community.

Many of the studies on diaspora communities focussed upon the anthropological accounts of the extended families and kinship network, particularly among the Punjabi families, who had migrated after independence to western countries for better prospects. Women in these works were described as the carriers of culture from the homeland. The anthropological accounts were qualitative and in-depth in nature. They discussed and narrated the concept of family honour (*izzat*), the traditions, celebration of festivals, arranged marriages, inter-generational conflicts, customs such as purdah, etc., women were seen as the link between the new and the old. According to Ahmad (2003):

> …some of the newer research on British second and third-generation diasporic subjects – the daughters and grand-daughters of these early pioneers – stresses issues such as 'identity', hybridity, agency and social change, and seeks to situate subjects as diverse and dynamic politicized individuals within both macro- and micro- contexts. Influenced by contemporary post-structuralist and feminist responses, researchers are further encouraged to engage with questions of subjectivity, power dynamics and self-reflection.[4]

Compared to the past women have, in recent years, a different set of experiences which have emanated from their identity and their status as women. According to Pandurang (2003):

> There are standpoints of women that are particular to their specific contexts. If for example we take the category of middle-class Indian woman, whose position is marked by certain class privileges, many women who migrate to the US are wives of green-card-holding professional men and these women are often themselves highly qualified professionals.

---

[4]Ahmad (2003), p. 45.

Yet because of technicalities of the visa issued to them, their dependence is sanctioned and enforced by law.

This status of dependency or lack of any formal position for educated women creates a complex of psychological, emotional and material problems. These frustrations and emotional problems often get accentuated when they are seen in the context of expectations that these women have about the host society. The western world is often portrayed as liberating space for women. The images that are shown particularly in the media, of western liberated, educated, empowered and free women, often tend to get settled in the psyche of many of the migrant women before they depart for their destination. But while facing reality, many of these images or constructions are challenged. Thus the gap between expectations and actual reality is often the source of much of the dissatisfaction for migrant women.

> Does the educated Indian middle-class woman, in the process of migrating, view the movement out of the geographical space of the home culture as an opportunity to go beyond her middle-class social status, and explore the possibilities of 'the agentive new woman', or is her role one of being a vital link in the continuum of culture of the sending society, largely already pre-defined? (Pandurang 2003)

For many of these young brides, the responsibility of balancing tradition with modernity, maintaining a cultural connect becomes a 'painful struggle' (Pandurang 2003, 89–90). These women tend to make several sacrifices in order to manage and establish families in the new land.

In contemporary times, with advanced means of communication and technology, remaining in touch with families is no longer an issue. With mediums such as whatsapp, skype, video calls, email, etc., there is a continuous contact among people and families who have migrated. The diaspora community does not feel disconnected with the family despite being physically located at a distance, unlike in the past when even a simple post used to take months to reach. Communication today has reduced the distance. Revolution in the means of communication technology has its own benefits but it generates stress as well. Indirectly it also acts as a binding force, and in some cases it becomes a source of constant vigil and checks on whether family practices are being followed, and among members in a family the onus/burden of following the family norms and traditions lies primarily on the women. Women in diaspora families are often caught between the two worlds or cultures, they find themselves torn between the freedom and liberty offered by the western culture and environment and the force of tradition binding them to their own value system, which is often backward. Mala Pandurang writes that:

> …the strong popularity of Bollywood films (popular Hindi films), and innumerable websites hosted for and by Indians abroad, which offer viewing of television serials in Indian languages (sonytv.com, numtv.com), bring the visual presence of the homeland right into the domestic space of emigrant homes. This in turn allows for the continued internalization of patriarchal constructs and ensures that, while the new Indian citizen may be physically dispersed within the boundaries of another state, s/he will remain culturally part of the homeland." (2003, 91)

The process of physical dislocation generates conditions of confusion among women. In patrilineal societies women tend to move to their husband's house after marriage. The new residence, environment and culture offer the joys of a new marriage and the sorrows of departing from the near and dear ones. Women have to continuously work in these new situations often making adjustments and compromises to create and sustain new relationships and maintain harmony with the self and with others as well. All these adjustments and compromises are interestingly expected from the new bride without questioning the established tradition. Similarly when women move out to other countries, they are expected to make adjustment and compromises even in hostile or discriminatory environment in order to settle a new household. For instance, places where one can come across instances or environment of racial discrimination, where the migrant population is well aware of the social tension and conflict in everyday life, in such situations, based on their experience from the past, women employ coping strategies to adjust to the new environment, which often poses adverse situations and conditions.

According to Jain (2006, 2312):

> In most cases in the north Indian families, a girl goes through experiences of various types in the form of anticipatory socialisation for her future adjustment in stable marriages. After marriage, she moves out to another set of living patterns with varying degrees of similarities and differences in values she has lived within her family of orientation. Coping with excitement of new experiences and both joys and traumas of new situations involves most women into constantly working on their capabilities of creating and then sustaining new relationships. Their social competence in the various arenas of action over the years keeps the cultural process of life-long learning alive.

In whatever role, women are expected to conform to tradition and maintain the cultural system.

It is interesting to note that the issue of the subjectivity of women in diaspora communities gets 'inextricably linked to nation-ness' (Bhattacharjee 1992). The connections between diaspora communities are important for maintaining the idea of the nation, and the cultural connect in foreign nations is created through the patterns of pre-defined roles that the woman is expected to perform. Women perform the rituals, follow the traditions, celebrate the festivals and act as a link between the home culture and the host nation. Emphasising the strong role of cultural socialisation shaping the mental constructs of women, Jain (2010, 52) describes that 'sustaining a given social structure over a period of time, social reproduction processes include complex social construction that is based on values and the social production of meanings. In this sense, straddling of transmigrant families being and belonging into two (or in some cases more than two) cultures poses a situation of conflict and tension with reference to the social space which is appropriated by a hegemonic class (the 'whites' in the case of South Africa) as a tool to reproduce its dominance'. Women are often also engaged in maintaining traditions because of the reason that the image of 'Indian culture' that community members want to portray to the host society. Bhatia (2007), writes that 'several scholars studying issues related to diasporic identity note that South Asian women are often the victims of the community's attempt to present itself as a spiritual, traditional, and homogeneous group with ancient cultural roots'. In the work Bhatia quotes Dasgupta (1998, 5), that, 'The main casualty of our communities' efforts to reformulate homogenous "authenticity" is women... South-Asian women in America are given the task of perpetuating anachronistic customs and traditions'. Mentioning the work of yet another scholar, Bhatia writes that 'thus, scholars examining the construction of South Asian women in the diaspora argue that they are struggling to "know" their place in society (Mani 1994). On one hand, they have to face racial discrimination from the larger American society and prejudice as brown minority women, but on the other hand, they have to deal with the oppression in their own communities' (Bhatia 2007, 38).

Identifying the struggles that women in diaspora face, Bhatia (2007, 38–39) points out that all the scholars indicate that 'it is essentially that the acculturation of many non-white, non-European/Western immigrants, especially women, to the US society is a painful, difficult, and complex process. Their acculturation process occurs at the intersection of race, gender, and nationality and represents the different personal and cultural 'I' positions of the diasporic self'. According to Anderson and Jack, 'Indian women often do not express their thoughts and feelings whenever or wherever they try to talk about their lives' (1991, 11). Indians as an ethnic entity are a very close-knit group, and there are chances that the personal or lived experiences of women will soon become public if they are discussed with one other. Thus, the personal and private experiences and their narratives remain within the family circle and any discussion with the outsiders is not encouraged, especially when women are outside their own country. It is feared that these stories will turn into gossip and it will damage the reputation of the family, its respect and social status. Women thus become bearers of family's honour and social pride despite the fact that they may be unduly subjugated under certain circumstances. Although there are many women migrants who have migrated because of economic reasons, a majority of them have accompanied their husbands who have taken up a profession in a developed country. Once these migrants settle in the new country, women remain confined to homes, managing household dutifully and also struggling to look for avenues to have a part time professional engagement or career. Thus even working and professional women back home are subjected to domestic division of labour and in the line of their husband's professional aspirations, they sacrifice their ambitions. The everyday life experiences of women are full of narratives of the struggle to strike a balance between and understand what they have achieved at the cost of what or one may say, rather taking account of what all they have lost?

Women in diaspora communities face a conflict in their lives because of dis-location from their home country. This conflict stems from the difference between their cultural setup and the cultural fabric of the host country. Faist (2004) remarks that, while actively participating in 'transnational space', transmigrant women negotiate many critical matters associated with the continuation of family rela-tionships which they shape, maintain and reshape through social networks. Most of the time such social networks include dispersed family members and the creation of new spaces for transnational households, by deploying new household strategies and practices. Further, Ramusack and Sievers express that in traditional Indian society, men have higher status than women, and 'Indian men retained the authority accorded to them by a patriarchal, extended family structure' (1999, 43). The patriarchal family structure implies that the very nature of the Indian families is male dominated, where women are accorded subordinate status to men and thus they are often not allowed to speak or express their views. Clifford (1994) writes that 'women in the diaspora remain attached to, and [are] empowered by, a "home" culture and a tradition—selectively…women sustaining and reconnecting diaspora ties do so critically, as strategies for survival in a new context'.

Along with maintaining the household and carrying out their domestic duties women of the diaspora confront yet another critical challenge, that of bringing up children. Brought up in a new country where language, cultural assumptions and norms largely differ from their home countries, children in migrant families often have to make a choice between the two cultures. It is often seen that growing up and socialising in a different culture these children are more comfortable with the culture of the host country rather than their 'home' country. This situation becomes much easier for the children when they are born there, in the host country. They tend to perceive the environment as a natural setting. In fact in such cases, the culture of the home country appears strange to them, as and when they come to know about it or experience it when they are back in the 'home' country. Women find it difficult to maintain or strike a balance in such situations. It is quite challenging for women/mothers particularly, to make children understand the importance and relevance of their own culture as against that of the foreign setup. They strive to maintain traditions by celebrating festivals, by also asking the children to participate, to observe the rituals, to perform prayers, etc. However, the third or fourth generation of migrants, even women, often tend to give preference to new ties and the practices of the adopted country. They become distanciated from their own cultural roots and are more part of the country of destination. In such cases, time and nature and degree of contact with people back home play an important role. If the relationship with families back home is intense, then still there are chances of survival of cultural affiliations to some extent. If it is less intense, then naturally these families tend to embrace the foreign culture without much hesitation. After a couple of generations, marriages also happen easily with people from other nationalities or culture. The families now do not oppose their children's wish to marry outside their cultural communities. In contrast, the first generation migrants tend to maintain the cultural links by forcing children to agree to alliances within their own community or at least the nation, which are mostly arranged. According to Jain (2010) 'first generation transmigrant parents tend to create— often through pressure tactics—a "home" culture for their children in the host country. Being and belonging spread out in such diverse situations and parents and children attach, in an unarticulated and unspoken manner, different meanings to the same social phenomenon'. Women in diaspora communities bear the prime responsibility of maintaining cultural continuity in their family in different ways and for different purposes.

Women in the diaspora community also feel a psychological pressure in having to cope with the altered ways of life. Migration to another country does not just change the economic role of a woman, it changes her whole life, her relationship with other members, her role and status in the family. Besides these changed roles, 'some studies of migration processes and its impact recognise that migration influences not only the person herself but also her family, especially those left behind. Their lives are reshaped in a complex manner by the departure of key household members…women who leave their families in order to support them are subject to a huge psychological and emotional burden. They provide love and affection to their employer's children or relatives in order to improve the quality of the lives of their own children, whom they sometimes never see for many years' (Caritas Europa 2009).

On the other hand, it is interesting to note that the strategies adopted by women also point towards the freedom or agency that these women have. No matter how little or limited in scope, these women tend to develop a lifestyle of their own, in which they combine or at least attempt to combine with varying degrees of success, the good elements of both the worlds. Flexible citizenship policies, legal loopholes and easier and faster means of money transfers across transnational spaces offer women's agency to creatively redefine/reshape established normative social practices and also to fulfil their long-cherished aspirations (Jain 2010). The patriarchal structure tends to guide the social behaviour and also poses challenges and limitations to the creative capacities of women. However, women have been quite successful in creating new goals and have the vision to sustain the intricate balance between tradition and modernity. Women with children and family have an all the greater responsibility of maintaining their family culture, at times even against the challenge posed by rebelling children, who wish to pursue their lives as per their own choice.

The stories about the experiences of migrant women are full of struggles, of adjustments, challenges, of compromises and at times of despair and frustration. With the growing quantum of migration, women constitute almost half the total number of migrants the world over. Yet studies continue to focus on the economic and spatial dimensions of migration only. Little attention is paid to the socio-psychological experiences of women in the whole process of migration. The entire journey involves separation from not just the place, but from culture, from near and dear ones, from families and cultural roots. Women and their feelings are often not accounted for in the entire journey of shifting from one location to another. Their presence, their indispensable contribution is often taken for granted. How they feel, how experience the transitions, the compromises they have to make, what challenges they face while settling down in new countries, what are the sources of their tension, how and when they feel frustrated, all these issues are conveniently ignored or are just not discussed. In the patriarchal set up, all this is expected from women. And when husbands move them, the women, are supposed to make these sacrifices—so what is the big deal, everyone makes such sacrifices. These are the explanations generally provided whenever women attempt to express their displeasure, their dissatisfaction while balancing their roles and their responsibilities.

From the constructivist perspective 'everyday life is the dominant site for making sense of the world and of ourselves. The taken for granted, the intersubjective (shared with others) and the ordered (both spatially and temporally) are features of everyday life, originates in people's language, thoughts, and actions' (Rydin and Sjöberg). Everyday behaviour and thoughts create routines and rituals, thereby providing us with what Giddens (1991, 44) calls 'ontological security'. Most of the research on migration and its related aspects focuses on the objective cause and consequences of migration and that too in the public sphere. A large part —associated with the experiences of the migrants, their lives, activities, thoughts, process of adjustments in their personal spheres or in private sphere—remains either under researched or not studied. Experiences in the private sphere have a direct implication on how migrants perceive and interact with the public sphere. Quoting Couldry (2006), Rydin and Sjöberg (2010) write:

> It is about connecting intimate and domestic spaces with the public, the home with society, the local with the national. It is also about asking the question, 'What are the practices that link private action to the public sphere, beyond the obvious act of walking down to the polling station to cast a vote?' And here the experiences of women in particular, are looked at in detail and their role of acting as mediators for creating and maintaining the agendas of social life, (dis) continuity with the homeland and adaptation in the new societies.

Conclusion

To conclude, it can be said that it is still easy to measure the number of migrants at the global level. It is easy to measure various aspects pertaining to their social, educational, demographic composition, remittances, etc. However it is almost impossible to fathom the subjective experiences, the pain and loss of bonding with family and friends when people move from one place to another. If one were to unravel these stories it would be almost beyond human capacity to even accumulate and narrate the experiences, let alone have an empathetic understanding. The quantum and intensity of these experiences increase manifold in the case of women diaspora. As discussed earlier, women face enormous challenges when they have to cope with the opposing forces of change and continuity in the new environment. It is immensely demanding for them to strike a balance and recreate an environment, which is a mix of both, the culture of their home and lifestyle of the host country. Women in the diaspora face these challenges on an everyday basis while dealing with family, children, work and other pressures. However, despite all these varying demands they still manage to take most of the challenges in their stride.

References

Ahmad, F. 2003. Dilemmas, Tensions and Contradictions in Theorizing South Asian Muslim Women. In *South Asian Women in the diaspora*, ed. Nirmal Puwar, and Parvati Raghuram. Oxford: Berg.

Anderson, K., and D.C. Jack. 1991. Learning to Listen: Interview Techniques and Analyses. In *Women's Words: The Feminist Practice of Oral History*, ed. S. Berger Gluck and D. Patai, p. 11–26. New York: Routledge.

Bhatia, Sunil. 2007. *American Karma: Race, Culture, and Identity in the Indian Diaspora*. New York: NYU Press.

Bhattacharjee, A. 1992. The Habit of Ex-nomination: Nation, Woman, and the Indian Immigrant Bourgeoisie. *Public Culture* 5(1): 19–44.

Brubaker, R.W. 2005. The 'Diaspora' Diaspora. *Ethnic and Racial Studies* 28 (1): 1–19.

Buijs, Gina (ed.). 1993. *Migrant Women: Crossing Boundaries and Changing Identities*. Oxford: Berg.

Caritas Europa. 2009. The Social Costs of Labour Migration, Caritas Europa Migration Forum, September 17–19. www.caritas.org/includes/pdf/backgroundmigration.pdf. Retrieved December 10, 2014.

Castles, Stephen, and Mark J. Miller, 1998. The Age of Migration: International Population Movements in the Modern World. In *The Feminisation of Migration: Dreams and Realities of Migrant Women in Four Latin American Countries*, by Cecilia Lipszyc. 2004. The Guilford Press: New York.

Clifford, J. 1994. Diasporas. *Cultural Anthropology* 9 (3): 314.

Couldry, N. 2006. Culture and Citizenship: The Missing Link? *European Journal of Cultural Studies* 9 (3): 321–339.

Dasgupta, Shamita Das. 1998. A Patchwork Shawl: Chronicles of South Asian Women in America. London: Rutgers University Press.

Faist, T. 2004. Towards a Political Sociology of Transnationalization. *European Journal of Sociology* 45 (3): 331–366.

Giddens, A. 1991. *Modernity and Self-identity. Self and Society in Late Modern Age*. Cambridge: Polity Press.

Jain, Shobhita. 2006. Women's Agency in the Context of Family Networks in Indian Diaspora. *Economic and Political Weekly* June 10: 2312.

Jain, Shobhita. 2010. Transmigrant Indian Women: Creators of Diasporic Spaces. *Journal of Social Sciences* 25(1–2–3): 51–57. http://www.krepublishers.com/02-Journals/JSS/JSS-25-0-000-10-Web/JSS-25-1-2-3-000-10-Abst-PDF/JSS-25-1-3-051-10-1150-Jain-S/JSS-25-1-3-051-10-1150-Jain-S-Tt.pdf. Accessed 12 Dec 2014.

Mani, L. 1994. Gender, Class, and Cultural Conflict: Indu Krishnan's 'Knowing her Place.' In *Our feet Walk the Sky,* ed. South Asian Women's Descent Collective, p. 32–36. San Francisco: Aunt Lute Press.

Pandurang, Mala. 2003. Conceptualizing Emigrant Indian Female Subjectivity: Possible Entry Points. In *South Asian Women in the Diaspora*, ed. Nirmal Puwar, and Parvati Raghuram. Oxford: Berg.

Ramusack, Barbara N. and Sharon L. Sievers. 1999. Women in Asia: Restoring Women to History. US: Indiana University Press.

Rydin, Ingegerd and Ulrika Sjöberg. 2010. Women in Diasporic Communities Tell Their Stories: a Generational Perspective. Paper presented at Migra Nord Seminar, Helsinki, Sept 1–3. http://www.diva-portal.org/smash/get/diva2:439521/FULLTEXT01.pdf. Accessed 12 Jan 2015.

Sharma, Sheetal. 2013. Immigrants in Britain: a Study of the Indian Diaspora. *Diaspora Studies* 5(1): 14–43. New Delhi: Organisation for Diaspora Initiatives.

Part II
Revisiting Historical Narratives

Chapter 5
Indian Indentured Women in the Caribbeans and the Role Model of Ramayana's Sita: An Unequal Metaphor

Archana Tewari

Migration or movement from one place to another in search of employment, a new home, etc., is a painful phenomenon. This pain increases manifold if the migrant is a female from an economically weak section, a manual labourer, a victim of fraud and deceit (when registering to move from her native place) and belongs to a society where the status of a woman is low and she is stereotyped as a deity of sacrifice. All these qualities would precisely describe the Indian women moving to the Caribbean islands to work in the sugar plantations during the British period.

The transportation of Indian men and women under the indentured labour system, a mechanism that had the sanction of the British Imperial Government, was arguably another of the very ugly, inhuman faces of the British colonial system. These numerous destitute, impoverished and ignorant men and women were the victims of circumstances beyond their control. By 1833, when slavery was abolished in Britain and her empire, the writ of the British administration was well entrenched in British India. By the dawn of the nineteenth century, the ever-expanding British colonial economy had increased the demand for labour which the British colonies were, however, unable to meet. The British government succumbed to the demand of the white planter class and sanctioned the indentured labour system, whereby the Indians could be recruited to work in its colonies overseas. The indentured system was designed to supply a cheap and docile work force to work in the plantations overseas as a substitute for African slaves. 'It was India's role within the British Empire to furnish a supply of cheap and disposable labour, units of production, not people were exported, across the seas to supply the demand but somehow they remained people all the same' (Tinker 1974, 38).

Keeping in mind the circumstances under which this system was born, one can surely (with a sense of regret) state that there was little room for any concern for the indentured men/women. The main concern of the planters in the colonies to which

A. Tewari (✉)
Department of Western History, University of Lucknow, Lucknow, India
e-mail: archanatewari1972@gmail.com

© Springer Nature Singapore Pte Ltd. 2018
A. Pande (ed.), *Women in the Indian Diaspora*,
https://doi.org/10.1007/978-981-10-5951-3_5

53

the Indians were transported was the acquisition of a relatively cheap labour force. George Arbuthnot stated that—'Their cost is not half that of slave' (Tinker 1974, 63).

The movement/migration of people is different from the migration of birds and animals or the transportation of other tangible items. 'Migrants carry with them a socio-cultural baggage' which identifies them as originating from and/or belonging to their homeland (Jayaram 2004, 16).

To state it in layman's language, one may say that while the body may be physically taken to a new land but his/her heart and mind stay in the parent country. Migration is a traumatic movement between different social and cultural systems and a migrant is required not only to adjust to a new (physical) environment but has to develop an internal adjustment and survival map in order to adapt to new social and cultural changes (Al-Balawi 2002, 271–278).

In the hostile and alien environment of the Caribbean (known for the sugarcane plantations), the indentured Indians desperately required a religious, social, cultural and an emotional anchor and this need was filled by the Ramayana and the Ramcharitmanas and other religious symbols and activities.

Geographic Origin and Religious Orientations of the Emigrants in the West Indies

Various studies on the emigration in the second half of the nineteenth century show that given the abysmal economic conditions in the United Provinces (now Uttar Pradesh), about 700,000 persons left in search of employment and not less than '100,000 were registered in 1908 as emigrants to the West Indies, Fiji and Natal' (Jha 1973, 28–50). The Ramcharitmanas, a version of the Ramayana was most popular among these indentured Indians as it was composed by the saint poet Tulsidas in a Hindi dialect spoken in Ayodhya (the birthplace and capital of Rama) in the heart of the United Provinces.

V.S. Naipaul who is 'the touch stone by which the literature of the Old Diaspora continues to be measured' (Misra 2007, 12) has described the Ramayana as something that 'lived among us and as something I had already known'. (Naipaul 2000). The basic difference between the Ramayana and the Ramcharitmanas is '… the Ramayana was written by Sage Valmiki, a contemporary of Rama in Vedic Sanskrit and is considered to be "Adi Kavy" (an ancient epic) whereas the Ramcharitmanas was written in the fifteenth century by Goswami Tulsidas in the local dialect Awadhi; the latter is the retelling of the original text. At least 300 Ramayanas are known to have been written…' (Bose 2014, 141–146).

According to the story of the Ramayana, King Dashratha, of Ayodhya, had four sons from his three queens: first Rama (to Queen Kaushalya), then Bharata (to Queen Keyikayi) and followed by Lakshmana and Shatrughana (to Queen Sumitra). Later, Rama married Sita, the daughter of King Janaka of Mithila in the swayamwara ceremony wherein a princess chooses her husband herself—from amongst several suitors—all kings and princes. King Dashratha, wished Rama to be his successor; however, the second Queen Keyikayi compelled him to send Rama on exile (*vanvaas*) to the forests for fourteen years and crown her own son Bharata as the King of Ayodhya. Thus, the blind devotion of a mother destroyed the peace and harmony of the kingdom. King Dasharatha died from the pangs of separation from Rama, Bharata as an affectionate and devoted brother refused to take over the reins of the kingdom directly but 'it is a step towards the destruction of evil incarnate Ravana in the future' (Adhikari 2011, 169–179). Sita and Lakshmana then accompanied Rama into exile and, while on exile, Sita (after a turn of several events) was kidnapped by Ravana (the king of Sri Lanka), Rama later rescued Sita by invading Sri Lanka (after crossing the seas) with the help of Monkey God, Hanuman and his *vanar sena* (or army of monkeys).

There are numerous reasons for a strong devotional feeling to the Ramcharitmanas in the India diaspora, especially the old diaspora. Apart from the moral teachings through the different characters of the epic, it was, specifically, the theme of exile which had a special appeal. The treatment of the theme of exile provided immense solace and emotional support (a balm for troubled minds) to the immigrants who considered their indentures as 'a type of exile, identified with the trials and tribulations of Rama in the text…' (Singh 2012, 25–41). The sacred texts are sources of inspiration and so is Ramayana 'Ram models what a man should be: the embodiment of right conduct what Hindus call dharma and Sita models what married women should be according to Hindu orthodoxy; faithfully obedient chaste' (Bahadur 2013, 106). Sita, wife of Lord Rama exemplifies 'implicit devotion self sacrifice and purity' (Naval and Hussain 2008, 189). The influence of Sita on social and cultural aspects of life in India is deep and is not limited to the Hindus. Nine Paley in a conversation with Malashri Lal commented, 'My Christian friend in Kerala told me her family always exhorted her to be like Sita' (Lal 2014, 127). It has been observed that even western countries such as the UK, Canada and the United States 'celebrate Sita as the ideal women…' (Bose 2014, 141–146).

The Image of Sita

The birth of Sita is a mystery (Hindu mythology has reference to Lord Ram and Lord Krishna as toddlers and their endearing activities; unfortunately there is no such reference to any girl child). 'Sita is the essential orphan; the girl child' (Sen 2014, 131–140). She is described as the daughter of the earth goddess Bhumi and the adopted daughter of King Janaka of Mithila and Queen Sunayana. According to Hindu mythology, Janaka found Sita while ploughing as a part of *yagna* and adopted her. The child was named Sita, a name derived from the Sanskrit word meaning furrow, and so literally, found in the furrow (Lal 2014, 55–61).

About 300 versions of the Ramayana can be found—all variants of the original version by Valmiki. The Sita of Valmiki is by no means a meek, silent woman; on the contrary she is a woman who not only knows her mind but also speaks it, often against the authority of her husband (Bose 2014, 141–146). There are abundant instances of Sita's strength in Valmiki's Ramayana and also in other versions. Sita, as a child, is said to have lifted Shiva's bow with her left-hand while she was cleaning the room in which the bow was kept. 'Witnessing this, Janaka faints, as he had never been able to lift the bow himself' (Sen 2014, 131–140).

Again when Sita asserts that she could accompany Rama to the forests and will not deter by the rigours of life in the forest, she is a symbol of strength. She says 'I shall remain in the path without any fatigue as though remaining in a palace of recreation or in a state of sleep…if you do not take me who is not alarmed of the forest as such. I shall drink poison now…' (Vijay 2014, 21–26).

In the critical episode of the abduction of Sita by Ravana, Sita's stubbornness, akin to that of an ordinary woman, is fully displayed. Even though Rama repeatedly asserts that the presence of a golden deer in the midst of the jungle appears to be a sinister omen, Sita forces him to go after it. She is equally vehement when Lakshmana is reluctant to go to Rama's aid. Sita blames Lakshmana for harbouring a desire for her.

Again, after the defeat of Ravana when Rama is reluctant to accept Sita for having stayed in the protection of other man and asks her to prove her chastity through a fire ordeal (walking through the fire: *agnipareeksha*) the episode has been presented by many critics of the Ramayana 'more as an act of defiance rather than as submission to Rama's tyranny' (Kishwar 2014, 101–111).

That Sita conceives only once Rama is secure on the throne of Ayodhya, is viewed by many (idealist) intellectuals as a proof of abstinence on the part of Rama and Sita during their stay in the forests. However, many intellectuals feel that this implies that she is at least in control of her reproductive cycle (Desai 2014, 3–9). The act of Sita forsaking her family (the sons Luv and Kush) and going back to her mother Earth when Rama demands a second ordeal by fire is the final symbol of her strength. Sita 'finally emerges as a strong woman with a will of her own…' (Desai 2014, 3–9).

The Indian psyche, in general admires Sita for her submissive and meek behaviour where '…a Sita like women is synonymous with a slavishly dutiful wife…' (Kishwar 2014, 101–111). At times one feels (especially women do so) as if the epic has been rewritten over and over again simply '…to brainwash Indian women into accepting servile status for themselves…' (Kishwar 2014, 101–111). The servile image of Sita has made such a deep mark on the minds of Indians that the image of the independent and decisive Sita of Valmiki has totally evaporated. This transformation of Sita's image is definitely a subject for research on the deliberate literary manipulation devised to serve religious and social ideologies and one can surely say that the '…odour of patriarchal management is hard to ignore in the reconfigured myth of Sita…' (Bose 2014, 141–146). Probably, the aim of the various literary intellectuals was (consciously or subconsciously) to glorify female victimhood.

The various versions of the Ramayana with the image of a voiceless Sita reached countless countries through the migration of Indians to the Caribbeans as well as to other regions to which they emigrated. The Indians carried with them a 'socio cultural baggage', where in the women were supposed to don the mantle of Sita. The indentured Indians may have been illiterate and ignorant folks but they were representative of a cross-section of the Indian community and of a culture that was centuries old (Kannabiran 1991, 53–57). The researches have amply proved that Indian women migrating to Trinidad were 'already independent women who made a conscious decision to move out of the difficult social situations which confronted them in India' (53–57).

Registration and Departure of the Emigrants

Since the beginning of the Indian indentureship one of its disturbing features was a numerical disparity between the sexes. Records show that the Indian population always suffered from an imbalanced sex ration 'In 1911, according to one source the ratio of women to man in the United Provinces was 915–1000, while in Punjab (including Delhi) at this time the ratio was only 817 women to every 1000 men. Recruiting, therefore, took place in a situation of an already existing unequal sex ratio' (Reddock 1985, 79–87).

As regards the composition of women indentured labour the researcher finds that the observation of the commissioners McNeill and Lal[1] merit to be quoted in detail:

> The women who came out consist as to one-third of married women who accompany their husbands, the remainder being mostly widows and women who have run away from their husbands or been put away by them. A small number are ordinary prostitutes. Of the women who emigrate otherwise than with their husbands and parents the great majority are not, as they are frequently represented to be, shamelessly immoral. They are women who have got into trouble and apparently emigrate to escape from a life of promiscuous prostitution which seems to be the alternative to emigration….

> …what appears to be true as regards a substantial number…is that they ran away from home alone or accompanied by someone by whom they were abandoned, that they drifted into one of the large recruiting centres, and after a time were picked up by the recruiter. (Reddock 1985, 79–87)

The basic aim of the British power was to derive maximum benefit from her colony, i.e., India and to impoverish her masses. The excessive land revenue demand, the practice of carrying away the best (raw) resources to the Mother country, and dumping machine-made (British) goods of superior quality led to the decline of local industries, and appointing British to posts of high salaries, etc., were some of the methods that led to the impoverishment of the Indian masses. Poverty and hunger could have led to 'an increase in the number of girls consecrated to the temple goddess as ritual prostitutes' (Reddock 1985, 79–87). This in turn, could have prompted emigration among some of the prostitutes as a way to achieve an honourable way of living. Though there were laws concerning the minimum number of women, these were just fallow announcements to satisfy the public. A constant feature of the Indian indentured labour throughout the period of

---

[1]James McNeill and Chimman Lal were deputed in 1912 to report on the conditions of indentured Indians in Fiji, Demerara, Trinidad and Surinam.

its operation was the imbalance in the sex ratio—fewer number of women registered as compared to men.

These ordinary Indian women who registered themselves as indentured labour (called coolies in the colonies) were far more disadvantaged than the Sita of the Ramayana. There were many Ravanas (symbolic) in the lives of these women: their circumstances, the *arkatias* (recruiters), the crew, Indian men and white overseers in the sugar plantations.

These recruiters or '*arkatias*' who used all the tricks of the trade were the 'key players in the indenture ship system' (Kannabiran 1991, 53–57). Maharania, a young Brahmin widow of Trinidad, who had run away from home (in India), recalled the recruiter's chant:

Chenne Chala

Chenne Chala

Going tappu

tappu may

sara bara anna.

Sifting sugar

Sifting sugar

To the island go

There in the island

Full Twenty-five cents. (Mahabir 1985)

All men and women bound for various colonies were lodged for some time in a depot near Calcutta port till the requisite number was collected to fill a ship. The journey of indentured women from Calcutta (now Kolkata) to their respective colonies on ship was also full of danger. These women could fall prey to the lust of crew members or the ship's surgeon or his junior compounder. Many a times 'marriages' or pairings were performed on the ships. Captains themselves performed marriages (couple up) for the emigrants. The indentured men were persuaded to get married so that they would get a woman who could cook and perform other chores for them. Recalling the marriage ceremony on a ship bound to Gayana, one Chanan Singh in an interview with Noor Kumar Mahabir said 'They (the man) say that they take this woman and the woman say that they take this man (Bahadur 2013, 73)'. The hastily conducted depot marriages and ship board marriages lacked the sanctity as compared to marriages solemnised by family members in India.

Life on the Sugar Plantations

The most severe trials indentured women faced began on their arrival at the sugar plantations. '...the Fatal Rozack brought the first 227 Indian immigrant labourers to Trinidad on May 30 (1845) 206 were men and 21 women" (Reddock 1985, 79–87).

Since the inception of the system no importance was attached to the issue of the imbalance in the sex ratio. Sir John Gladstone (father of the future prime minister of England) who was greatly instrumental in the commencement of the indentured system wrote to Messrs. Gillanders Arbuthnot & Company (one of the firms that recruited indentured Indians) in 1837 that if the firm could not manage a large proportion of women, one woman to every nine or ten men 'for cooking and washing is enough!' (Bahadur 2013, 79)

The indentured men and woman were supposed to live in the barracks of the former slaves, or in the 'relics of the past' as the Reverend C.F. Andrews called them. These dwellings were small and cramped, unfit to support a healthy married life. The barracks contained a row of rooms raised from the ground on short stumps. The rooms had partition that did not reach the roof—thus every sound was 'communal'. The floors were made of mud or clay and the rooms were bereft of any furniture. The roofs were made of corrugated metal sheets which made the rooms totally inhabitable in the afternoons. One planter of Trinidad 'defended his iron roofs as a check on laziness'. The people, he said, '…ought to be in the field all day long. I do not build cottages for idlers'. Asked about people forced to stay at home such as pregnant and nursing women he said, 'I only want working hands' (Bahadur 2013, 79). The planters had imported Indians only to work on the sugar plantations and there was no concern for any of their humane needs. The dwellings also lacked latrines and had no source of clean drinking water; as such they were derisively compared to stables and often called *narak* (hell) and *kasbighar* (brothel). With a role emphasis on hard labour and frightening living conditions, the indenture system did not promote traditional stable families. The planters did not separate couples or children from parents as was done during the enslavement of the Africans. Most of the Indians lacked family ties, apart from the friendships they had forged on the ship during their middle passage: *jahaji-bhai, jahaji-behan*.

Bahadur has identified six patterns of relationships/households that proved beyond doubt that 'there was no room for morality in the cramped immigrant quarters' (2013, 79).

1. A woman living alone except, perhaps for children
2. Several men succeeding each other in a woman's home
3. A woman passing from the home of one man to another
4. Traditionally monogamous
5. Much less frequently polygamous and
6. Some combination of three or more men and women living together; without marriage.

Monogamy is one of the essential messages of the Ramayana—whether it was Rama or Sita. However life on the plantations rendered the institution of monogamy redundant. Still, keeping in mind the patriarchal nature of the Indian society, on Indian indentured women lay the burden of upholding the glory and value of an ancient civilization. The numerical scarcity of Indian women put pressure on them, as the Indian men indentured or free, refrained from interacting with women of

African descent. Despite the shortage of Indian women, very few Indian males married women of African descent.

The coolie women were also supposed to protect their honour from various officials of the plantations. The Indian women being Sita 'the significant unknown other or potentially threatening agents such as white colonial oppressor and Trinidadian of African descent were referred as "Ravana"' (Singh 2012, 25–41). It was not unusual for overseers or even managers to cohabit with coolie women. There was a feeling of jealousy and a sense of competition when a coolie woman was summoned to the overseer's or the manager's lodge.

Sita Under Duress

Disputes over women (for possession charges of infidelity or jealousy over betrayal/rejection etc.) often led to horrific, violent and at times fatal incidents. The decision to emigrate to the colonies (if not a result of deceit and fraud) was an independent one in the case of single women. However, the Indian men adhering to their culture in letter and spirit, albeit more stringently, wanted the Indian women to follow the path of the 'slavishly dutiful wife'. Thus, in many cases, women were killed for rejecting the advances of men. Even husbands were rejected for errant behaviour. As Gaiutra Bahadur reports, 'One woman was nearly decapitated by her husband because she couldn't return from her mother's (place). Rather than greed or libido what the victims had in common was choice. They had all exercised a choice to say yes or in more cases than acknowledged to say no' (2013, 119).

The very fact that, women were scarce and wage earners, put them in a position of relative strength, and thus many tried to assert themselves from the restrictions of patriarchy. The Indian women definitely used the numerical scarcity to their advantage. Speaking on the issue Ron Ramdin narrated: 'when the last immigrant ship came in, as a Brahmin widow is said to have told Morton',[2] 'I took a man. If he does not treat me well I shall send him off at once...' (2000, 218). For a Brahmin woman to have spoken in this manner is a bit intriguing as of all castes of the Hindus for a widow to re-marry could amount to sacrilege. The reason a Hindu widow emigrated was probably to give her life a new start as Hindu widows led a miserable life in India.

The quest for economic security many a times was the main reason for a women's urge to look for a new partner in the exploitative environment of the sugar plantations. A few lines of Gaiutra Bahadur merit to be quoted:

In early 1890s (Sarah[3]) Morton met a group of women returning from the fields. One a recent Christian convert had just left one man for another. The women

---

[2]John Morton, a Canadian Presbyterian Minister was a pioneering missionary, who worked for the education of Indians and opened a first primary school at Iere village [South Trinidad] in 1868.

[3]Sarah, wife of John Morton.

singled her out for Morton's attention. 'Your disciple is going to church now', they said. The missionary's wife answered, 'That will do her no good unless she changes her living'. One of the women then shot back, capturing pitch perfectly the paradox that many Indian women found themselves living out what can she do? 'This husband takes better care of her than the other did' (2013, 138).

The scarcity of Indian women had one more significant effect on the social life of the Indians in the Caribbeans. A female child was undervalued in India, in the Caribbeans they were greatly appreciated. The female infants were brought up with great care. However, the explanation for this is not simple and 'did not really represent an improvement in their position per se' (Reddock 1985, 79–87). The scarcity of girls led to the practice of child marriage (of girls, as young as 10 years became the rule) and bride price (i.e. improving the marketability of girl child by their fathers). 'In 1893 Sarah Morton noted a case where a father had sold his daughter nine times for money and goods and on each occasion had refused to deliver her' (79–87). This particular case if true triggers the question was the girl's father behaving like Janaka? If not why were women expected to be Sita? Did all men who committed (wife/female partner) murder behave like Rama? Rama had simply banished his wife to the jungle; remained unhappy never remarried and even took *Jal Samadhi* in river Sarayu; such questions will remain and arguments will continue.

Analogy to Sita: Positive Effect

Like all historical events of negative nature begetting some positive output, the analogy between Sita and the coolie women had a positive outcome. If the abduction of Sita led to end of the demon king of Lanka (a country of gold), similarly the sullying and vilifying of the images of coolie women had a significant impact on the nationalist campaign to end the indenture system. The end of the indenture system was perhaps the first question to be settled by the protests of colonial India, although the system was born in the British Parliament (The role of exigencies of World War I and protests by natives to the entry of Indians in their country were also important factors).

The comparison of indentured women to Sita was misplaced. Sita is said to have been blessed with the power of burning down to cinders any one that dared touch her body against her will. This power was circumvented by Ravana who kidnapped her by pulling her by her hair. These ordinary women had no such power. They had simply wanted to shape their own lives with dignity: however, they were pitted against the 'monstrous' indenture system, where the white planter class enforced laws that impinged on their freedom and the men of their own race had unfair expectations. The stories of these unnamed, countless women could move even the most stony-hearted person, …the majority of them had led an impoverished, unhappy life in India before they were lured or may take the decision to escape their miserable conditions which ended in, what Rev. C.F. Andrews called, the 'death traps' of the sugar plantations in far-off colonies. 'The commonest epithet for Sita in Bengali (also found in Maithili) is Janam-dukhini (born to suffer)' (Sen 2014, 131–140). This phrase aptly describes the plight of Indian indentured women. Despite the blame and slanders and innumerable 'wife' murders many Indian women laid the foundation of the Indian social life in the alien and often hostile environment of the Caribbeans.

The deep-seated traditions of ancient Hindu civilization helped the later generations to overcome such a shaming abnormality. Patricia Mohammed has studied the role of the Ramayana in restoring gender relations in the Caribbeans. Mohammed's findings are rather interesting as Indian women fully supported the Indian community's effort to restore the norms, despite the fact that many of these norms were oppressive for them, so that the Indian community could emerge from the derision and ridicule they faced during the period of Indentureship. This was considered absolutely necessary to erase the memory of the indentureship period where there were innumerable instances of women reneging on patriarchal orders by disobeying the rules of monogamy and indulging in other acts of infidelity. The Ramayana was chosen as an instrument to bring erring women back to the fold of the Hindu culture, and with this end in mind the public recital and performance of the Ramayana (or the Ramleela), Mohammad observes: 'The lesson to women was one of monogamy, chastity and devotion to the husbands chosen by their parents and elders' (Vogt-William 2014, 252).

The institution of arranged marriage which is considered to be an essential part of the Indian culture became a norm in the Caribbeans. Gaiutra Bahadur who visited her relatives in 1997 talks about her cousin who had an arranged marriage (Bahadur 2013, 12), Ron Ramdin too stated: 'By and large most Indian marriages in Trinidad were (in many cases still are), arranged by parents or family elders' (2000, 219).

Thus, the abnormality that the indentured system had brought into the lives of Indians ended with the growth of the female population, the termination of the indentured system and the gradual improvement in the economic conditions of the Indian community. Indian women slowly assumed their traditional roles and their respectability restored: '...they were constrained by an acceptance of docility, passivity and dependence: the glorification of motherhood and an acceptance of the androcentric ideal of Indianness being coterminous with subordination' (Kannabiran 1991, 53–57).

References

Adhikari, Madhumalati. 2011. Journey Through the Ages: The Ramayana and the Alchemist. In *The Asian Conference on Arts and Humanities, Official Conference Proceedings.* ISSN 2186-229x, 169–179. http://iafor.org/acah_proceedings.html.
Al-Balawi, R. 2002. Migration Related Stress and Psychosomatic Consequences. *International Congress Series* 1224 (1): 271–278. Accessed January 21, 2016.
Bahadur, Gaiutra. 2013. *Coolie Woman.* Hachette India.

Bose, Mandakaranta. 2014. The Portrayal of Sita in Two Bengali Ramayanas. In *Search of Sita: Revisiting Mythology*, ed. M. Lal, and N. Gokhale, 141–146. Delhi: Penguin Books.

Desai, Meghnad. 2014. Sita and Some Other Women from the Epics. In *Search of Sita: Revisiting Mythology*, ed. M. Lal, and N. Gokhale, 3–9. Delhi: Penguin Books.

Jayaram, N. 2004. *The Indian Diaspora, Dynamics of Migration*. London: Sage Publications.

Jha, J.C. 1973. Indian Heritage in Trinidad, West Indies. *Caribbean Quarterly* 19 (2): 28–50.

Kannabiran, Kalpana. 1991. Mapping Migration, Gender, Culture and Politics in the Indian Diaspora, Commemorating Indian Arrival in Trinidad. *Economic and Political Weekly* 53–57.

Kishwar, Madhu. 2014. Trial by Fire. In *Search of Sita: Revisiting Mythology*, ed. M. Lal, and N. Gokhale, 101–111. Delhi: Penguin Books.

Lal, Malashri. 2014. Sita's Voice. In *Search of Sita: Revisiting Mythology*, ed. M. Lal, and N. Gokhale, 83–88. Delhi: Penguin Books.

Mahabir, Noor Kumar. 1985. *The Still Cry: Personal Accounts of East Indians in Trinidad and Tobago During Indentureship, 1845–1917*. New York: Calaloux Publications.

Misra, Vijay. 2007. Voices from the Diaspora. In *The Encyclopedia of the Indian Diaspora*, ed. Brij V. Lal, 120–139. Oxford: Oxford University Press.

Naipaul, V.S. 2000. *Reading and Writing: A Personal Account*. New York: Review Books.

Naval, Uday C., and Sofia K. Hussain. 2008. *Striped Zebra, The Immigrant Psyche*. New Delhi: Rupa & Co.

Ramdin, Ron. 2000. *Arising from Bondage*. New York: New York University Press.

Reddock, Rhoda. 1985. Freedom Denied: Indian Women and Indentureship in Trinidad and Tobago, 1845–1917. *Economic and Political Weekly* 20 (43): 79–87.

Sen, Navneeta. 2014. The Essential Orphan: The Girl Child. In *Search of Sita: Revisiting Mythology*, ed. M. Lal, and N. Gokhale, 131–140. Delhi: Penguin Books.

Singh, Sherry Ann. 2012. The Ramayana in Trinidad: A Socio-Historical Perspective. In *Indian Diaspora in the Caribbean: History, Culture and Identity*, ed. Rattan Lal Hangloo, 25–41. New Delhi: Primus Books.

Tinker, Hugh. 1974. *A New System of Slavery*. London: Camelot Press.

Vijay, Tarun. 2014. Janaki: The Fire and the Earth. In *Search of Sita: Revisiting Mythology*, ed. M. Lal, and N. Gokhale, 21–26. Delhi: Penguin Books.

Vogt-William, Christine F. 2014. *Bridges, Borders and Bodies: Transgressive Transculturality in Contemporary South Asian Diasporic Women's Novels*. Cambridge Scholar Publishing.

Chapter 6
'The Men Who Controlled Indian Women'—Indentureship, Patriarchy and Women's 'Liberation' in Trinidad

Radica Mahase

Introduction

From 1845 to 1917 approximately 147,600 Indian labourers immigrated to Trinidad under the indentureship system. Of these, female labourers formed 29% or roughly 42,800 women and girls. In 1917, when the Indian indentureship system was officially ended, only about 25% of the total number of these female labourers was repatriated to their homeland (Reports n.d.). The majority remained in the colony and eventually made Trinidad their home.

From the time of recruitment/registration until their settlement in Trinidad, female labourers were constrained by the prevalence of patriarchal social norms. At every step of the indentureship system, they were faced with patriarchal structures which hindered their ability to register and emigrate freely; regulated their behaviour on the 'coolie' ships and dictated their lifestyles on the plantations. Despite the efforts of men to control these women, female Indian labourers were able to claim some extent of agency, often contesting patriarchal structures and renegotiating gender roles through labour, education, social behaviour, culture and economic opportunities.

Reddock's seminal work is probably the most notable literature to discuss the gendered experience of indentureship in the Caribbean. In this article, she questioned the extent to which female indentured labourers migrated 'under the power, authority and control of their male relatives and were docile and tractable'. She argued that a large proportion of Indian women made a conscious decision to emigrate and they did not submit to patriarchal dictates (1985). Chatterjee's (1997) doctoral thesis explores the manner in which gender influenced the indentureship system from the time of recruitment to settlement in the colonies of Trinidad and

R. Mahase (✉)
College of Science, Technology and Applied Arts of Trinidad and Tobago,
9-11 Melville Lane, Port of Spain, Trinidad and Tobago
e-mail: radica.mahase@gmail.com

© Springer Nature Singapore Pte Ltd. 2018
A. Pande (ed.), *Women in the Indian Diaspora*,
https://doi.org/10.1007/978-981-10-5951-3_6

British Guiana. Other works have sought to show variations of the gendered experience in the Caribbean often focusing on the imbalance in the ratio of males to females and the impact of this on society, the degree of 'independence' of Indian women and the part Indian women played in preserving Indian culture.

The Indian Side of the Story

The conditions propelling women's migration and their experiences during the process and settlement have always been different and very specific to them. The Indian indentureship scheme was introduced solely to provide a cheaper source of labour on the plantations in Trinidad and other Caribbean countries. As it came in the aftermath of the abolition of African slavery, a labour system that had received much criticism from humanitarian groups in Britain, the British Imperial government and the Government of India realised that it was imperative to ensure that Indian indentureship was not perceived in the same manner as African slavery. Consequently, various stipulations were put in place so that indentureship would be seen as a completely new system, one in which all parties were protected, labourers had rights and privileges and the entire scheme was not disruptive to the lives of the Indian labourers. Most of this occurred at only a theoretical level and was not actually practiced, with the result that abuses were prevalent throughout the indentureship period. However, the Imperial Government was concerned about the presence of female migrants and the emigration of families. This may have been only to show that the labourers were simply taken from their rural villages and transported to a new environment, with families and cultural practices intact, with little actual disruption to their everyday lives. Thus, they would be able to marry, have a family, socialise and so on. In this way, indentureship would be different from that of African slavery. Simply put, Indian women were 'allowed' to migrate because it suited imperial/colonial policies.

Interestingly enough, while the British Imperial Government preferred the migration of Indian women under the indentureship scheme, India's patriarchal society did not always favour such a move. Thus, Indian women were simply not at liberty to register for the indentureship system or to leave India on their own. The patriarchal system placed restrictions on Indian women in the recruitment/registration process, which resulted in lower numbers of female emigrants for the duration of the labour system. At one level, women were even controlled legally. For example, after 1879, magistrates refused to register single women and attempted to confirm that they had the permission of a male relative before they could be registered. Some magistrates insisted that local police enquire into the background of those single women who wanted to register for the labour scheme (Seenarine 2011).

Indian women, however, developed very creative ways to negotiate the patriarchal controls exerted over them. A clear example of this is the fact that some women married Indian men at the depots so that they would still be able to migrate, as a couple rather than as single individuals. In 1890, 436 marriages were recorded under '*The Immigrants' Marriage and Divorce Ordinance, 1881*'. Of this number, 282 were 'marriages of immigrants who, on arrival here, declared themselves to stand in the relation of husband and wife' (Comins 1893, 30), while 64 were marriages recorded by District Registrars under clause 11 of the Ordinance. Marriage at the depots was a trend that occurred throughout the indentureship period.

During the whole period of indentureship, there was an entire colonial discourse with rhetoric of gender discrimination as is evident in the debate on the inferior status of Indian women. The colonial officers dealing with emigration have emphasised that some of the women who emigrated were prostitutes, although substantial figures and intensive information regarding this claim have not been recorded. This was especially visible in all levels of colonial communications; in discussions between and amongst the British Imperial government, the Government of India and the colonial governments in British colonies. It was reflected in both the language and context of the communication. 'Coolie' women were always perceived as problematic; there was a need to protect them so as to protect the entire labour scheme from its critics. Single Indian women were deemed prostitutes and women of 'irreputable character'. The authorities were afraid that these women would cause problems between married couples and chaos amongst the single men. Hence, there was a need to keep them separate from these two groups at the depots and on the ships.

This whole notion of single women being equivalent to low class/immorality was perpetuated by the colonial authorities. They believed that only immoral women would emigrate on their own and hence, single women were perceived as trouble-makers. In 1891, Comins noted that in Trinidad:

> A good-looking young woman receives much admiration, and many are no doubt polyandrous and some regular prostitutes, which cannot be wondered at, as women are drawn from the same class in India…. I think more women of a respectable class should be encouraged to emigrate with their husbands and children…but there is no occasion to increase compulsorily the proportion of women who accompany the men, which would only result in a greater number of loose women being recruited in the Indian bazaars. (1893, 37)

The supposedly low character of Indian women occupied a large space in the communication amongst colonies and between colonial officers. These officials felt obligated to suggest ways to get rid of this 'problem' and to ensure that 'a better class of women' arrived in the colonies. Comins, for example, suggested that:

> To encourage the emigration of women of respectable character with their families, and to do away with the objectionable practice of filling up the complement of females by the recruitment of women of doubtful character in the bazaar, I would recommend that the indenture of women be limited to two years, and that when helpless during, immediately preceding, and after child-bearing, they should be considered as sick and receive food from the estate hospital. A woman who has been two years under indenture will be able to earn good wages in the field and will have acquired habits of industry, and there is little fear that

when work is plentiful and good wages are to obtained that the husband will allow her to sit idle. (1893, 49)

Another colonial officer, Sir Neville Lubbock, Chairman of the West India Committee noted:

I think in the first place it would enable us to get a better class of men, and in the second place, and more important still, I think it would enable us to get a better class of women. The question of the recruiting of women is always a difficulty, and there is no doubt that the class of women who go out are not the very best class. (Sanderson Cd. 5193, 95)

The fact that single women were labelled and condemned in such a manner illustrates the lack of understanding of Indian society and the distorted perceptions of colonial officers operating in a land culturally unfamiliar to them. It is imperative to remember that colonial officers in British India were operating in a Victorian Age when it was extremely easy to affix stereotypes to women. In the Indian situation, given the patriarchal nature of the society it was rather easy for colonial officers to label single women as prostitutes. This led them to the conclusion that single women who were emigrating by themselves were, therefore, running away from their homes and from their male guardian/protector. For example, one report on emigration stated that 'the women who come out consist as to one third of married women who accompany their husbands, the remainder being mostly widows and women who have run away from their husbands or have been put away by them. A small percentage is ordinary prostitutes' (Mc Neill and Chimmanlal 1915).

Interestingly, despite the colonials' aversion to allowing such low caste/class women to emigrate, they were always seeking to increase the number of female labourers. The ratio of males to females was always an unequal one and this was not good for the image of the labour scheme as a whole. Ships were, therefore, mandated to carry 40 women for every 100 male labourers (Proceedings, 1870), and, as an incentive, recruiters were paid more to recruit female labourers. Sanderson noted that 'A fixed gratuity, generally Rs. 25 for a man and Rs. 35 for a woman, is paid for each duly qualified emigrant to the sub-agent at the up-country depot...' (1910, 17). Despite this, the ratio of males to females remained unequal throughout the period the indentureship system was in force.

Regulating Women on the Plantations

A study of the lives of Indian women on the plantations of Trinidad is a study of complex issues, a sometimes ambiguous freedom and the desire to create their own space while negotiating the colonial and often patriarchal gaze. According to Mohapatra (1995):

The position of Indian indentured women on the plantations was marked by what may be called an ambiguous freedom. It is true that constraints on women were the same as those on the men in so far as the labour process was concerned, perhaps even more onerous. But certain factors of this labour regime provided the basis for the greater exercise of independent choice by women, when compared to the situation from which they had emigrated.

Indian women were required to negotiate a world where every attempt was made to control and regulate their behaviour but at the same time the intricacies of the plantation society did not always encourage patriarchal values to dominate. Thus, a conflicting situation existed where, on the one hand, the female labourers were expected to follow values and traditions imported from the Motherland, but on the other hand, new opportunities were presented in a different environment which consequently influenced changes in social behaviour as well as in economics and politics. Thus, Indian women played a significant role in structuring and restructuring the cultural formats of patriarchy and gender relations.

This was especially visible in the economic sphere where a contradicting situation existed as Indian women were able to achieve some amount of economic status while at the same time they operated in a regulated environment. On the one hand, female labourers were given an opportunity to earn wages, separate of their husbands and fathers. Generally, the Indian woman may have felt better about herself. Her wage earning status may have given her a sense of self-worth. Whereas in India her labour went unrecognised in Trinidad she was actually compensated in monetary form for her efforts. Nonetheless, constraints exerted over the female labourers through contract regulations reflected the patriarchal nature of the world society in that specific period. The female indentured worker was to work a full 9-hours day, at what was termed the 'lighter field tasks', that is cutting grass, hoeing the fields, cutting cane, looking after animals, etc., but what she actually did was the same work as her male counterparts. The only difference was that she could not be employed at any of the skilled tasks. However, wages were paid according to how 'able-bodied' an immigrant was. The Indian Ordinance Act stated that 'the minimum daily wage for an indentured labourer is fixed at 25 cents (1 s. 0½ d.), if able-bodied, and not less than 8 d. per day if other than able-bodied' (Sanderson Cd. 5192, 65). Comins (1893, 9) noted that, 'women, boys and weakly men were given permanently some sum less than 25 cents per task, because it has been decided that they are unable to do a full task'. Women were not seen as 'abled-bodied' as they were considered physically weaker and hence, they were paid lower wages. Therefore, while most women worked alongside the men in the fields, at the same tasks, the wages they received were actually lower.

In 1910, Mr. Oliver William Warner (Emigration Agent in Calcutta and former Protector of Immigrants in Trinidad for 12 years) was asked the question, 'Do the Indian coolie women do any work?' His response shows the willingness of Indian women to be gainfully employed. He noted: A great many of them work, but all the more sensible planters as a rule told me that they did not care whether the women worked or not. The great idea was that the presence of the women kept the men contented, and they did not force them to work. If they did not care to work they let them alone. But many of the women like to work because they like to make money too; they are very ambitious but they are not forced to work to any great extent (Sanderson Cd. 5193, 28).

Once their wages were fixed at a lower rate, the capacity of women to save the same amounts as their male counterparts was affected. Mc Neill and Chimmanlal (1915) noted that a good worker could easily have saved two shillings a week while everyone else (except the inferior workers) could have saved an average of one shilling per week. They stated:

> A steady man of ordinary industry and physique works on average about 260 days in the year. The average earnings for women varied very greatly because first women cannot be ordered to work after three years' residence and second, throughout the five years of their indenture, the employer seldom uses pressure to exact work except to reinforce the wishes of the husband. Their earnings were normally about one half to two thirds of those of the male immigrants.

The female indentured labourer earned from an average of half a crown to three shillings per week. According to Mc Neil and Chimmanlal, a woman's wants may cost from half a crown upwards and if this is the case then there appears to be a rather limited prospect of the woman saving part of her wage. The other point brought out by their observation was the idea that the employer would 'reinforce the wishes of the husband' (1915). Although it is not clear now why a husband would have wanted to pressurise his wife to work, the mere fact that the employer could be an enforcer of such wishes of the husband shows the ambiguous independence of the Indian women on the plantations.

At a social level, there were always systematic attempts to regulate women's social behaviour in the plantation society. However, the overriding factors of the perpetuation of patriarchal philosophy and the domination by male Indians were continuously evident at all levels of the society. The systematic attempts and continuous efforts to regulate women and their behaviour were in force at several various levels in the plantation society, for different reasons:

(i)   At the base level these efforts started within the home, because—naturally and logically—the joint family system prevalent in the then contemporary India was continued on the plantations. This family structure was a form of a patriarchal institution as the members of the household, including the women, were under the authority of the oldest male in the family. The system did not allow for a female member of the family to be in 'control' over male members, except of course when a woman, as a single parent, lived alone with her minor sons. This scenario itself was not common in those days as many single mothers took up residence with male partners.

(ii) Outside the home, at the level of the village, the patriarchal domination was manifested in the *panchayat* system, where men continued to dictate the law-making process and women were not permitted to sit on the village council.

(iii) At an even wider level, were laws of the colony, which were used to ensure that women could not be taken away from their husbands. The obvious indicators of these restrictions were the laws, imposed in Trinidad, against seducing a man's wife, and those which prevented a man from harbouring an immigrant's wife.

(iv) Attempts were also made to control the lives of Indian females by denying them access to educational opportunities. Although there were schools established by Presbyterian missionaries and the Trinidad colonial government, Indian parents were often hesitant to send their girl children to these schools. This was so partly because they were suspicious of the proselytising activities of the missionaries. However, more importantly it was due to the patriarchal value system which dictated that the education of females was irrelevant for the most part, as the girls would learn to cook and take care of the home and their marriages would be arranged when they became teenagers. The unspoken diktat of Indian society was that an Indian girl was reared to be a faithful wife and a good mother. Hence, she would learn how to carry out the duties of the home and when she was 'of age' she would be married to a suitable Indian man. According to the Protector of Immigrants, Trinidad in 1893, 'the female children of Indian descent are generally married about the age of ten years, under arrangements made for them by their parents' (Comins 1893, 31). In the host society many parents also saw it unnecessary to send their girl children to school as the plantation economy allowed the girl child to do minor tasks for a small sum of money. This supplemented the family's income and was only possible if she stayed away from school. Added to this, the Indians were always suspicious of the work of the missionaries and feared that their children would forsake their own cultural heritage and convert to Christianity.

Educational opportunities were indeed made available for children of the Indian indentured labourers in general and schools were established both by the government and various missionary groups. In fact, Mc Neill and Chimmanlal noted that in 1915 there were 252 schools; only 52 of which were run by the government, while 200 were denominational schools assisted by government grants providing free education. They also noted that 43 schools were special Indian schools where both Urdu and English were taught. Of these 40 were managed by the Canadian Presbyterian Missionary, two by the Anglicans and one was Roman Catholic. The Census of 1921 states that 531 girls were attending government schools, 1,895 were enrolled in government-assisted schools and 171 were in private schools. Therefore, a total of 2,597 Indian girls were attending school (Census 1923). Also, Mc Neill and Chimmanlal noticed that more than one-quarter of the estates had schools located on or very near to the estates while more than a half of the estates were within one-mile radius of a primary school. Of the remaining estates most of them were within two miles of a school, while only ten estates had no school within a two mile radius and some of these had either very few or no children at all on them. Unfortunately however, 16,477 Indian girls—a significantly higher number—were not enrolled in a school. This figure is a clear indication of the extent to which Indian parents denied their daughters access to education opportunities.

(v) At yet another level, there were the religious laws carried over to the host
     colony, which resulted in successful controls over women through religious
     and personal laws. This was particularly so when it came to Hindu law.
     Eighty percentage of the immigrant population were Hindus, with the natural
     result that Hindu religious laws were transported to the colony and so
     dominated the everyday lives of most of the indentured population.
     Marriages which were regulated by Hindu personal law and religion provide
     the most visible example of this control as they impacted on inheritance;
     particularly so when a man died, when in the case of an inter-caste marriage
     (as was most often the case) his widow and the children could not inherit his
     property (Comins 1893, 31).
(vi) Making the lives of women yet more difficult were the Hindu marriage laws
     which conflicted with the civil laws of the colony. For example, 'Under
     Hindu and Muslim personal law and religion, a man may marry more than
     one wife'. However, under the laws of the colony a man could be given
     heavy penalties for '...harbouring, enticing or having illicit intercourse with
     any of the females registered as a wife' (Comins 1893, 31). Therefore, the
     colony needed to do something to legalise the unions between those of
     different castes and consider those who have been living together to be
     legally married. This would then enable the wife and children to inherit the
     property of parents.

Renegotiating Patriarchy

Despite all the attempts made to control Indian women on the plantations of
Trinidad, these women were often able to renegotiate gendered structures and to
create their own space in the colony. They gave themselves agency and in the
process they created opportunities where they were able to assert their independence, redefine their roles and perceptions of self and deconstruct male/female
barriers. They found creative ways to address and redress the complex issues faced
by them, renegotiating their domestic roles and embracing new professional and
educational successes in the process as is stated in the introduction of this volume.

One of the most visible ways in which they asserted their independence could be
seen with economics. As mentioned previously, female indentured labourers were
paid for their labour as individual workers. Many of them took advantage of the
opportunities offered by the Trinidad colonial government to become landholders
which in turn led to a higher status for them individually in the colony (as property
holders). In Trinidad, Indian women were able to acquire Crown land through the
commutation system, which was implemented in 1869 to encourage time-expired
Indian labourers to remain and settle in the colony. Under this scheme, they could
forego the right to a free return passage to India in return for a grant of land or a
sum of £5 in cash or, alternatively they could purchase land independently of the

commutation system. This prospect of becoming landholders was eagerly grasped by several Indian women who probably saw it as a positive economic move and an indication of economic stability as well as an increase in their status in the community, given the fact that in India, land ownership in the colonial state placed the individual at a high social position. In 1875, as many as 223 women accepted commutation grants and from the period 1869 to 1889, 1,873 Indian women had opted for the land grant rather than a return passage to India.

Many Indian women took advantage of other opportunities that existed and, upon completion of their contracts, they moved towards the town areas seeking employment. Comins noted that '… among the women there are midwives and seamstresses and domestic servants' (1893, 18). On another note he said that, some Indian women returned to India and then remigrated as ordinary passengers, paying their own passage back to the colony. 'During the period 1881–1892, 141 men paid their passages to Trinidad while 97 women did the same along with 25 boys and 20 girls'. Some of them returned to India and remigrated with their relatives (25).

The renegotiation of patriarchal controls by Indian women also became evident in their social behaviour. As discussed previously, patriarchal structures in Indian society restricted the migration of female labourers. Consequently, throughout the indentureship period there was always a disparity in the sex ratio in Trinidad. Throughout the period of emigration, there were a lower number of female Indians in the colony and it was obvious that the root of this disparity lay with the Indians coming directly from India. For example, in 1851 there were 512 native female Indians for every 1,000 native male Indians. Amongst the Indians born in the colony, however, the relative proportion of the sexes was much more balanced with a ratio of 930 females to every 1,000 males (Census 1891).

Interestingly enough, while on one hand the lower number of Indian females helped to increase the status of Indian women, on the other hand it created a situation whereby the behaviour of women was strictly 'regulated'. While female infanticide may have been practiced in India—it was simply unnecessary and impractical in Trinidad as a female child was not a burden on the family. In fact, as Indian girls were allowed to work on the plantations, as mentioned earlier, this meant an additional income for the family. Also, in Trinidad the Indians did not have to worry about finding spouses for their daughters and since Indian females were 'scarce' and Indian males were not inclined towards inter-racial marriages, parents were now able to demand a bride price rather than pay a dowry upon the marriage of their daughters. According to the Protector of Immigrants for Trinidad in 1893:

> The proportion of Indian females in the colony is so much smaller than that of the males that it is impossible for every man to have a wife of his own, even if he wishes to have one. This evil is also increased by the fact that in some cases Indians, such as shopkeepers, landholders, etc. who are in comfortable circumstances, have more than one wife, and though they may perhaps be married to one, keep another as a concubine. (Comins 1893)

This was in addition to the fact that Indian men were not inclined towards inter-racial marriages. With this in mind, Indian women were able to give themselves a sense of agency when it came to marriage and children. This was evident in the fact that some changed partners, left marriages in which they were not happy and had children from more than one man. Sara Morton, a Presbyterian missionary who played a very active role in conversion activities amongst the labourers, cited the case of a visit to a village where she asked a female indentured labourer where the father of her children was at that moment. The woman calmly replied that as he had misbehaved she sent him away and taken 'another papa', who if he misbehaved as well, would also be sent away by her (Comins 1893). Unfortunately, for the Indian women, when faced with the situation where women had some amount of leverage in marriage and where infidelity was possible, the Indian men were unable to deal with this change and many retaliated with violence as seen with the cases of wife murders and physical abuse. In fact, from the period 1872 to 1879 there was of a total of 102 murders, 76 were of women, 59 of which were murders of wives (Mohapatra 1995, 232).

The age for marriage was now no longer in the prepuberty range and the knowledge that they could find another 'husband' was sufficient for Indian women to experience increased self esteem/self confidence as they could leave one husband but not become an outcaste. In the same way widows were no longer ostracised from society but were in fact able to find other husbands. This knowledge was sufficient to empower Indian women. The Indian men on the other hand had to devise methods of 'controlling' their women and settle for women from castes lower than their own. Consequently, there was a disjuncture in the caste system as inter-caste marriages were now prevalent, something that was possible only with severe consequences in Indian society. At the same time there was a change in the male–female relationship to some extent. This can be seen with respect to the Hindu wife who was still expected to be a replica of the Goddess Sita in a society, where the Ramayana tradition became the dominant cultural tradition. F. Gibbon, Acting Protector of Immigrants, reported on 20th August 1909, that Indian men "are jealous with respect to their womankind—of whom only 40%, accompany them— and swift to avenge infidelity" (Sanderson Cd. 5192, 136).

Conclusion

There was a common agreement by the colonials that the Indian females who arrived in Trinidad were the ones who benefitted the most from the indentureship system. Generally, they saw Indian women who had lived in the colony for long periods as less traditional, with better appearances and increased status. One colonial officer described the Indian women as '... bright-eyed, well-proportioned women, clad in their picturesque costume, a white or coloured skirt, a robe thrown over the head and shoulders, and sometimes literally hanging over with jewels— bangles, necklaces, nose jewels, etc.'" (Comins 1893, 20). Comins also noted that 'Females who on their arrival here would veil their faces with their *ornie*[1] at the

---

[1]*ornie*: veil.

approach of a man, not being their husband or one of the household, after some years' residence in the colony, merely touch the *ornie* with the hand, and in many cases neglect to do so altogether' (38).

After the Indian indentureship system ended in 1920, there continued to be a change in gender dynamics in the colony. This was a period in which Indian women/Indo-Trinbagonian women continued their struggles to create a space in society. It was also a period when the voices of the middle-class women began to emerge in a colony where it had always been subsumed. There were a small number of women who were educated and were employed as professionals—as teachers, clerks and so on. This small group became visible when they demanded political participation at the level of the legislative council and with their outspokenness against men's attempts to control them.

Almost one hundred years since the abolition of the Indian indentureship system the position of Indian women in Trinidad and Tobago has changed drastically. Presently, Indo-Trinbagonian women in Trinidad and Tobago are integrated into society at all levels. They occupy top positions in almost all professional fields: in politics, medicine, law, business and economics amongst others. They account for the most educated proportion of the population and Indo-Trinbagonian girls have been awarded the highest number of scholarships and awards over the past ten years. They are leaders in the society, like former Prime Minister and current Leader of the Opposition, Mrs. Kamla Persad-Bissessar who is of Indian ancestry, and they provide strong competition in every area for their male counterparts.

References

Census. 1891. *Census of Trinidad and Tobago, 1891*. Registrar General.

Census. 1923. *Census of the Colony of Trinidad, 1921*. Port-of-Spain: Govt. Print. Office.

Chatterjee, Sumita. 1997. Indian Women's Lives and Labor: The Indentureship Experience in Trinidad and Guyana: 1845–1917. Ph.D. dissertation, University Massachusetts at Amherst.

Comins, D.W.D. 1893. *Note on Emigration from India to Trinidad*. Calcutta: Bengal Secretariat Press. West Indiana and Special Collections Division, UWI Main Library, St. Augustine.

Mc Neill, James, and Lala Chimmanlal. 1915. *Report to the Government of India on the Conditions of the Indian Immigrants in Four British Colonies and Surinam*. Indian Commerce and Industry Department, Government of India. National Archives of India, New Delhi.

Mohapatra, Prabhu. 1995. 'Restoring the Family': Wife Murders and the Making of a Sexual Contract for Indian Immigrant Labour in the British Caribbean Colonies, 1860–1920. *Studies in History* 8 (11): 227–260.

Reddock, Rhoda. 1985. Freedom Denied: Indian Women and Indentureship in Trinidad and Tobago, 1845–1917. *Economic and Political Weekly* 20 (43): 79–88.

Reports. n.d. *Annual Reports on Emigration from the Port of Calcutta to British and Foreign Colonies*. Calcutta, Bengal Secretariat for the periods 1845–1917.

Sanderson. Cd. 5192. *Report of the Committee on Emigration from India to the Crown Colonies and Protectorates*. 1910. Series: Cd. (Great Britain. Parliament), 5192–5194. London: H.M.S. O. (West Indiana and Special Collections Division, UWI Main Library, St. Augustine.).

Sanderson. Cd. 5193. *Report of the Committee on Emigration from India to the Crown Colonies and Protectorates. The Minutes of Evidence.* 1910. London: H.M.S.O. (West Indiana and Special Collections Division, UWI Main Library, St. Augustine.).
Seenarine, M. 2011. *Indentured Indian Women in Colonial Guyana: Recruitment, Migration, Labor and Caste.* http://mosessite.blogspot.com/2011/05/indentured-indian-women-in-colonial.htm.

Chapter 7
Tamil Women of the Diaspora: Indentured to Independence

Bernard D'Sami

One can clearly see three major trends or waves of migration by Tamils to other countries. The first wave witnessed the Tamils being taken to sugar colonies in far-off countries as indentured labourers. The 1830s witnessed the emergence of the 'coolie migration', when a large numbers of Indians, particularly Tamils, were forcibly taken from their homeland to work as indentured labourers in British plantations in the Caribbean Islands (West Indies) and to countries in Asia and Africa such as Burma, Ceylon, Malaysia, Mauritius and South Africa. Tamil women of the diaspora were once part of the indentured labour doing hard work besides looking after the family in the most unfamiliar of conditions. The plantation settlements were followed by the process of assimilation and integration in the host countries. This wave was followed by the decolonisation process or the second wave, in which Tamil women participated in the liberation wars for India that were fought from outside India. The third and final 'wave' being the postcolonial emigration which had taken Tamil women professionals to western countries. The modernisation process of Gulf countries with the rise in the oil prices (petrodollar) witnessed labour migration as Tamil women went to Gulf countries some as skilled, but many as unskilled labour. Thus, Tamil women were part of the process in all the three 'waves' of emigration.

The legacy of this mass-migration is clearly reflected in contemporary demographics. As of 2004, 'Indians' comprised 8.4% of the population of Singapore, with Tamil as one of Singapore's four official languages. Tamils comprised 80% of the two million strong Indian population of Malaysia, they formed almost a quarter of the total population of Réunion, and were seven per cent in Mauritius. Around half of South Africa's Indian population are

B. D'Sami (✉)
Loyola Institute of Social Science Training and Research,
Loyola College (Autonomous), Chennai, India
e-mail: bernarddsami@gmail.com

© Springer Nature Singapore Pte Ltd. 2018
A. Pande (ed.), *Women in the Indian Diaspora*,
https://doi.org/10.1007/978-981-10-5951-3_7

of Tamil descent, while small Tamil populations can reportedly be found in Indonesia, Burma, Vietnam, Cambodia, Fiji, the Seychelles, Guyana, Suriname and the Caribbean. (Jones 2013)

First Wave—The Beginning of Tamil Emigration

Britain, through colonialism, controlled both the sending and the receiving country. By abolishing slavery in 1833 through the Slavery Abolition Act which came into force in 1834, some 700,000 slaves were freed in the West Indies, 20,000 in Mauritius and 40,000 in South Africa. The exceptions were the territories controlled by the British East India Company where slaves were legally freed only in 1843. However, by 1838 most of the slaves in the British colonies were freed, as a result, particularly in the West Indies, the sugarcane plantations suffered the most. The British also suffered when the slaves in Mauritius—which was known as 'Sugar Island'—were freed. The British also wanted to manage the macroeconomic problem of unemployment through emigration (Finkelman and Miller 1998). As early as 1819, Britain decided to send the Tamils to Mauritius, though they were taken across as indentured labourers only from 1834 onwards. In 1838, 400 workers in two ships emigrated to British Guayana. In 1844, they went to Trinidad and in 1845, they were sent to Jamaica. Tamils also went to the islands of Grenada, St Lucia and St Vincent in 1856, 1858 and 1861, respectively. They started emigrating to Natal in South Africa in 1860. Those who worked for the abolition of slavery called this new type of 'indentured labour' as a new form of slavery. Though the first phase of Tamil emigration was temporary in nature, those who returned were small in number compared to those who emigrated. The volume of emigration required was decided by the receiving country based on its demand for labour in the plantations. It may be clarified here that those who went to distant countries in the West Indies, or to Fiji, Mauritius and South Africa went as indentured labourers, while those who went to nearer ones like Ceylon and Malaysia went on free migration. They were not required to produce any documents either at the point of departure or at the point of entry. It is estimated that nearly a lakh of people at the time were emigrating from the then Madras Presidency from, predominantly, the Telugu and Tamil districts. The districts from which the Tamils emigrated were Arcot Chennai, Chingleput, Coimbatore, Madurai Nilgiris North, Salem, South Arcot, Tanjore, Tinnevelly and Tiruchirapalli (Mani 2001).

Tamil Women in the Indentured Labour Force

Through the 'indentured' (or legally enforced 'debt bondage') labour system workers were sent abroad. According to this system, a labourer had to work at least for 5 years. They could not be changed from one plantation to another. They had to work in groups with the workers allowed to take their families with them who would also work. It is also through the *Kangani* system that Tamils migrated to Ceylon and Malaysia to work in the tea, coffee and rubber plantations. *Kangani* means 'to take responsibility' in Tamil, and the 'Kangani', also a worker, was so called because he had under him workers in small groups, and he was responsible for them. The Kangani was from a dominant caste but the workers were mostly from the oppressed castes.

Women emigrated for a variety of reasons. There were widows escaping *sati*, others escaping forced marriages, some escaping the twin structures of a patriarchal and caste-ridden society. Most came as ordinary migrants, 'did their time' and then became part of the settled communities, with many taking advantage of the new opportunities offered. This was, however, doubly difficult as their status was not equal to that of indentured men (Desai and Vahed 2010). Many women emigrated during this period. The owners realised the importance of women workers. Some young men when they emigrated individually saved money and returned. In order to stop the young men from returning after the contract period, women too emigrated so that the chances of the young men returning would cease and they would stay in the colonies itself permanently. The host countries too wanted the colonists to settle down permanently and to become citizens of the respective countries as temporary emigration put them to great difficulties. So the owners tried to send them (emigrate) as families instead of individuals. In the initial stages, there were few women and more men on the plantations and this led to many problems. So the British passed laws which provided for one woman to three men (1:3) and this was strictly adhered to by the ships carrying them to the destination country with the plantations.

In the French colonies, the number was 1:2 and only this law adhered at the port they were sent to. The Madras Port Trust cleared the ships from the port only after ensuring that the stipulated number of women and men were going to the colonies. Agents in the destination countries were finding this difficult, as women were not accompanying men as stipulated by the law. This led to women who were not involved in agricultural work, women who had been cheated and those in dire poverty, being sent to the plantations. Many women were cheated, some remarried, the incidents of violence and murder increased on the plantations, and women were treated worse than prostitutes. There were different categories of women, like those who went with their husband, widows, deserted women and girls accompanied by their parents. Women also re-emigrated to other places from the plantations to which they had been sent. Young girls deserted by their lovers were also part of the women who made their way to plantations. The different kinds of women were all attracted by the promises of the agents who were keen to send them abroad to maintain the ratio fixed by the British and French. The Madras Presidency ensured that there were at least 35% women on its ships carrying indentured labourers to the colonies, with less than that number, the ship was not allowed to leave the port. The British also ensured that women leaving the Indian ports did not have sexually transmitted diseases (STD). Women workers were difficult to get, so the official in Mauritius asked for 25–30% women of a 'good' character and in the course of time the ratio of women would increase. As the Indian government refused to change its formula of 3:1, therefore women were trafficked from different parts of Tamil Nadu. In the French Indian colonies, women were allowed to leave only after entering into a written contract by the agent. They encouraged family migration and couples moving out to colonies. Those who guaranteed to work and return between 3 and 5 years were allowed to emigrate. This is how Tamil women migrated as married, single, deserted or trafficked to the plantations developed by the English and French in the eighteenth century (Mani 2001). The Emigration Act that was passed in the year 1883 regulated the indentured labour. Their registrations were now made mandatory. Apart from the government, through the district collector, some others were also recognised to register (agents) and allowed to send labourers for emigration. The district collector was empowered to supervise the emigration at all stages of migration. This also prevented women from leaving alone. Women were allowed to emigrate only with their parents or with the husband. Indians were sent only to British colonies, (Mauritius, Jamaica, British Guyana, Trinidad, St Lucia, Grenada, St Vincent and St Kitts.); to French Colonies (Martinique (Caribbean) Guadeloupe, French Guyana); to Dutch Colonies (Dutch Guyana, Surinam) and to the Danish colony of Saint Croix.

Second Wave of Emigration

This phase was a period in which Tamils started integrating with the people of the host countries. Many of them participated in the liberation movements against colonial governments. They were part of the trade unions. They fought for the rights of labourers and for justice and dignity. They moved from 'confrontation' to the 'negotiation' period with the political parties and influential associations for their rights. During the nineteenth century, several million Tamil speaking people moved to the Straits Settlements (Singapore and Malaysia). Almost 28 million migrated from South India to South-East Asian countries. This was a melting pot because Europeans, Chinese, Indian and other ethnic groups of South-East Asia were constantly passing through this territory. Tamil Muslims and traders from the Hindu religion were moving out of the Madras presidency and this place became the connecting point for the South India (particularly from Tamil Nadu) and South-East Asia. A '…sense of Tamil diasporic consciousness emerged…. The colonial state identified plantation workers and urbanites alike as "Tamils"…' (Amrith 2009). The colonial state recognised both the plantation worker as well as those who settled in the ports for various works as 'Tamils'. The elite urban Tamil tried to identify more directly with the masses in the rubber estates and thereby moved towards a diasporic community. This consciousness became more profound during the 1930s with the rise of the Malay nationalism when Tamil intellectuals highlighted the plight of the plantation workers and other living and working conditions of Tamils.

> ...Tamil diasporic consciousness was a product of the shifting balance between mobility and immobility across the seas: a sharper sense of diasporic consciousness emerged as a consequence of immobilization, rather than mobility. Diasporic connections, on this view, solidified when oceanic connections attenuated. Until the 1870s, the intensity of oceanic connections across the Bay of Bengal forestalled the sense of separation—between home and abroad—at the root of the diasporic experience. (Amrith 2009)

Another outcome of the 'Tamil' consciousness that was taking place in the Straits was the 'diasporic consciousness' that literature has dealt with the inward looking picture of the diasporic communities isolated from contact with others. The diasporic consciousness was forged through the interaction between multiple diasporas in the port cities of South-East Asia. In the port cities of South-East Asia, shaped to an unusual extent by mobility, being part of a diaspora was, by the 1930s, an essential part of what it was to be modern. During the 1930s, however, significant numbers of women began to migrate to the port cities of the Straits Settlements for the first time, leading to the establishment of settled families. This applied more to the Chinese than to Tamil communities; the gender ratio within Singapore's Tamil communities, for instance, remained at fewer than 400 women for every 1000 men at the end of the decade. Nevertheless, the 1930s did see the arrival of more Tamil women in Singapore and Malaysia, lending a more settled character to the population (Amrith 2009).

Professor Sunil Amrith (2009) of Harvard University has stated that the Bay of Bengal facilitated the migration of Tamils to the Straits Settlements and the Tamils who went as plantation workers and those who went to do business assimilated to create a Tamil diasporic consciousness. As Singapore was a place frequented by Europeans, Chinese and Tamil traders of Hindu and Muslim religious backgrounds, they created together a diasporic consciousness.

When Britain granted independence to the colonies (decolonisation process), the Tamils were left in the lurch. They lost the support of the governments in power and the locals became hostile towards them. Many countries such as Sri Lanka and Burma repatriated them through political agreement with the country of origin. Some of them became 'stateless' in that process. Tamil women of the diaspora were once part of the indentured labour doing hard work besides looking after the family in the most unfamiliar conditions. They were also part of the liberation struggle against colonialism. Thillaiyadi Valliammai was a South African Tamil woman who worked with Mahatma Gandhi in her early years when she developed her non-violent methods in South Africa fighting its apartheid regime.

One of the earliest formal attempts to get women involved (in South Africa) was the Indian Women Association (IWA) formed in 1907 by Tamil Christian women. The IWA did sterling work in Tamil vernacular education, including forming and

running The Durban Tamil School (Desai and Vahed 2010, 278). Gandhi started a
Patriotic League Fund to collect funds from Indian merchants. Indian women
prepared pillowcases and handkerchiefs from cloth provided by merchants for
Ambulance Corps and Women's Patriotic League (327).

The Rani Jhansi Regiment—The First All Women's Military Wing

Lakshmi Sahgal also known as Captain Lakshmi (born 24 October 1914 in Madras,
Madras Presidency, British India) was an ex-officer of the Indian National Army,
and the Minister of Women's affairs in the Azad Hind Government. Lakshmi
decided to study medicine because she wanted to be of service to the poor, especially to poor women. As a result, she received an MBBS degree from Madras
Medical College in 1938. A year later, she received her diploma in gynaecology
and obstetrics. In 1940, she left for Singapore where she established a clinic for the
poor, mostly migrant labour, from India. She became one of the most popular and
prosperous gynaecologists in the city. She was not only a competent doctor but also
played an active role in the India Independence League which contributed greatly to
the freedom movement in India. In 1942, during the historic surrender of Singapore
by the British to the Japanese, she worked hard in serving the injured prisoners of
war. In the process, she came in contact with many Indian Prisoners of War
(POW's) who were thinking of forming an Indian liberation army. Subhash
Chandra Bose arrived in Singapore on 2 July 1943. In the next few days, at all his
public meetings, Netaji spoke of his determination to raise a women's regiment, the
Rani of Jhansi Regiment, which would also 'fight for Indian Independence and
make it complete'. Lakshmi wasted no time in joining this new regiment. She was
given the rank of Colonel. The unit had the strength of a Brigade. In a regular army,
this women's army unit was the first of its kind in Asia. The army fought on the side
of the Axis powers against the British (Chhabra 2015).

It was Captain Lakshmi Swaminathan Sahgal who went to Ipoh (Malaysia) and
convinced the parents of Janaki Thevar. First, she went to Singapore and joined the
force meant exclusively for women. They were trained to do all that a soldier had to
do like night marches, swamp marches. There were some thousand girls and
according to her 'there were members of Rani Jhansi Regiment who were ready to
be members of the 'Jaan Baaz' a suicide squad'. She trained many and the INA
officers escorted them. After the end of the Second World War, she joined the
Women's Council in the Women's Movement (Malaysian Indian Congress) and
was made as its Senator in which capacity she served Parliament for 5 years.
S. Dhannalakshmi joined the *Ranis* at the age of fourteen as she was very young and
also sick, she had to stay back in Singapore and after the war, she was given the
duty of taking back girls to Kuala Lumpur and Ipoh in a truck. Anjaly Suppiah was
trained in the Waterloo Street camp in Singapore and received a rigorous training

by walking miles and miles and in rifle shooting. She said in an interview: '*some of us were given special training to go to India, shot guns, grenades, first aid etc.... when INA was disbanded it was difficult to accept the civilian life again*'. Back in Kuala Lumpur, I also met several other women freedom fighters including Anjali Punnuswami and Muniammah Rangaswamy. I met Anjali Punnuswamy, also a member of the Rani Jhansi Regiment, in Rangoon. She spoke neither English nor Hindi. She spoke only Tamil, so we communicated through an interpreter. Here was a young girl who at the age of 18 had been fired by Netaji's call for freedom—'*tum mujhe khoon do, mein tumhe azaadi doonga*'—you give me blood and I will give you freedom. She had gone to Burma and undergone both hardship and military training. Muniammah Rangaswamy, also a member of the Rani Jhansi Regiment said '*I heard Netaji at the Selangor club. I got inspired and I joined him*'. She studied only up to fifth standard and received rifle training. Returning after the war, she married and settled in Malaysia (Chhabra). As the names indicate that they are all mostly women who went from Tamil Nadu to Malaysia, Singapore and Burma. Netaji established an exclusive women's wing to fight for the independence of India. The Tamil diaspora actively participated in it.

The Third Wave of Emigration—Postcolonial Migration

In the postcolonial era, Tamil migration witnessed two phases. The first phase from the 1960s to the 1980s witnessed migration by professionals and students. Many women went abroad from Tamil Nadu for higher studies and settled in the industrialised countries such as scientists, engineers, doctors, lawyers, academics and researchers. Tamil Nadu was also the source area for the IT wave of the highly skilled migrants in the 90s. The IT 'wave' also took Tamil women to non-western states such as Singapore, Malaysia and to some Gulf countries.

The majority of Tamils in the United States are from the middle- to upper income backgrounds and are well educated, often in English-medium schools in India. It is estimated that of the 20,000 Asian Indians now migrating to the United States each year and currently a notable number of Tamil speakers form a small and distinctive minority. They are different from other South Asian groups emigrating to the US. The vast majority of the Tamils in the US are Brahmins, (till the IT wave in 1990s) the community at the top of the Hindu caste hierarchy. Brahmins attributed 'affirmative action' as the main reason for their emigration. Non-Brahmins claimed that Brahmins always take the best opportunities and have the knowledge and ability to take advantage of political conditions in Tamil Nadu and tried to go to developed and industrialised countries such as the US (Underwood 1986).

1916 forms an important year for the emergence of two movements in Tamil Nadu, namely the Home Rule Movement and the Non-Brahmin Movement. The latter movement engineered 'a revolt of the masses' against 'the tyranny of caste'. Through the Justice Party, the non-Brahmins of Tamil Nadu asserted themselves against the intellectual oligarchy of the upper caste people. The Tamil Renaissance heralded by EV Ramasamy Naicker in Tamil Nadu was attributed by them for their flight to the US. The rationalist party with its ideology of self-respect movement condemned those who were commercialising religion, particularly the priestly class. Rituals and religious practices were declared irrational (Rajaraman 1988). Initial emigrants to the US from Tamil Nadu were the professionals such as doctors, engineers, scientists, etc. The 1990s witnessed the 'IT wave' which took several Tamil families irrespective of caste and religion to the West Coast of America particularly to the Silicon Valley. The Tamils on the West Coast and elsewhere are heterogeneous and from different parts of Tamil Nadu with their knowledge base being software.

Tamil immigrants have in the process come to question certain aspects of their traditions, even as they try to preserve other aspects. They are now actively engaged in renegotiating long-held cultural identifications. This renegotiation is symbolically expressed in various forms which demonstrate some of the situational and social variation that occurs in the process. Two examples of this renegotiation and translation of Tamil identity can be seen in the use of Tamil names and the practice of Indian dance (Underwood 1986). Tamil families in the US did not change their names (which are usually long when combined, customarily, with that of the father), rather they shortened them for ease of others to address them by. Most of the Tamil families train their children in the music and dance which they consider as keeping in touch with their country, religion and culture.

Celena Costa-Pinto of Monash University in her paper 'Constructing Identity, exercising agency in the diaspora: Narratives of Indian women migrants in Melbourne' (2007) talks about the second wave of Indian migration which started in the 1970s and continues to this day. It includes Anglo-Indians and ethnic Indians. In the 2001 census of Australia, 95,452 India-born migrants were identified as the second largest group of migrants from Asia after the Chinese. The migrants were from urban backgrounds, seeking white collar jobs and representative of the skilled cohort favoured by Australia's skilled immigration policy. Most Indian women migrate as brides, wives and mothers. This paper examines the narratives of 24 women—eight each from three major ethnicities the Sikhs, Tamils and Anglo-Indians. She narrates the experience of one Tamil emigrant who migrated when she was young and all of a sudden became a widow, in order to escape the social stigma she migrated to Australia and after almost 20 years she decided to remarry by that time her children were adults and she was working as a senior executive in IT industry. She surfed Internet sites targeted at seeking Indians and made her choice. The author had focused on three areas—the impact of technology, the assignment of household activities and sociocultural reproduction—to show that women create coherence in their lives through flexibility, autonomy and self-reflexivity.

There are many studies done on the UK's Tamil population which have focused on Sri Lankan Tamils. The UK is also home to Tamil migrants of other countries (state origins) mainly Indian, but also Malaysian, Singaporean, Mauritian and South African. This study *Diversity and Diaspora*: *Everyday Identifications of Tamil*

Migrants in the UK (Jones 2013) is the first to give a detailed account of the narratives and experiences of Tamils in the UK from diverse state backgrounds, and to address the question of their identification with a 'Tamil diaspora'. The study conceptualises diaspora as a process and considers the actual embodied practices through which migrants enact diasporic identifications, which vary in different contexts and before different audiences. This study is about the lives of migrants, their social relationships, the domestic space of home and the performances of faith and ritual, which are considered not as discrete sites, but as interrelated components of a complex landscape upon which 'being Tamil' and 'doing Tamil-ness' is enacted. The UK's Tamil population also incorporates diversity on other bases which cross-cut statehood; religion, migration impetus and the subject positions of gender, class and age.

Outstanding Tamil women of the diaspora include Ms. Navaneetham Pillai (South African of Tamil origin) an outstanding lawyer, who contributed substantially as UN High Commissioner for Human Rights (2008–2014). In the corporate sector there is Indira Nooyi of Pepsico, then there is the first Special Rapporteur on Violence against Women (VAW), Radhika Coomarassamy, who is of Sri Lankan Tamil origin, and a host of authors most of them young, whose works are considered for the Booker Prize and other prizes who are all of Tamil origin. In Fiji, Mauritius, La Réunion, South Africa, Singapore, Malaysia, the US, the UK and Canada, Tamil women of the diaspora are law makers and administrators, playing a significant role in the development of the host countries. It is a major departure for the Tamil women diaspora whose journey across the seas started as indentured labourers then moved on to protest movements for liberation from the clutches of colonialism and imperialism, and now they are an integral part of the host societies contributing to the growth of governance, society, the economy and culture. Take the case of Renuga Veeran who is an Australian badminton player. She has represented both Malaysia and Australia internationally as a badminton player. As part of the Australian Olympic Team, she paired with Leanne Choo and reached the quarter-finals in the women's doubles at the 2012 Summer Olympics. Renuga was born on 20 June 1986 in Kuala Lumpur, Malaysia. Her mother, father and brother (Raj Veeran) all played badminton, representing Malaysia in international competitions. She is an ethnic Tamilian and speaks Tamil fluently. She gave an interview in Tamil on the Australian Special Broadcasting Service (SBS) Tamil Radio a week after returning from the London Olympics. Ambiga Sreenevasan (born 1956) is a prominent Malaysian lawyer and human rights advocate and is one of the eight recipients of the US International Women of Courage Award in 2009. She formerly served as the President of the Malaysian Bar Council from 2007 to 2009 and was former co-chairperson of Bersih, an NGO Coalition advocating for free and fair elections.

The postcolonial era Tamil migration was the labour migration from India. Millions of Indians work overseas, particularly in the six oil-rich Gulf Arab countries of Bahrain, Kuwait, Oman, Qatar, Saudi Arabia and the United Arab Emirates. As many as 6 million Indian expatriates send home 20 billion dollars a year from Gulf States. Three-fourth of them were migrated from four southern states (Tamil Nadu, Karnataka, Kerala and Andhra Pradesh) of India, But reports abound that the migrants are mistreated, according to workers' associations and human rights groups. 'Reports of foreign women working in domestic positions being beaten or sexually abused by their employers and recruiting agents were common (in 2006)', said a US State Department report on Bahrain, where 130,000 Indians work. The Tamil Nadu Migration Survey estimates 2.2 million Tamils as emigrant workers. According to the TMS, the number of women emigrants is estimated to be 3.3 lakhs or 15% of the total emigrants. Most of them leave for Gulf countries, Singapore and Malaysia to work as domestic helpers, cleaners and to do odd jobs. The higher proportion of women emigrants is found in Qatar (11.8%), Oman (11.2%), United Arab Emirates (10.4%), Kuwait (9.2%), Singapore (8.8%) and Malaysia (8.7%).

Tamil Diaspora Consciousness to Diasporic Consciousness

Tamil women have been moving out of the country from the beginning of the eighteenth century. They were taken as part of the 'indentured' labour force and through agents such as the 'Kanganis'. Tamil women who accompanied men went with the hope of return but only very few could make it and most of them settled in the places to which they emigrated. It is also interesting to note that Tamil women participated in the struggle for freedom from the destination countries. The 'second wave' of emigration saw them as fighters for their own rights as well as fighters for the liberation of their own countries of origin. Many Tamil women settled in the destination countries and received education. It is clear from the literature scanned for this study that Tamil women—be they in the US, Canada, Australia, Singapore, Malaysia or the Middle East—continue to learn the Tamil language (their children are told to keep the ethnic identity by learning Tamil) and keep some of the cultural expressions like Carnatic music dances such as Bharatanatyam. In the article on 'Transmigrant Indian Women: Creators of Diasporic Spaces' Shobhita Jain (2010) sums up the experience of women diaspora:

> ...lessons may be learnt through the story of their vicissitudes as transmigrant Indian women for the creation of new spaces for themselves and hence for women empowerment globally. Participating actively in 'transnational spaces' (as explained by Faist 2004), transmigrant women negotiate many critical matters associated with the continuation of family relations which they Shape, maintain and re-shape through social networks.

Tamil women according to Jones (2013) are an 'aesthetic community' in the preservation of social lives, their homes, and performances of faith and ritual and as a 'moral community'. Non-Sri Lankan women's solidarity with the 'pain' of Sri Lankan Tamils in the civil war period is well documented and it is a proof of being a 'moral community'. So the Tamil women of the diaspora play the role of being an 'aesthetic and moral' community in the destination countries.

Tamil Women diaspora who started their journey as indentured went to the colonies as single, widowed, married and some escaping the violence against them (women). Two centuries after their journey to a new and unknown destination woman created a space for themselves. In the period of indenture, they worked along with men, earning money and thereby asserting their economic independence. They were not cut-off from the home country when it was fighting the liberation war. Associations were started and women in the Strait settlements even went militant under Netaji Subhash Chandra Bose's INA (Indian National Army) and patriotic feelings were running high in the colonies with the visit of Indian leaders. Enough and more support for India's independence was coming from outside India and Tamil women did their best in the colonies to create this pressure on the colonial power. They also started contributing to the host country with their education and professional training. Tamil women are in large number software engineers, doctors, scientists, chartered accountants and involved in administration of various kinds in the host country both in the private and public sector. In the feminist writing of *Kala pani,* the author Mehta (2006) says the widows, adolescent girls....such women 'transformed social marginality into personalized historicity when they embarked on a ...journey in search of redefinition and subjective visibility'. The Tamil women of the diaspora achieved a triple win—one for the host, one for the home and one for themselves.

References

Amrith, S.S. 2009. Tamil Diasporas Across the Bay of Bengal. *The American Historical Review* 114 (3): 547–572.

Chhabra, Sagari. 2015. In *Search of Freedom: Journey Through India and South-East Asia.* HarperCollins Publishers.

Costa-Pinto, Celena. 2007. Constructing Identity, Exercising Agency in the Diaspora: Narratives of Indian Women Migrants in Melbourne. Monash University *Eras,* Edition 9, Number. http://www.arts.monash.edu.au/eras.

Desai, Ashwin, and Goolam Vahed. 2010. *Inside Indian Indenture: A South African Story, 1860–1914.* Cape Town: HSRC Press.

Finkelman, and Miller. 1998. *Macmillan Encyclopedia of World Slavery,* 1:293.

Jain, Shobhita. 2010. Transmigrant Indian Women: Creators of Diasporic Spaces. *Journal of Social Science* 25 (1-2-3): 51–57.

Jones, Demelza. 2013. *Diversity and Diaspora: Everyday Identifications of Tamil Migrants in the UK.* School of Sociology, Politics and International Studies, January: University of Bristol, Faculty of Social Sciences and Law.

Mani, Marimuthu. 2001. *Socio-Economic History of Tamil Nadu Emigration 1840–1920,* Salem: Balamma Press. (A Book written in Tamil).

Mehta, Brinda. 2006. The South Asian Woman's Kala Pani Journey. In *Borders: Bridges and Bodies.*

Rajaraman, P. 1988. *The Justice Party—A Historical Perspective, 1916–1937.* Chennai: Poompozhil Publishers.

Underwood, Kelsey Clark. 1986. Image and Identity: Tamil Migration to the US. *Kroeber Anthropological Papers* 65 (66): 65–72.

Part III
The Contemporary Challenges

Chapter 8
Fitting in: The Joys and Challenges of Being an Indian Woman in America

Mahua Bhattacharya

'मैं तो संग जाउं बंवास'
('I would like to go to your exile with you')
(Bhupen Hazarika's lyrics for the Hindi film 'Ek Pal')

'I think how I just want to feel at home, where people know me. Instead I remember, when I meet Mr. Boone, that home was a place of forced subservience, and I know that my wish is that of an adult wanting to stay a child: to be known by others but to know nothing, to feel no responsibility. Instead I recognize, when I walk out in my neighborhood, that each speaking-to another person has become fraught, for me; with the history of race and sex and class' (Pratt 1988, 28–29).

'Whether we are individuals or groups, we are made up of lines and these lines are very varied in nature. The first kind of line which forms us is segmentary—of rigid segmentarity... At the same time, we have lines of segmentarity which are much more supple, as it were molecular...At the same time, again, there is a third kind of line, which is even more strange: as if something carried us away, across our segments, but also across our thresholds, towards a destination which is unknown, not forseeable, not pre-existent...' (Deleuze and Parnet 2002, 125).

Marriage in a multicultural country like India is akin to being in a diasporic situation for a woman who takes a leap of faith into the unknown. She is held together by pride in her heritage, a faith in *karma* and a belief in her *dharma*: to follow her karma, no matter where and with whom it is carried out. This prospect of being a '*paraya dhan*' (a keepsake for someone else) always casts a shadow on her upbringing. Her body, from the moment she is born, is always under surveillance. If she is not the 'perfect' woman, she is subject to rebuke and ridicule. This situation used to be particularly difficult when arranged marriages were the norm; but today, when a woman has a little more say in who she marries, the pressures to be qualified and procure a 'good' job have mounted. This complicates the notion of 'home' for Indian women that Pratt so eloquently describes in the above quote.

M. Bhattacharya (✉)
Elizabethtown College, One Alpha Drive, Elizabethtown, PA 17022, USA
e-mail: bhattacharm@etown.edu

© Springer Nature Singapore Pte Ltd. 2018
A. Pande (ed.), *Women in the Indian Diaspora*,
https://doi.org/10.1007/978-981-10-5951-3_8

A woman in India lives in the liminal space of the Deleuzian molar and molecular identities, given the pressures she faces never to be comfortable in her home.

The reference to the Hindi song mentioned above is from a film, *Ek Pal*, which could be called somewhat 'feministic,' since it engages with the agency of a woman who decides to keep her child, even though the child is not from her husband but from an extramarital affair. This movie, in the late 1980s, marked the beginning of a feministic phase in Indian popular culture that tapped into a sense of independence that marked the serious entrance into the job market by middle class women. Several woman-centred films, like *Paroma, Arth, Fire*, etc., explored a woman's independence and her sense of identity in modern Indian society. Women film directors like Aparna Sen, Kalpana Lajmi, etc., were the trailblazers in this context (Kalpana Lajmi 1986).

But while the Hindi film *Ek Pal* stopped short of having the woman truly question her agency in the film, the Bengali film *Paroma*, which explored the same subject matter, went further and attempted to explore the awareness of a woman who decides to live life without the support of a man.

These two films reveal a chasm in the sensibilities of the two cultures that form the context of my own marriage. This makes me come to the conclusion that marrying out of one's community, even if it is to an Indian, resembles the situation when women marry diasporic men or men who might be born in a foreign culture.

This chapter explores the joys and challenges of a diasporic Indian woman who chose to live in the US after marriage. It also engages the research done by Brah (1996), who shows how political contexts in their adopted countries shape South Asian women's struggles when they try to fit in. This paper will also bring into this dialogue the issue of subjectivity formation, as explored in the research of Deleuze and Guattari (1987), which often shapes the way Indian women in the US try to assimilate in American society. Finally, it also complicates the idea of 'home' that women settling in the US feel about their homeland, India. This idea is akin to what Pratt (1988) calls a place of 'forced subservience' that hides forms of repression, exploitation and violence which one may not be conscious of till they come flooding in when contexts change in a diasporic situation.

Much of this chapter is autobiographical, but will also include the results of interviews with Indian diasporic women spanning three generations and living in or near Harrisburg, the capital of Pennsylvania.[1]

It is extremely difficult to pick a moment in one's life in an alien culture that marks the feeling of 'arrival' or the moment of having 'made it,' since the life of a diasporic person in an alien environment is always in flux. Is it the moment of arrival at the airport, the perennial liminal space between two cultures, where a total stranger in a forbidding uniform with suspicious eyes peers at you and then miraculously stamps your passport, saying 'welcome to America'? Or is it the moment one chooses to present oneself at an embassy to leave one's familiar land to take the proverbial leap of faith to a territory to which one is forced to move or to

[1]The author would like to thank the women of Harrisburg and Lancaster County who participated in the survey conducted for this paper. Their names have not been included to protect their privacy.

which one feels inexplicably drawn? Or is it the moment when one carries home a paycheck over which one is in complete control?

Brah's (1996) influential monograph that explores discourses spanning several cultures shows how political contexts affect women's agencies. Brah's situation is powerful in showing that the more repressive a country is, the more difficult it is for women to assert themselves. In such a situation, narratives of women tend to be very different from situations where women find themselves valued.

The political context surrounding the entry of Indian women into the US in the 60s is illustrated by the fact that it followed the lifting of a ban on the entry of Asians. Asian Americans experienced exclusion by law from the United States between 1880 and 1965, and were largely prohibited from naturalisation until the 1940s. Since the Immigration and Nationality Act of 1965, a new wave of Asian immigration has occurred, and nearly 40% of all new immigrants to the United States in 2010 were from Asia (Pew Research Center 2015).

When women were finally allowed entry, it was largely to follow their husbands who had come to the US for work. Initially, this was not seen as a prestigious move. There were horror stories filling the news that men would bring these women under pressure from their parents who would believe that having a bride from India would keep their sons tethered to their roots and family in India. However, the same stories would also describe how these women would often become maids in the homes that their husbands would set up with western wives. These Indian women would be unable to escape their situation, trapped in a foreign country without the support of their families or communities.

Even when they came under better circumstances, Indian women's lives were full of uncertainties, loneliness and exclusion from the mainstream American life. This was despite the fact that there was an Indian wave during that time which allowed for the flowering of a certain kind of spirituality inspired by the Beatles, the civil rights movement, and later, the protest against the Vietnam War. Some of the women who form part of the survey in this paper eloquently describe how their lives centred around their husbands in part because their entry into the job market in the US was difficult. This difficulty was due to several reasons, including non-recognition of their academic degrees from India by the institutions in which they wanted to work. Not only was this factor affecting their acceptance into American life, but their home life was also complicated by the unavailability of materials required to create the home culture that they were used to in India, and a resulting difficulty adjusting and integrating into an American lifestyle that included differences in dressing styles, food habits and cultural values.

One participant stated:

> Frankly, I did not know at the time of my graduation that I would come to the USA, although I always wanted to study abroad. But the only way I could come would be after marriage since coming to the USA as a single person was not an option. Parents, especially father, were strict and conservative and not open to this idea.

Subsequent waves of Indians, coming to the US and the generations of Indians growing up in America created gaps in the experiences of Indian women in the US.

As more women came to the US to study and mingled with women growing up here, their experiences started merging when it came to choosing life partners. Some of them became more comfortable accepting both American and diasporic men and creating lives for themselves here that differed substantially from life in India. Of course, many also went back to their families and joined the work force in India that valued their advanced degrees procured here, marrying men who respected them for their qualifications.

The Deleuzian concepts of the molar, the molecular, and the line of flight of subjectivity formation, quoted above, allow for exploring how on the one hand, some women find it easy to settle in a foreign land, marking a clear break with where they had grown up, while on the other, some women find it difficult. The molar tendencies in this description can be described briefly as behaviours that are learned within a certain context that gets so ingrained within us that it prevents us from accepting change. The molecular, on the other hand, refers to 'connections with others and objects at the micro-level of interactions ... that involves a letting go of molarised roles and rigid identifications' (Ellwood 2011, 964). Finally, Deleuze and Parnet refer to the third kind of movement as 'lines of flight', which is completely different from the first two. In this situation, the subject is carried away 'towards a destination which is unknown, not foreseeable, not pre-existent' (2002, 125). This movement allows one to accept new ways of being that make for better assimilative practices if one is encountering a foreign culture. Of course, one can remain a molarised personality even while living in a foreign culture, and one can experience the lines of flight even if one has never left one's native place of birth. Also, if I were to speak from personal experience, the seeds of this movement are sometimes planted long before the movement to go abroad is made.

The Deleuzian concept of lines of flight explores the desire to be free (Rayner 2013). Says Rayner, in his analysis of Deleuze and Guattari's books, that, this idea links human creativity to flight. 'It is our desire to escape the status quo that leads us to innovate. Like the prisoner, we dream of being anywhere but here. We coordinate, form alignments, combine our powers and innovate. We remake the world on creative new trajectories'. This desire to leave to be 'free' is also the spirit of the globalised soul, a spirit that sees itself as belonging here, there and everywhere. Rayner (2013) opines that it is not an accident that Deleuze and Guattari aligned their ideas with the New Left movements in the 60s and 70s France, which they perceived as attempts to open up different and more liberated ways of living.

So while the counterculture in the US was at its height in the 60s, Indians were also being inundated with ideas on the different ways of 'being'—that gushed in from the US and other western countries. Growing up with a woman prime minister, Indira Gandhi, ruling India from 1966, I personally felt at one with the women of a particular class who felt empowered and liberated. This also echoes the sentiments of the women surveyed who had come here in the 70s.

This is where I would like to unpack the threads of my life that have impacted my experience of being in the US as a woman from India. While I have chosen to adopt US citizenship, I have also retained an Indian identity, formally, through the OCI status that recognises my desire to stay connected with my heritage, while also extending that right to my American husband.

Personal Life: A Narrative of Both Rootlessness and Stability

As Avtar Brah has demonstrated so admirably in his *Cartographies of Diaspora*, our lives are never formed in a vacuum.

I was born in the late 1950s into a privileged middle-class family of a doctor in the Indian Air Force. My father was an officer and was thus able to give his daughters a convent school education. This education laid emphasis on an Indian heritage and entailed learning about the formation of the Indian state and British history in a way that fudged the exploitative nature of the Indian colonial past. Similarly, we learned about the story of Jesus in our visits to the church and public ceremonies conducted in the school while remaining engaged in visits to the temples and religious festivals in which our parents were involved. This was the nature of our Indian identity. It did not really question the significance of the westernised education that was part of our privileged existence.

My parents did not have an arranged marriage. My father fell in love with my mother who was not a very educated lady, but belonged to royalty in Bangladesh before partition. Though my mother was relatively uneducated, she could speak English, which she had to pick up due to my father's profession. She was determined to have me educated and lead a life that allowed me to have choices different from hers.

While we did live a life of some privilege, it also entailed hardships. We were frequently transferred to different parts of India. I was born in Pune, Maharashtra, in western India, for example, while my younger sister was born some 1500 odd km or more east, in Kolkata, West Bengal. This meant that we not only did not feel rooted to one place, but that we also had a rough academic life since we had to change schools frequently. I do not remember any of my childhood friends. I remember flitting from one school to another—collecting the addresses of classmates with whom I rarely exchanged any letters later. This was, however, the beginning of a change—a change from my molar identification to one in a homogenised space and culture.

My cousins who grew up in Delhi (unlike me, travelling all over India) loved western music and introduced me to Elvis, The Rolling Stones, Bob Dylan, and Joan Baez. I loved them all and would sing their songs in public venues whenever I got a chance.

I majored in Japanese in Jawaharlal Nehru University, a leading university in Delhi, in the 1970s on the advice of my father, who dissuaded me from following in his steps to become a doctor, but who agreed that women should not merely be housewives but may want to think of working if their married life necessitated it. His words were, 'A foreign language will allow you to be employable even when you are saddled with responsibilities of home and children after marriage'. These experiences that filled me with a strange excitement could be considered 'molecular', since I could feel myself transforming from the molarised, inward-looking person that I was until then.

While I did not have much choice to refuse my father's dictum, I enjoyed studying a foreign language and was even more pleased when I got to travel to Japan in my second year of study, when I was only 17 years old. This visit changed my life. It marked my turn from the Deleuzian molecular to the line of flight that I describe above.

I wanted to return to Japan, and I would get that chance soon after my marriage to my first husband. Without going into too many details, I would like to state that the kinds of experiences women today face over family versus career were very much also my own. My ex-husband needed me to work and support him while not being supportive about household chores. The situation became unbearable and a divorce resulted soon after. This happened in the 80s, when divorces were still a social taboo, and I had to prevaricate whenever the issue of my marital situation came up.

However, this was also the point at which my Deleuzian 'desire to be free' was at its peak. My professional life in JNU, where I taught after completing my studies, while protecting my financial status, was also filled with challenges that propelled me to seek out newer, more liberated ways of being.

I did not go to America in search of a job or career, family migration or seeking exile. I went there because I fell in love. I married an American whom I met at the University of Chicago in the summer of 1993, where I initially went as a Visiting Fellow. My husband was doing his doctorate in Indian religions and philosophy and was attracted to the philosophy of Hinduism.

My husband grew up in a small town in Missouri as a Catholic. His family consisted of his grandparents who were married for about 60 years and his mother, who lost her husband in a train accident and raised her only son while pursuing a degree in nursing. His mother raised him single-handedly and sent him to college on her salary, as well as a generous scholarship. Divorces are not common in his family, so they were a little nervous when they heard that I had had one. In some ways, they are as traditional as any Indian family.

My father was also initially concerned when I told him I was marrying Jeff. While he had supported my decision to divorce, he was not enthusiastic about my second marriage. However, when he met Jeff, he was charmed by his personality. Jeff and I got married at an Arya Samaj *mandir*, where to Jeff's great joy; he was able to convert to Hinduism. This led to me rediscovering my Hindu roots through Jeff!

My departure for the US preceded the migration of the new 'transnational class' of IT professionals, and so I was inducted into the diasporic Indian community by the generation that had gone during the 60s and 70s, whose culture is described quite eloquently in Jhumpa Lahiri's *Namesake*. But my liminal position between the wider American community and this Indian community also shielded me from the subtle nuances of what it meant to be a 'traditional' Indian woman and a westernised Indian woman.

It is true that I went to America with some baggage. My Indian upbringing had made a feminist out of me. Patriarchy reigned supreme in both my father and my ex-husband. Meeting my American husband, however, made me realise how healthy, loving and communicating a relationship could be. I felt supported and cared for and never felt that I had to be or do something to 'win' his love or to be 'accepted'. His family is a traditional American family with strong family values, which means that we give each other our individual space and accept who we are. His family was fascinated by my cooking and my late grandmother-in-law felt Jeff had married a 'traditional American girl', since I did not mind helping out in the kitchen.

Professional Life: A Narrative of Global Education and Adaptation

While the conditions of one's family life can be debilitating if they prove to be beyond one's control, professional lives are even more difficult to manage, since they are in the hands of hierarchies that seem to have no limit. My professional life in JNU allowed me access to worlds that were already transnational in nature, since I was teaching Japanese. Even though my first 8 years in JNU were full of uncertainties, they did provide me the financial independence that shielded me from the experiences I was facing in my first marital home.

I had a brief teaching experience in Japan that would have changed my life had I let it. I was quite successful there, due to the convent school education I received in India. However, I felt that my Indian-ness was never in doubt. I could not hide either my skin or my accent and it was precisely because of that that I was welcomed or shunned in certain contexts. Since I was not considered to be a 'native' speaker, I was paid considerably less than speakers from the US and UK. However, since that money was more than I was used to getting in India, it served me well. Due to my knowledge of Japanese, I was considered to be very successful in the company that hired me and they offered me a full-time job to teach English in Japan. I had to refuse, due to the part-time job I was offered in JNU upon my return to India.

Going to the US as a Visiting Fellow to the University of Chicago, which boasted of centres in postcolonial studies with Homi Bhabha and Dipesh Chakrabarty, and South Asian scholars such as Sheldon Pollock and Wendy Doniger, Bernard Cohn, Arjun Appadurai, etc., changed my life. I used my status as a Visiting Fellow to acquire as much knowledge as possible. I was fascinated by the reading lists that professors in various courses would prescribe and tried to read as many as I could. I was excited beyond belief. I went above and beyond what I was required to do in my excitement—and not having any obligation to any institution allowed me to overdose on my knowledge acquisition. It was pure pleasure, described eloquently by Deleuze and Guattari as 'moments in which the subject's sense of self disappears in the face of new, as-yet unknown, possibilities' (Cited in Ellwood 2011, 965).

Since I was on extraordinary leave with no pay, I was able to take up a part-time teaching position at DePaul University in Chicago, and I noticed how poor the conditions were for learning foreign languages in the US. I saw how professors made the most of the situation by devising techniques of teaching languages that were successful in imparting usable skills in practical situations.

I was also able to put to use, my skills as a warden in JNU, in the residential halls at the University of Chicago and was quite successful in being a caring 'resident head', as they called us and learnt a lot about the popular American culture through the undergraduate students. It was there that I learnt what a great chasm existed between US and Indian students of the same age in how they treat their teachers and their education.

Life changed drastically when I left Chicago for a small, insular, sleepy town in Pennsylvania, where Jeff was given his first full-time teaching position. In Chicago, people at least knew where India was and did not confuse me with the Native Americans. The town to which we moved was different. It reminded me of the small towns that Stephen King writes about: gun shops, churches that proselytise, sus-piciousness and closed-mindedness.

The town I moved to, had another dimension that people in India are not usually aware of. The character of Midwestern people in the US differs greatly from that of the Mid-Atlantic region. My husband describes the difference as 'Midwesterners love you till you give them a reason not to. Mid-Atlantic people distrust you till you give them a reason not to'. This meant that people on the street were not very welcoming. Similarly with some of the people in the college where my husband worked: we were an interracial couple that attracted suspicious looks (Ninian 2012). Being faculty at the local college protected us somewhat, since the college is quite respected in the community, but we faced problems amongst some staff that worked at the lower level administrative positions. We felt alienated at first in our new surroundings and it was the Indian community that we turned to for moral support.

The other cultural shock that we experienced at our new college was the intel-lectual gap that existed between it and the University of Chicago. Postcolonial studies were relatively new here, and the study of India was restricted to the study of religion. The study of Japan was virtually non-existent. Jeff was a fresh graduate of the University of Chicago and he wanted to explore some of the ideas he had acquired there at the college. While the students were very enthusiastic, he found that some of his colleagues felt threatened by his rigour. But the emphasis on student evaluation in the college, which is considered a 'teaching college', came to his rescue. He was so popular with the students that the senior administrative staff felt that he had to be given an incentive to stay—and soon after they started talking about a teaching position for me.

Despite the 13 years that I had spent teaching Japanese at JNU, I had to start as an adjunct teaching one intermediate course in Japanese and ESL (English as a

Second Language) to the foreign students who came to study at the college. This might not have happened to a native-born American with similar qualifications. Despite the need to start a full-fledged program in Japanese, the department where I was based felt the elementary level of Japanese that was being offered was enough. I started looking around and accepted a similar position teaching Japanese in a nearby university. Since my evaluations at both institutions were also very good, I was hired by our local college in the department of sociology and anthropology, as well as the program in women's studies. Soon I was teaching six courses a semester, when the normal load was three courses for regular faculty. This resulted in my getting a lecturer's position within a year and then a tenure-track position in teaching Japanese. The tenure-track position was the result of my teaching Japanese at the nearby university, which senior administrative personnel at the college felt would lure me away, so they wanted to create a position to hold me.

The experience of getting a tenure was quite novel for me, since that practice did not exist in India. Since a tenure meant a career for life, and not getting one was quite a disgrace, I had to throw myself into this experience. At the end of the 5 years that I got to 'prove' myself, I created a major in Japanese language for the college that now started to grow exponentially. I soon had more majors in my program than the French, German and Spanish courses put together, which was quite surprising for me too. A major is a student who studies a certain subject for 4 years in college. If we were to calculate the tuition required at our college, i.e. at $50,000 a year, it is a considerable figure—and in a private institution where students are the customers, it speaks volumes. Both my husband and I had achieved our goals and received our respective tenures. Both of us learnt to work for the cause of India and Japan, and through the Asian Studies program that we helped set up, were able to create the environment where we could be comfortable and help dispel some of the stereo-types about India and Japan from our students.

Our success has, however, created other problems for us. We feel that there is resentment and anxiety about giving us more resources. We are currently facing a zero-sum game where we feel that our colleagues feel that 'they have given us too much', not recognising that ultimately our success is their success in a private college setting.

Indian women have been coming to the US to study for a long time, and the situation in Pennsylvania is no different. Many of the respondents to my survey have done so. Some have come to graduate programs here for clinical psychology or education or to gain more experience as an IT professional. Says one that her motivation to come to the US was that she:

> ... wanted to work with client directly at onsite (I was an IT consultant), learn business in more detail. Basically the motivation was to improve as a professional. (10 April 2016)

In my professional life both at the University of Chicago as well as currently, being a minority woman had its pluses and minuses. While it is easy to empathise with women of colour, my background of privilege did make it difficult for me to appreciate fully the discrimination minority women experience on a daily basis in the US. While my non-white colour protected me from certain kinds of violence on the streets when I travelled alone in Chicago, it increased the pressure on me in my workplace. I was expected to be better, work harder and be more tolerant of workplace hardships than the people around me. I became a stronger person as a result of it. My experiences have kept me feeling grounded at all times.

Diasporic Life for Women: A Supportive Role

How does the Indian diasporic community in our area function? And how does it benefit me? Well to me, whose life is connected with a native of the host country, I feel it plays a supportive role. While Indian grocery stores and shops provide all the necessary tools for one to create an 'Indian' life, the people help create an environment that understands what it means to miss family, miss births, marriages, and deaths and miss the cultural ties that one grew up with. So, Indian get-togethers are a site for speaking in one's native tongue, watching movies that are popular in India, celebrating festivals and wearing Indian clothes. We do get quite passionate about what we consider to be 'our' culture. We define it variously and we use it to exclude people, to include people and also to selectively ignore it when it proves to be cumbersome. The definition of what constitutes Indian culture also varies with who is in the authoritative position to do the defining. For instance, if the person who is in that role happened to have arrived in America in the 60s, that person's understanding of Indian culture is determined by what was happening in India during that time. So the community might coalesce around those notions or split up, when the generations, which came later, challenge that definition.

For me, personally, the community has become somewhat of a hobby. It provides entertainment and also an opportunity to speak my mother tongue. In the beginning, it was like a piece of home, providing moral and emotional support. In Chicago, it was an opportunity to demonstrate one's talents and eat good, home-cooked Bengali food, which was not available in the Indian neighbourhood restaurants. We hung out with other Bengalis and celebrated pujas, which was something I missed when I was unable to go back to India because of the high airfares and our relatively low income in the early days.

Later on, it became a routine affair in Pennsylvania, where one hung out with like-minded people and shared experiences in the workplace and discussed current issues both in India and the US. However, because interpersonal politics and divisive infighting became, after a certain point, commonplace, it became very distressing to me. Since I live in the liminal space between the American and Indian social milieu, it is possible for me to switch off and insulate myself from the negativity that has, at various times, threatened to overwhelm me. It is, therefore, easy for me now to say that the diasporic community is a hobby for me and has stopped being the emotional blanket that it once was. And I have also, of course, developed a handful of deep and enduring friendships, distinct from my experience of the community as a whole.

The rich body of literature that analyses the diasporic community has been particularly useful for my own understanding of the diaspora. In my own profession where I teach Japanese language and culture and, when necessary, provide the 'authentic' voice to an Indian narrative, I have a vast body of texts to choose from, both in the print and visual form. When required, I have used movies like *Mississppi Masala* and *Mr. and Mrs. Iyer* to illustrate certain issues that I have felt needed to be highlighted. I have analysed Jhumpa Lahiri's *Namesake* and Aparna Sen's *Japanese Wife* for professional conferences, etc.

But when I reflect upon my own story, I feel that most analyses focus on the experiences of families that are internally homogenous, despite there being 3.7% Indian females who have married Americans (as opposed to 7.1% Indian males marrying American females (Ninian 2012). I do not find myself reflected in them except negatively, as Lahiri does with her one-dimensional character in *Namesake* who chooses to leave the protagonist for a Frenchman. She is portrayed as an ultimate traitor whose motives for leaving this 'nice' but 'confused' Indian man is not explored.

Radhakrishnan (2011), in her recent work on IT professionals, similarly makes an extensive study of Indians she believes are the new face of India, arguing that the transnational Indians are redefining for both Indians at home and abroad what the image of India should be. According to her:

> The new form of Indianness realized by the Indian IT professionals strengthens a bond to India as an eternal, unchanging source of cultural belonging and forges a sense of unity with Indians around the world. Yet this sense of belonging is necessarily divorced from the divisive messiness of everyday life in India. The appropriately different version of Indianness that emerges, then, is self consciously distinct from the cultural behemoth of the 'western' while at the same time compatible with a western, cosmopolitan life style. (p. 22)

While this may be true for the globetrotting IT professionals who are dependent on a volatile market in the US, the Indians who have been settled here for several generations are in no mood to return and have no desire to create an image for the Indian nation state. In fact, many feel alienated from their lives in India and feel that their return, albeit for short periods, do not result in feelings of regret about leaving India. Their ties are mainly with their families in India to whom they make regular phone calls or visits. But except for wishing their elderly relatives were with them, where they could take care of them, there is no desire for a long-term stay in India. These sentiments have been repeated over and over again by the members of my survey. One even said that,

> As a single woman, I have no "nosy neighbors" and "well wishers" trying to get into my business. (10 April 2016)

Many have children who have married Americans and face no reprisals for doing that. And Americans who form part of their families have been very serious about adopting Indian lifestyles without any demands being made on them from the Indian side.

My own experience of short-term trips has led me to believe that while there is a great preoccupation in the media about life in the US, people in India are not particularly happy with the diasporic community in the west, which has complicated the idea of 'home' for many. It appears that the economic power that this class brings with them creates inequalities and insecurities that unbalance the structure that the local Indians have created (Zhu 2007). While we hear of 'strategic partnership' between India and the US in foreign policy forums, there is a great chasm that separates the two peoples which some of us who live in the US have stopped experiencing. Whether it is multiculturalism or the new political environment where the voices of the minority communities have started mattering, the Indian community does not feel so sidelined anymore. Indians are rated quite highly in opinion polls (Newport and Himelfarb 2014) and there are several very successful Indians who feature quite prominently in the media.

One of my interviewees said:

> Initially my only outlet of interaction with American people was at my daughter's school. They would not talk to me at first. I am very social person, so I was kind of lost and was curious to know why they would not talk to me. I started initiating small talks with my daughter's friend's moms. Later, after knowing them well, I questioned them and to my surprise I was told that they thought I do not speak or understand English. Now, I have many good American friends that I can count on. I work with American people around me. My neighbors are all American and I feel blessed around the people I live. (10 April 2016)

Since I know many of the members personally, it seems that both molarised and lines of flight personalities exist in the community. There is a resistance to returning, whether they have come to the US in the 60s or in the 90s, and very often their children who grow up here clinch the deal for them.

Conclusion

Life in the US for many Indian women can be both challenging and rewarding, as I have experienced both in my life as well as in the lives of the people I have interviewed. Obviously, the political context that shapes the entry of women into the US does present some challenges. Very often it is shaped by the visas under which they come. But once they settle down to a job I found most of them celebrating the cleanliness, better standard of living, freedom of movement, better education for children, religious freedom and access to American and other cultures in this country. The challenges they express come from a certain sense of loneliness when they are older, the distance from the family, the lack of household help, and of course, a certain kind of discrimination that emanates from living in a foreign country. Interestingly, sometimes, Indians face discrimination from other Indians when they do not conform to what their understanding of being 'Indian' should be. Deleuzian subjectivity does a good job of analysing what happens when women face such situations. A molarised person would retreat into her shells and express her agency in hanging out with other people with similar ideas. People with a strong sense of their lines of flight would abandon this community and find different avenues to express their agencies.

It might be surprising to some that there is nothing in India that is not available in the US. From *chats* to *dosas* to *paan*, we get everything we want—so it is not for material satisfaction that we visit India. Our lives, both as women with opportunities to advance professionally and emotionally in our workplace and at home, and as people with certain unique cultural attributes, do enrich the cultural life of the US. In many respects, we feel that our lives, especially those of us who have chosen Americans as our spouses, are like 'bridges' that help the Americans with whom we come in contact understand who we are as Indians, and also explain to the Indians why we have chosen to make America our home (Zhu 2007).

References

Brah, Avtar. 1996. *Cartographies of Desire: Contesting Identities*. Abingdon, Oxon: Routledge.
Deleuze, G., and F. Guattari. 1987. *A Thousand Plateaus: Capitalism and Schizophrenia*. London: Continuum.
Deleuze, G., and C. Parnet. 2002. *Dialogues II*. New York: Columbia University Press.
Ek Pal. Directed by Kalpana Lajmi. 1986.
Ellwood, Constance. 2011. Undoing the Knots: Identity Transformations in a Study Abroad Programme. *Education Philosophy and Theory* 43 (9): 960–978.
Japanese Wife. Directed by Aparna Sen. India: Saregama Films, 2010.
Lahiri, Jhumpa. 2003. *The Namesake*. New York: Houghton Mifflin.
Mr. and Mrs. Iyer. Directed by Aparna Sen. India: MG Distributors, 2002.
Newport, Frank, and Igor Himelfarb. 2014. Americans Least Favorable toward Iran. *Gallup Politics* Accessed March 7, 2014. http://www.gallup.com/poll/161159/americans-least-favorable-toward-iran.aspx.
Ninian, Alex. 2012. The Indian and the Pakistani Diaspora in the US. *Contemporary Review* 294 (1706): 317–324.
Pew Research Center. 2015. The Rise of Asian Americans. *Pew Research Center's Social & Demographic Trends Project*. Accessed October 26.
Pratt, Minnie Bruce. 1988. Identity: Skin Blood Heart. Accessed July 2, 2016. https://activismtoolkitcu.files.wordpress.com/2014/04/identity-skin-blood-heart-minnie-bruce-pratt.pdf.
Radhakrishnan, Smitha. 2011. *Appropriately Indian*. Hyderabad: Orient Blackswan. Pvt. Ltd.
Rayner, T. 2013. Lines of Flight: Deleuze and Nomadic Creativity. *Philosophy for Change*. Accessed April 18, 2016. https://philosophyforchange.wordpress.com/2013/06/18/lines-of-flight-deleuze-and-nomadic-creativity/.
Zhu, Zhiqun. 2007. Two Diasporas: Overseas Chinese and Non-resident Indians in Their Homelands' Political Economy. *Journal of Chinese Political Science* 12 (3): 281–296.

Chapter 9
Three Tamil Diasporic Women's One Mission: *Discover New Identities*

Gopalan Ravindran

Introducing the Three Diasporic Women

Susheela Raman, the British Indian/Tamil rap singer, was born to parents who migrated from Thanjavur (Tamil Nadu) to U.K. From U.K., the family moved to Australia and eventually settled in U.K. She is an acclaimed pop singer who takes her inspirations from Murugan Bhakti[1] songs and Sufi[2] songs and articulates the innovative diasporic imaginations of her generation. Mathangi Arulpragasam was born in London and is popularly known as M.I.A (Missing in Acton/Action). She lived in Jaffna, Sri Lanka and Chennai, India, before settling in U.K. She is a leading British pop singer of Sri Lankan Tamil origin, who has been articulating her

---

[1]*Lord Murugan* is a Tamil God of yore. He is one of the ancient Gods worshipped by Tamils since the last *Sangam age* (600 BC-300 AD). Referred to as *Ceyon* during the *Sangam* period, *Murugan* is a God associated with the *Kurinchi* or Hill country—one of the five *thinais* or geographical divisions of the ancient Tamil landscape. *Murugan Bhakti songs* are employed in various modes during major *Murugan* festivals like *Thaipoosam*, which attracts lakhs of devotees in all the countries to which Tamils have migrated. *Kavadiattam* is a ritual dance (which also transforms into a *trance* dance) performed by devotees to the accompaniment of *Murugan* songs. The aesthetic practices woven around the *Murugan Bhakti movement* in Tamil Nadu since the *Sangam* age signify the essence of Dravidian/non-*Vedic* religious traditions of Tamils. The well-known Czech Tamil Scholar, Kamil Zvelebil's work *The Smile of Murugan: On Tamil Literature of South India* and the well-known Tamil scholar, writer and orator of twentieth century, Thiru. Vi. Kalyanasundaram's work *Lord Murugan or Beauty* are very significant resources to explore the *Murugan Bhakti movement*.

[2]*Sufi* songs represent the musical traditions of the Islamic spiritual movement that originated in thirteenth century. The *Sufi* singers yearn for the inner spiritual awakening of themselves and their fans/subjects.

G. Ravindran (✉)
Department of Journalism and Communication, University of Madras,
Chepauk Campus, Chennai 600005, Tamil Nadu, India
e-mail: gopalanravindran@gmail.com

© Springer Nature Singapore Pte Ltd. 2018
A. Pande (ed.), *Women in the Indian Diaspora*,
https://doi.org/10.1007/978-981-10-5951-3_9

missing identities in her place of dwelling, Acton London, as well as her longing for her lost homeland in Eelam[3] through her voices, songs and interviews vociferously. Ahalya Dharmalingam was born in Malaysia. Unlike the other two, she does not have a history of migrations. Unlike the other two, she is not into pop music, but is leading a pop version of Tamil Bhakti Movement[4] in Malaysia, by leading a trend where traditional exteriors of a religious person are erased/subverted by a radically different attire of a young female who is in love with the Tamil scriptures, Thevaram and Thiruvasagam.[5] In exploring the past and ongoing works of the three Tamil diasporic women, this paper seeks to examine their diasporic subjectivities outside the realm of the macro frameworks such as colonialism, globalisation, migration, cultural identity, etc. This paper wants to explore their multiple subjectivities through the application of disparate theoretical frameworks from the sides of material rhetorics, Deleuzian film philosophy, Foucauldian philosophy of knowledge/power and Vertovian concept of 'cine-eye'.

Rethinking Diasporic Studies/Subjectivities

There has been a growing interest in diasporic subjects in India in recent times. The reasons are manifold. Important among these are the recent waves of cultural globalisation mediated by the sectors of the internet and transport, the continuing flows of Indians and people of Indian origin across borders, the establishment of

---

[3]References to *Eelam* (the Tamil region of Sri Lanka) occur widely in *Sangam* literature (including *Pattinapalai*, *Akananuru*, Kurunthokai and *Narrinai*) and ancient and mediaeval epigraphs. The earliest reference is to a dweller of the land of *Eelam* in *Thiruparankundram* epigraph (1 BC). *Erukatur Eelakutumpikan Polalaiyan* ("Polalaiyan, (resident of) Erukatur, the Husbandman (householder) from Eelam"). After the emergence of *the Liberation Tigers of Tamil Eelam (LTTE)* during 1980s, the term refers to the state proposed by the organisation in the northern and eastern Sri Lanka.

[4]The *Tamil Bhakti Movement* spans the period between the sixth and the eleventh centuries when there was a revival of the literary and aesthetic practices of the *Sangam* age Tamils on an entirely different plane, rather as counter site of the then major religions, *Tamil Buddhism* and *Tamil Jainism*. The *Tamil Bhakti Movement* resulted in two major literary corpuses, *Nalayira Divya Prabandam* (4000 sacred verses) and *Pannirandu Thirumurais* (12 sacred texts). The first represents the works of 12 *Tamil Vaishnavite saints,* known as *Azhwars.* The latter represents the works of *Nayanmars*, the 63 Tamil *Saivaite saints.*

[5]The fourth, fifth and sixth *Thirumurais* were authored by *Thirunavukarasar* and the anthology is known as *Thevaram.* The eighth *Thirumurai* was authored by *Manickavasagar* and is known as *Thiruvasagam.*

centres of diaspora studies in Indian Universities[6] and the growing 'cultural identity crises'[7] of members of the Indian diaspora in their places of domicile.

For a long time, scholars in the field of diasporic studies have engaged themselves with their diasporic subjects through a typical prism: cultural identity as a given attribute. Hall (1993) broke the ice when he conceptualised 'cultural identity' as a dynamic and evolving one for the diasporic subject rather than as a 'given identity'. Hall also said that '… identities are about questions of using the resources of history, language and culture in the process of becoming rather than being: not 'who we are' or "where we came from", so much as what we might become, how we have been represented and how that bears on how we might represent ourselves'. As a diasporic subject of Caribbean origin, he was bristling with the voice of authority in this seminal paper.

Naficy (2001) located the emergence of 'accented' expressions of cultural identity of exilic subjects to be their experiences and imaginations journeyed between their homelands and their places of settlement. Here, again, the concept of a 'cultural identity' is seen as the relevant prism of engagement. However, for Naficy this 'cultural identity' is not tied to a fixed, primordial place of origin/belonging, but as a marker of the negotiations in the spaces of 'liminality', as Bhabha (1994) posited.

Gilroy (2000) located the logic of 'contemporary appeals to identity' in the process of globalisation and how it has been reconfiguring the relationships of diasporic subjects in their worlds of the colonial/nationalistic past and their reemergence in supranational and subnational versions. He further states that '…the growth of nationalism and other absolutist religious and ethnic identities, the accentuation of regional and local divisions, and the changing relationship between supranational and subnational networks of economy, politics, and information have all endowed contemporary appeals to identity with extra significance'. In an earlier landmark work, Gilroy (1993) asserted that the diasporic subject constructs its present location on contemporary terms rather than banking on the linkages with macro-entities such as nationalism and pan-cultural identities. According to Gilroy (1993), the diasporic subject '…opens up a historical and experiential rift between the locations of residence and the locations of belonging…. Consciousness of diaspora affiliation stands opposed to the distinct complexity of nation-states. Diaspora identification exists outside of and sometimes in opposition to the political forms and codes of modern citizenship'.

---

[6]At least five *Centres for Diasporic Studies* were established during the last 5 years in India in Tamil Nadu, Goa, Punjab, Gujarat and Kerala.

[7]Cultural identity crises in countries as varied as South Africa and Malaysia were a cause for concern for the members of Tamil diaspora. The emergence of *Hindraf (Hindus' Rights Action Force)* in 2007 as a rallying point for securing rights and privileges for the Indians in Malaysia was in fact the effect of the growing cultural identity crises faced by the Indians/Tamils in Malaysia on account of reports alleging the demolition of Hindu temples in the country. In South Africa, the cultural identity crises were fueled by reasons ranging from lack of Tamil schools to the removal of Tamil channels from local cable networks to the odds against securing audiences for releases of new Tamil films.

Like Gilroy (2000), Appadurai (1996) had before him also rooted for the primacy of the process of globalisation in the construction of the subjectivities. For him contemporary globalisation causes the emergence of flows, disjunctures and scapes, and results in a cultural process where the logic of centre and periphery does not hold water anymore. He said

> The suffix –*scape* allows us to point to the fluid, irregular shapes of these landscapes, shapes that characterize international capital as deeply as they do international clothing styles. The terms with the common suffix –*scape* also indicate that these are not objectively given relations that are the same from every angle of vision but, rather, that they are deeply perspectival constructs, inflected by the historical, linguistic and political situatedness of different sorts of actions: nation states, multinationals, diasporic communities, as well as sub-national groupings and movements (whether religious, political or economic), and even intimate face–to–face groups, such as villages, neighbourhoods, and families." (1996)

> Fanon (1963) was the first in the long line of scholars who succeeded in revealing the falsity of realities sought by the subject of "pan-identities". The location of the colonial subject as a subject of *misrecognition*, psychoanalytically speaking, was exposed by Fanon when he sought to use the Hegelian notion of "intersubjectivity" with a rider. According to him, the Black subject is not as privileged as the White subject in achieving recognition. Said Fanon (1963), "… the white master recognized *without a struggle* the black slave. But the former slave wants to *have himself recognized*. There is at the basis of Hegelian dialectic an absolute reciprocity that must be highlighted." Fanon further also disputed the logic of "pan-Africanism" as Appiah (1992) did later. "…We say the black Frenchman because the black Americans are living a different drama. In the United States the black man fights and is fought against. There are laws that gradually disappear from the constitution. There are other laws that prohibit certain forms of discrimination. And we are told that none of this is given free." (Fanon 1963)

In the logic of Fanon (1963), the idea of 'cultural identity' is tied to the 'idea of freedom' from the yoke of coloniality in the same geographical location. In the logic of Hall (1993), the idea of 'cultural identity' is tied to the idea of 'becoming' a new subject in a new geographical location, the settled homeland, while retaining the imagination of 'being' a subject that flowed in as a migrant. In the logic of Naficy (2001), the idea of 'cultural identity' is 'accented' as the imaginations and experiences flow between the axes of homeland and the settled homeland. In the logic of Gilroy (2000, 1993), the idea of 'cultural identity' is tied with the processes of globalisation, particularly, the domains of supranational and subnational identities. In the logic of Bhabha (1994), the logic of 'cultural identity' is tied with the location of the diasporic subjects in their 'liminal spaces'. In the logic of Appadurai (1996), the idea of 'cultural identity' is tied with the notion of 'disjunctures/flows/scapes' in the contemporary times of globalisation.

In all these notions, the key terms are colonialism, post-colonialism, nationalism, globalisation, migration, displacement, flows, scapes and cultural identity. In all these notions, the idea of the diasporic subject, who can be a self-determined site of individuated agency and performative identity, is missing. In all these notions, what succeeds is the idea of the macro-processes such as colonialism, post-colonialism, nationalism, globalisation, migrations, flows, scapes, etc. In all these notions, the need for a new theoretical/disciplinary lens is missing as they are largely located in the fields of post-colonial or cultural studies. Even if the objective is to engage with the idea of 'cultural identity', there are relevant alternative methods of enquiry such as material rhetorics to understand the negotiations of 'cultural identities' by the individual diasporic subjects. The material practices, as sites of Deleuze in 'molecular intensities' shall also count as much as the 'molar' intensities caused by the macro-entities (Deleuze and Guattari 1993).

This paper seeks to locate the negotiations by the individual diasporic subjects in the performative identity seeking acts of three women of Tamil origin. This paper seeks to engage with the logic of 'pure perception', in both Deleuzian and Vertovian senses to relate to the works of Susheela Raman, M.I.A and Ahalya Dharmalingam. Further, this paper seeks to engage with the theoretical prism of material rhetorics to relate to the material practices of the three Tamil women and their rhetorical implications and characteristics. The Foucauldian perspective on subjectivities provides an additional dimension to explore the diasporic subjectivities of the three women.

Susheela Raman, M.I.A and Ahalya Dharmalingam as *Deleuzian, Vertovian* and *Foucauldian* Subjectivities

Both Blair (1999) and Dickson (1999) drew the attention of scholars engaged in rhetorical studies to a familiar and yet unrecognised direction when they leveraged the fact of materiality over the fact of *symbolicity* in their works. For a long time, rhetorical studies located the *rhetor* and his acts in verbal and written discourses. The meanings were said to reside in the speech and written acts and the rhetorical act looked more like a closed circle wherein the causes and effects of the rhetorical act were seen to be more on the side of the *symbolicity* of the rhetor than on the materiality of the rhetor and his/her texts. Material rhetorics argue the case of the materiality of the *rhetor* in terms of his corporeality, his/her texts (words and acts) and the long running presence of the materiality, in comparison with the short life of the *symbolicity*. The *symbolicity* is said to have a short life as its meaning making potential vanishes in the absence of the rhetor.

There are two strands of theoretical wisdom in material rhetorics. Blair (1999) argues that the characteristics of consequences and partisanship are to be found in both the sites of *symbolicity* and materiality. She says that materiality is a fact in *symbolicity* as well—as the rhetor and his verbal acts have the essence of materiality and consequently the ability to have consequences or effects. But the nature of consequences can be unintended as well, particularly in the absence of the *rhetor*. This results in what she labels as the characteristics of partisanship. The materialities of the text have lives of their own in the absence of the *rhetor* as in the case of the virtual bodies in *Youtube* videos. Dickson (1999), on the other hand, argues a straightforward case of the material rhetorics. According to her material rhetorics is interested in looking at '...how multiple discourses and material practices collude and collide with one another to produce an object that momentarily destabilizes common understandings and makes available multiple readings.... reads for the ways persons inscribe on their corporal bodies the culture that produces them and that they mutually produce'.

Whether we seek to apply Blair or Dickson's notions of material rhetorics, Susheela Raman, M.I.A and Ahalya Dharmalingam would emerge as subjectivities borne of their material practices. They are *rhetors* engaged with the elements of *symbolicity* and *materiality*. Their material subjectivities are made possible by both linguistic and non-linguistic elements. We find in their works testimonies of what Dickson (1999) articulated as the highpoint of material rhetorical approach. Their works testify '...how multiple discourses and material practices collude and collide with one another to produce an object that momentarily destabilizes common understandings and makes available multiple readings' (Dickson 1999).

As *rhetors*, Susheela Raman, M.I.A and Ahalya Dharmalingam represent a cultural/religious constituency. Their rhetorical discourses, though divergent, converge on a common ground as they are all in the process of cultivating multiple subjectivities on the strength of their diasporic subjectivities as Tamils of Indian, Sri Lankan and Malaysian origins.

Susheela Raman and M.I.A share the similarity of being pop singers of Tamil origin. But they have wide-ranging differences in terms of their individual roles as diasporic *rhetors*. The crucial difference is due to the divergent rhetorical content they employ in the course of the formation of their rhetorical/material subjectivities. While Susheela Raman seeks to engage with a range of *Bhakti/*Ethnic/*Sufi/*Pop music from different parts of India such as Tamil Nadu and Rajasthan, from Pakistan and also from Europe and Africa, along with her collaborators from India, Pakistan and Europe, M.I.A is engaged with her own version of pop music that slams genocides of different kinds. While Susheela Raman is known for her radical approach in universalising the *trans* qualities of the *Murugan Bhakti* music of Tamil Nadu, M.I.A is known for taking the campaign against the genocide of Sri Lankan Tamils to the Western pop music stage and the media there. Their material subjectivities have their locations in these rhetorical planes which they have been constructing with passion. Their material practices on stage are, however, set to a tune different from the characteristics of these rhetorical planes.

Susheela Raman enacts her diasporic material subjectivity as a Tamil Indian of Australian and U.K. lineage. As she sings the famous *Murugan* songs *Ennapane* and *Vel Muruga*, her earthy voice flows along the meadows and climbs uphill, her corporeal body sways in antithetical fashion to the accompaniment of her swaying curly hair. Susheela Raman is not without her share of detractors or admirers. The conservatives among her online audience dubbed her *Murugan Bhakti* music as sacrilegious as can be seen here. No changes have been made in the comments of either her detractors or of her fans. Here are the comments of her detractors:

(i) 'Lord *Murugan* will get shocked of his life and run away with his peacock',
(ii) 'Yet another of Susheela Raman's sounds that come across like a drunken and chemical-laced daze than any thing else',

(iii) 'the way u presented is amazing and ur performance is extra ordinary, but why the hell did u choose *Murugan* songs for u becoming popular',

(iv) 'You are not showing any respect to god'.

Others have praised her music as being true to form:

(i) 'Great imagination! Susheela Raman must ignore all negative comments!',

(ii) 'Elder Sister, Susheela, I am proud that you are a Tamil',

(iii) 'I am sure Lord Muruga is resting on his peacock and shaking his head slowly to this song' and,

(iv) 'She is taking us (Tamilian) to next level' (*YouTube* Susheela Raman 2011).

The exposition of Susheela Raman's material subjectivity is found, very clearly, in her domains of *symbolicity* and *materiality*. Her ideological postures are not just in her words or statements, but specifically in the creative deployment of her *Murugan* songs alongside *Sufi/Qawali* songs of Pakistani origin and Rajasthani drumming, along with ethnic African music and the pop music traditions of the West.

Now, if we take this a step further and ask (sic) rhetorically: 'How can we relate to her rhetorical plane in terms of the linguistic and ideological constructs?' Well, in this case, Susheela Raman's deployment of Western materialities hides the genuine urge—on her part—to find the truth, through the choice of her Tamil *Bhakti* songs. Says she

> The Tamil influence came from the fact that I was studying music with (late) Dharmapurma Swaminathan, who was a professional singer of *Murugan* songs and learning *Bhakti* music from Kovai Kamala. The music of legends like K. B. Sundarambal and Bangalore Ramani also influenced me immensely. I got a lot of the English music from my dreams. When the band and I combined both these elements, something very powerful and intense came out of it.
>
> On the one hand Kunnakudi Vaidyanathan's music is a big driving force and on the other, Bjork's work is hugely motivating. Both of them didn't pander to market demand and I don't want to either. Because, when you pander to external pressure, you lose the truth." (TOI 2010)

In a sense, her rhetorical and ideological purpose as a diasporic subject appears to be *not to lose the truth/live with the truth/find the truth.*

She does not wish to pander either to the populist market demands or to external pressure, and this wish becomes evocative and passionate on stage when she deploys her corporeality alongside the bodies of her White colleagues on stage (some of whom are with Indian instruments, some with Pakistani instruments and others with Western instruments). Her Western colleagues appear to swoon as they belt out their musical support to her singing of *Vel, Vel, Vel Muruga Vel.* Her Western audiences show their love for her music through their positive corporealities. The lights, sounds, bodies, machines and spaces communicate in their material versions in sync with her in her quest: *not to lose the truth/live with the truth/find the truth.* Her diasporic subjectivity is more a creation of her individual journeys as a diasporic subject that wishes *not to lose the truth/live with the truth/find the truth.* Her diasporic subjectivity is not the construction of the macro-entities which are deployed by diasporic studies scholars in their theoretical invocations. She seeks to build connections between the past and present roots of Tamil *Bhakti* music in a sincere way, outside the various spaces of the *Murugan* temples, the temple festival grounds and the concert circuits in Tamil Nadu. She seeks *not to lose the truth/live with the truth/find the truth* in the radical twists and turns she lends to *Murugan Bhakti* music to an audience who live far away from Tamil Nadu and the *Murugan Bhakti* music 'milieu'.

The case of M.I.A is vastly different from that of Susheela Raman as she locates herself as a person suffering from the pangs of the Sri Lankan Tamil genocide. Her video, *Born Free* (2010), was banned for violent content. She is a songwriter, rapper and painter. She sings only in English, unlike Susheela who sings in both Tamil and English, and again, unlike Susheela Raman, M.I.A loves politically charged views and strong notes of dissent against Sri Lanka and the USA. She has been a strong supporter of *Wikileaks* and its founder, Julian Assange. M.I.A said

> So obviously I love *Wikileaks* because, after I'd gone through the whole backlash, they were the first news information site to confirm any news on the Sri Lankan war in the truest form; they were the first to release information stating the truth about what had happened to the Tamils as I knew it and to reveal that the United Nations was aware that the Sri Lankan government was lying—war crimes had been committed, but their hands were tied because any time anyone tried to impose sanctions, governments would walk out. I support *Wikileaks* because of that. (Wikipedia 2016)

M.I.A's rhetorical plane, as it is in the case of Susheela Raman, is also structured around her quest for the truth. But unlike the cultural truth which Susheela Raman wishes to find and nurture, M.I.A wishes to find and nurture political truths through the medium of her musical journeys. M.I.A said

> All that information floats around where we are – the images, the opinions, the discussions, the feelings – they all exist, and I felt someone had to do something about it because I can't live in this world where we pretend nothing really matters. …Nobody wants to be dancing to political songs. Every bit of music out there that's making it into the mainstream is really about nothing. I wanted to see if I could write songs about something important and make it sound like nothing. And it kind of worked. (Wikipedia 2016)

> When she was dubbed a "terrorist sympathiser" by Oprah Winfrey, M.I.A retorted angrily: "She didn't talk to me. She shut me down. She took that photo of me, but she was just like, 'I can't talk to you because you're crazy and you're a terrorist.' And I'm like, 'I'm not. I'm a Tamil and there are people dying in my country and you have to like look at it because you're fucking Oprah and every American told me you're going to save the world.'" (Cantor 2015)

Born in London, M.I.A spent her early childhood in Jaffna, while incidentally, the civil war was raging. Sometimes later she moved to Chennai, then to Jaffna, and finally back to London. She carries with her very strong imprints of her early childhood in a violent Sri Lanka and her pictorial albums are full of acidic statements against violence by the State, identity politics and immigrant policies. Her first album, *Arular*, engaged with these and other issues. Her banned video, *Born Free*, is read as a violent statement against state-sponsored violence. Her famous single, *Paper Planes*, was a mocking statement on the immigration policies of Western governments.

Her materialities are in her statements as well as on her body and the bodies of the children and adults of Tamil, Asian, African lineage featured in her albums. She either deploys materialities of violence, as in *Born Free* or deploys anti-immigrant motifs as in *Paper Planes*. She deploys the LTTE (*Liberation Tigers of Tamil Eelam*) logo in *Bird Flu*. She deploys scores of bodies rushing up through barbed wire fences in her album *Borders*. Here she seeks to redefine freedom as a right for immigrants to rush across borders over land, by sea and by air. She makes liberal use of children in many of her albums. In *Bird Flu*, her diasporic subjectivity borne of her displacement and homelessness as a child, amidst the civil war, comes to surface as she dances—to the delight of street children—to her rap song and its soothing music even as she positions them against the backdrop of LTTE motifs. This album is obviously set in a Tamil speaking location in Sri Lanka. The jubilant children, panicking hens/cocks, pensive onlookers, a very vibrant M.I.A and the banners in Tamil make a political statement on her rhetorical terms and with her choice of materialities. It will be apparent from the above that Susheela Raman and M.I.A source their diasporic subjectivities from their wish to find and nurture *their* versions of cultural and political truths, respectively. Their rhetorical and material subjectivities are also reflective of the same.

Compared to Susheela Raman and M.I.A, Ahalya Dharmalingam wishes to find and nurture her version of Tamil *Saivaite* religious truth in the multiracial contexts of Malaysia. Unlike her counterparts, who are pop singers, Ahalya does not engage herself with pop concerts. She holds Tamil *Saivaite* discourses on her *Youtube* channel. She wants to appeal to the youth who cannot be satisfied by the traditional modes of religious discourses. She wants to be a liberal and non-superstitious type. Ahalya in an interview with the author on March 25–26 2016 stated:

> Older generations have their religious class conducted in the temple for hours sitting on the floor. We are not allowed to laugh. This class has only limited number of audience and the target group is all old folks after retirement, you can't ask questions to the speaker nor raise comments. People are wearing multiple garlands of *ruthiraksham* beads and loads of *thiruneeru* (sacred ash). These practices have not attracted youngsters to pursue his/her interest in spiritual matters. In my *Youtube* videos, I have a very modern outlook and I am trying to give out the same old stuff in a new packaging. This mode is more flexible for youngsters. They can hear this video anytime, anywhere, in their own phase. They can dress in the way they want.

Unlike Susheela Raman and M.I.A, Ahalya is faced with a different challenge as Malaysia, while being closer to the cultural homeland of Tamil Nadu in India, also happens to be a multiracial country. Malaysia, home to one of the largest Tamil diasporas in the world,[8] has over 500 Tamil schools. In the course of the interview Ahalya, during the interview, also pointed out:

---

[8]With nearly two million Indians, the majority of them Tamils, Malaysia has the second largest population of Tamils outside Tamil Nadu, the first being Sri Lanka.

We face a lot of challenges being in a multiracial country. Tamil spoken in Malaysia is a blend of all languages found in Malaysia. For instance, we refer to zero as *kosam* (which was derived from the Malay word *kosong*); to refer to 'easy', we might say *senangu* (derived from the Malay word *senang*). We also add '*la*' at the end of sentences, following the Chinese conversational mode. Thus, speaking Tamil without mixing other language is already a challenge. When it comes to dressing, multicultural interference occurs again. It's a great challenge to wear *sarees* or Tamil traditional dress when we prefer to wear them as they are too expensive compared to what Chinese and Malay wear in their daily lives. Tamil traditional dress has become a party wear. Eating Tamil food is also a great challenge, as the Malay and Chinese food items such as *Nasi Lemak*, *Mee Goreng*, *Char Koew Theow* are available for less than RM 5.00 while the Tamil food cost you RM 7-9. Living along with Chinese and Malay people, who share a different way of life, is challenging, for example in matters of marriage also. Chinese practice "living together" culture before marriage, Malays prefer "love" marriage culture. In such a context, it is a great challenge for us to just tell our youth why we should not follow others' culture in matters of marriage.

Ahalya is working against superstitious practices, which she thinks were brought from Tamil Nadu by the first migrants. She is also working against the corruption of the Tamil language caused by the assimilation of words and meanings from Chinese and Malay. She wants to promote authentic Tamil food culture, and does not want the traditional Tamil modes of dressing to fade away from the everyday lives of Malaysian Tamil youth.

Her material subjectivities are borne of the above concerns. As a *rhetor*, her ideological postures reflect the above concerns. Her *Youtube* videos project her as a different kind of Malaysian youth: very modern in outlook and dress and yet down to earth in teaching Tamil *Saivaite* philosophy to suit the mindsets of young Malaysian Tamils without invoking superstitious beliefs and practices. Her corporeality is devoid of the material practices that are the forte of traditionalists. She does not apply sacred ash or wear garlands.

In the works of the Susheela Raman, M.I.A and Ahalya, we find very meaningful contexts to relate to the divergent rhetorical accompaniment provided by the material subjectivities of themselves, machines and cultural artefacts, in the company of their chosen elements of *symbolicity*. Their existence as innovative diasporic subjects is made possible by the coming together of these in perfect unison. Their existence as individual diasporic subjects is made possible by their material subjectivities. Their material subjectivities, in turn, are made possible by the coming together of the elements of *symbolicity* and *materiality*. The above can be revealed only by the application of the Vertovian intra-image montage approach contained in his notion of 'cine-eye'.

Gilles Deleuze valued the concept of Dziga Vertov's concept of 'cine-eye' as much as he valued Bergson's notions in his two works (*Cinema I* 2005a and *Cinema II* 2005b) on film philosophy. In *Cinema I*, Deleuze said 'In the "cine-eye", Vertov was aiming to attain or regain the system of universal variation. All the images vary as a function of each other, on all their facets and in all their parts'.

The Vertovian logic has a natural affinity towards the objectives of material rhetorics as it leverages a material location for perception images and perceptions as they are seen to be an integral part of things and matter. In this sense, the materialities of the three women who are enacting their own perception images are key to the working of the 'cine-eye' as well as the emergence of the pure perception image, which seeks to empower the three women as well as their audience through linguistic and non-linguistic markers of rhetorics.

According to Dickson (1999, 297–98), material rhetoric is 'a mode of interpretation that takes as its objects of study the significations of material things and corporeal entities—objects that signify not through language, but through their spatial organization, mobility, mass, utility, orality, and tactility…material objects that represent the human body, because of the way these representations are then taken up by and inscribed upon corporeal bodies'.

Alongside the Vertovian 'cine-eye' and the Deleuzian 'perception-images', one can also explore the presence of Foucauldian subjectivities in the images constituted by Susheela Raman, M.I.A and Ahalya. For Greene (2009) in the Foucauldian logic of subjectivities, the technologies of self, the technologies of power and the technologies of sign systems, together with the technologies of production, determine the birth of subjectivities outside the domain of *symbolicity*. In the case of the works by Susheela Raman and M.I.A, the coming together of human beings, musical instruments, audio, video, lighting and numerous electrical/electronic equipment makes possible the Foucauldian material subjectivities in Susheela Raman and M.I.A as technologically grounded selves. The subjectivities caused by the technologies of power can be found in their ideological constructions of *Murugan Bhakti* music and *Ginger Genocide* music, particularly in their ethnic as well as their universal versions of appeal. The subjectivities caused by the technologies of production are to be located in the transnational collaborations between Susheela Raman, M.I.A and their collaborators from different cultures of the world. Another kind of Foucauldian subjectivity is made possible by the technologies of sign systems which are visible everywhere on stage, on human bodies which are on stage, in their words and deeds, on the faces of the members of the audience and in the ongoing sites of relationships between Susheela Raman and M.I.A and their fans.

The above-mentioned Foucauldian subjectivities are also accompanied simultaneously by the three kinds of Deleuzian perception images as well as the Vertovian intra-montage images of 'cine-eye'. For Deleuze, perception images come through three different stages in three different variations. They are solid, liquid and gaseous perceptions. What emerges as gaseous is pure perception in his logic and what Dziga Vertov postulates in his notion of 'cine-eye' is pure perception—a state of perception that is beyond the grasp of those who are enacting it, and of those who are making it possible as a collaborative event, as also of those who are watching it. Those who are enacting it and those who are making it possible are seen as biased as they work from a single location. But those who are watching it have the advantage of acquiring the vision of 'cine-eye' wherein the images enter images in a perpetual/eternal cycle and gain for the audience the power of 'intra-image' montage.

According to Deleuze (2005a):

> …what the French school found in water was the promise or implication of another state of perception: a more than human perception, a perception not tailored to solids, which no longer had the solid as object, as condition, as milieu. A more delicate and vaster perception, a molecular perception, peculiar to a 'cine-eye'. This was the result of starting from a real definition of the two poles of perception: the perception-image was not be reflected in a formal state of consciousness, but was to be split into two states, one molecular and the other molar, one liquid and the other solid, one drawing along and effacing the other. The sign of perception would not therefore be a 'dicisign' but a *reume*. While the dicisign set up a frame which isolated and solidified the image, the *reume* referred to an image in the process of becoming liquid, which passed through or under the frame. The camera-conscious became a *reume* since it was actualised in a flowing perception, and thus arrived at a material determination, at a flowing matter.

And finally, 'Camera consciousness raises itself to a determination which is no longer formal or material, but genetic and differential', resulting in a perception that is gaseous and pure.

What Deleuze said with reference to the nature of causation of perception images and their characteristics can be gainfully employed in exploring the diasporic subjectivities of Susheela Raman, M.I.A and Ahalya. As Susheela Raman and M.I.A enter the concert stage or the frame of the video, we are made to realise the presence of a solid perception image, which later transforms into a liquid perception image and later a gaseous image. Susheela Raman, M.I.A and Ahalya transform from their 'dicisigns' (solid perception images) into *reumes* (liquid perception images) as they pass through the early frames and enter the field of flowing perceptions made possible by the coming together of the acts of the performers on stage as well as the performers among the audience. These acts are to be located in the logic of camera consciousness; Deleuze refers to in an entirely different (filmic) contexts. In this paper, this consciousness goes beyond the logic of camera apparatus and material logic, as it is applied to film analysis, and becomes rather 'genetic and differential' as Deleuze posited.

The above-mentioned theoretical contexts of the lived experiences of the three women are very emblematic of the 'agency' for change and empowerment that each one of them has embodied in their words and deeds. The role and power of their 'agency' is evident in their unique practices as performative women seeking performative identities. What Butler (1993) envisioned as 'performativity' as the 'reiterative power of discourse to produce the phenomena that it regulates and constraints' is at full play in the cases of the three performative women. Susheela Raman, for instance, is powered by her performance as well as by her deeply entrenched urge to be the hunter of the 'truth' through the repertoire of *Murugan Songs*. Here, her 'agency' resides in her as well as in the *Murugan Bhakti Songs;* she seeks to fuse with her Western repertoire.

In a similar vein, M.I.A seeks to expose the truth about the genocidal crimes against Tamils by the Sri Lankan Government through the 'agency' provided to her by her lived conditions as a Sri Lankan Tamil in Sri Lanka, India and the West as well as by the radical content she packs in her Western albums. The case of Ahalya

Dharmalingam is no different as she is empowered by her 'agency' to see red in the traditional modes of *Saivaite* discourses in Malaysia and create innovative platforms to reach out to the Tamil youth of Malaysia who wish to learn *Tamil Saivism* online.

Conclusion

This paper wishes to conclude that the negotiations by the individual diasporic subjects namely Susheela Raman, M.I.A and Ahalya Dharmalingam have little in common with the macro-processes of colonialism, post-colonialism, nationalism, globalisation, migration, displacement, flows, scapes and cultural identity. The 'agency' gained by each of the three women is in fact emerging from the micro-processes engendered by their performative identity seeking acts, and also from their individual visions of the change they wish to bring about not only in their own lives, but more particularly in the lives of others. New theoretical prisms are the need of the hour in diasporic studies. The engagements with Deleuzian, Foucauldian, Vertovian and Dicksonian perspectives have proved that the diasporic practices of the three women are in fact material practices with significant rhetorical implications for their subjectivities. Their subjectivities are not to be read as being singular. They are very much multiple having been located in this paper as Deleuzian, Foucauldian, Vertovian and Dicksonian in nature. Hence, their 'taken for granted' identities as diasporic subjects become a deceptive facade in the face of their true/multiple subjectivities.

References

Appadurai, Arjun. 1996. *Modernity at Large: Cultural Dimensions of Globalisation.* University of Minnesota Press.

Appiah, Kwame Anthony. 1992. *My Father's House: Africa in the Philosophy of Culture.* Methuen.

Bhabha, Homi. 1994. *The Location of Culture.* London: Routledge.

Blair, Carole. 1999. Contemporary U.S. Memorial Sites as Exemplars of Rhetoric's Materiality. In *Rhetorical Bodies*, ed. Jack Selzer and Sharon Crowley. Madison: University of Wisconsin Press.

Butler, Judith. 1993. *Bodies that Matter: On the Discursive Limits of "Sex".* New York: Routledge.

Cantor, Paul. 2015. *Arular 10 Years Later: M.I.A Reflects on Her Globe-Shaking Debut.* Accessed on March 20, 2016. http://www.rollingstone.com/music/features/arular-10-years-later-m-i-a-reflects-on-globe-shaking-debut-20150320.

Deleuze, Gilles. 2005a. *Cinema I.* Athlone Press.

Deleuze, Gilles. 2005b. *Cinema II.* Athlone Press.

Deleuze, Gilles, and Felix Guattari. 1993. *A Thousand Plateaus—Capitalism and Schizophrenia.* Minneapolis: University of Minnesota Press.

Dickson, Barbara. 1999. Reading Maternity Materially: The Case of Demi Moore. In *Rhetorical Bodies*, ed. Jack Selzer and Sharon Crowley. University of Wisconsin Press.

Fanon, Frantz. 1963. *The Black Skin*. White Masks: Grove Press.

Gilroy, Paul. 1993. *The Black Atlantic: Modernity and Double Consciousness*. London: Verso.

Gilroy, Paul. 2000. *Against Race*. Harvard University Press.

Greene, Ronald Walter. 2009. Rhetorical Materialism: The Rhetorical Subject and the General Intellect. In *Rhetoric, Materiality and Politics*, ed. Barbara A. Biesecker and John Louis Lukaites. Peter Lang.

Hall, Stuart. 1993. Cultural Identity and Diaspora. In *Colonial Discourse & Postcolonial Theory: A Reader*, ed. Patrick Williams and Laura Chrisman. Harvester Wheatsheaf.

Kalyanasundaram, Thiru. Vi. 2012. *Lord Murugan or Beauty*. Chennai, India: Sri Shenbaga Publishers.

Naficy, Hamid. 2001. *An Accented Cinema: Exilic and Diasporic Filmmaking*. Princeton University Press.

TOI (*Times of India*). 2010. *Susheela Raman a Global Genre*. Interview with Anusha Vincent, August 24. http://timesofindia.indiatimes.com/entertainment/hindi/music/news/Susheela-Raman-a-global-genre/articleshow/6421174.cms.

Wikipedia. 2016. *M.I.A Rapper*. Accessed on March 20, 2016. https://en.wikipedia.org/wiki/M.I.A._(rapper).

YouTube. 2011. *Susheela Raman*. Accessed on March 20, 2016. https://www.youtube.com/watch?v=axBsv9aywKw.

Zvelebil, Kamil. V. 1997. *The Smile of Murugan: On Tamil Literature of South India*. Leiden: Brill Academic Publishers.

Chapter 10
Gender Differentials of Indian Knowledge and Service Workers in the US Labour Market: A Comparative Analysis in the Context of 'Age, Wage, and Vintage' Premia

Narender Thakur and Binod Khadria

The Context

In 2015, the ranking of India in the Global Gender Gap was the 108th of 145 countries (WEF 2015). In the sub-rankings, India ranked 139th for economic participation and opportunities, 125th for educational attainment and 143rd for health and survival (WEF 2015). In India, a mere 5% of senior-level workers are women, and their share of wages is 62% that of men (Inderfurth and Khambadda 2012). Further, India is also ranked fourth as a most dangerous country for women, behind countries such as Afghanistan and Congo (2012). This implies that India has to do more to provide equal playing field for women in the education and labour markets so that it can lead to their economic and social empowerment. The United Nations has launched 17 sustainable development goals (SDGs) for the period 2016–2030, to enhance the development process in the developing as well as the developed economies (UN 2015). Specifically, the gender equality targeted in SDG-5 is to achieve gender equality and empower all women and girls. However, the gender and migration perspective is not addressed in the SDG, whereas in the increasingly global mobility of people in the era of globalisation, gender equality is

N. Thakur (✉)
Department of Economics, Bhim Rao Ambedkar College, University of Delhi, New Delhi, India
e-mail: narender224jnu@gmail.com

B. Khadria
School of Management and Labor Relations, The State University of New Jersey, Piscataway, NJ 08854 - 8054, USA
e-mail: bkhadria@gmail.com

B. Khadria
Zakir Husain Centre for Educational Studies, Jawaharlal Nehru University, New Delhi, India

© Springer Nature Singapore Pte Ltd. 2018
A. Pande (ed.), *Women in the Indian Diaspora*,
https://doi.org/10.1007/978-981-10-5951-3_10

not only an important issue for women empowerment in the countries of origin (India) but it is also crucial in the destination countries of the migrants (US). The International Monetary Fund (IMF) is also concerned about the issue of gender equality in terms of the economic empowerment of women, as has been highlighted in a report:

> In recent years, extreme economic inequality has become a growing concern to a wide range of actors who have highlighted its negative effects on growth, poverty reduction, and social cohesion. The concentration of wealth is rising. In 2010 the combined wealth of the world's poorest half was equal to the wealth of the 388 richest individuals; in 2016 it was equal to the wealth of only 62 individuals. The gender dimensions of this inequality are undeniable - just nine of these 62 are women, whilst women make up the majority of those on low wages and in the most precarious forms of work. The IMF has voiced concerns, calling "widening income inequality... the defining challenge of our time" and the Managing Director Lagarde stated in June 2015 that addressing it is "not just morally and politically correct, but ... good economics". (Rhodes 2016)

To improve their living and working conditions, people move abroad to substantially increase their human capital and earnings, by acquiring higher educational qualifications and—consequently—work of a better standard in foreign countries. Developed countries are preferred. The United States, for example, has educational institutions of a higher quality, and also better living and working conditions as compared to India. Indian demography is widely diversified in its nature in terms of class, caste, religion, region and gender (Khadria 2000, 2016). The diversity of population groups also determines the different levels of returns from any gained human capital and wages in the labour market of the destination countries. Especially in the era of globalisation, the movement of people along with capital, finance and technology has increased (Thakur 2016). However, the global mobility of people has been dominated by temporary migration rather than a permanent one. The developed countries have introduced more stringent immigration laws and policies to control their borders for the inflows of immigrants. Since 2007 and 2008, the global financial crisis has also adversely affected the movement of people.

In the times of the ICT revolution and globalisation, there is a higher demand for high-skilled workers in the global labour market. There has been and is competition among companies and countries to attract and retain high-skilled talent to become a global technology leader through the use of the embodied knowledge of high-skilled workers. The developed country, mainly the United States, manages talent better and more efficiently. Since the 1980s, IT professionals contributed in the development of the IT sector of Silicon Valley in the United States. However, since the late 1990s, after the crash of the dot.com bubble, Indian IT professionals returned to India and developed its national IT sector which resulted in higher inflows of foreign exchange through higher IT and ITES production and exports. The Indian IT companies not only have contributed to Indian exports but also invested in foreign countries like the United States, the European Union and the other developed countries. Because of a higher presence of Indian IT companies abroad, they have a higher demand for Indian high-skilled workers. So the Indian professionals are in great demand in the developed destination countries both by

Indian and foreign companies. Thus, the ICT revolution and the globalisation process have contributed to enhance the demand for Indian high-skilled people abroad, although the global financial crisis halted this demand to some extent. This phenomenon of the higher demand for high-skilled workers in comparison to that for the low-skilled workers by the companies (national and multinationals) is also known as skill-biased technological change (SBTC) in the theoretical literature of international economics (Berman et al. 1994; Krugman 2000). So globalisation has resulted in winners as well as losers (Stiglitz 2012; Piketty 2014). For example, a significant number and share of Indian high-skilled workers (about 70% in 2014) successfully entered the United States and earned higher wages in the American corporate sector. In contrast, the share of high-skilled workers in the Indian organised sector has remained constant at a low of some 10% between 2001 and 2011. This reflects the skill-biased technological change (SBTC) in terms of higher demand for high-skilled workers along with higher wages. This results in wage inequality between the high-skilled and low-skilled workers, eventually leading to an expansion of income inequality between the developed (the United States) and the developing economies (India).

With a higher presence of Indian professionals in the United States, the gender disparities in Indian society are also transposed in the migrant population there. For example, India is basically still a male-dominated patriarchal society. This reality is reflected in the lower ranking of gender gap in India as per the report of the World Economic Forum, 2015. Of the female knowledge workers who go to the United States, some do start to work, but the majority of them go as a result of marriage or to join their spouses, who are US-based Indian male professionals. It is interesting to examine whether Indian highly educated females are going to use their higher education credentials in the US labour market or will stay at home to support their spouses in family responsibilities, i.e. to look after food, health, education, etc., of children and husbands.

To examine the SBTC in the context of gender, this chapter examines the numbers and shares of Indian male and female workers in comparison to the Chinese, Asians, foreign-born and natives, by using recent data from the American Community Survey (ACS 2016) and Census for the year 2014. Three aspects of skill premium in SBTC would be looked into, viz., 'age-premium', 'wage-premium' and 'vintage-premium'. According to Khadria (2009), the larger presence of Indian high-skilled or knowledge workers[1] in the United States is characterized by, what he called the age, wage and vintage effects. Khadria (2010) identified new emerging contours from three dynamic conflicts of strategic interests among the countries of origin and those of the destination. He explained that the stereotype benefits from the brain drain of high-skilled migration, viz. remittances, technology

---

[1]The high-skilled workers defined as 'knowledge workers' are mainly those engaged in *management, business, science and arts* occupations, as per the US census nomenclature. Further the 'service workers' are defined as non-knowledge workers and it means they work in the low-skilled *occupations, namely, service, sales and office, natural resources, construction, and maintenance and production, transportation and material moving occupations* (Khadria 1999).

and return migration to the countries of origin (like India), can be weighed against the three benefits that accrue to destination countries (Khadria and Thakur 2016). The benefits from the higher circulatory and temporary immigration of highly skilled people in the destination countries like the United States are (1) younger migrants to balance their ageing population (age-premium), (2) lower wages, perks, pension commitments (wage-premium) to replace older migrants and (3) stock of latest vintages of knowledge embodied in younger cohorts of overseas students (vintage-premium). To undertake a comparative gendered analysis of age, wage and vintage effects of Indian workers with the Chinese, Asians, foreign-born and natives in the United States, the rest of this chapter is divided into the following sections: (2) Gendered distribution of Indian workers in the United States in terms of numbers and shares, (3) the wage-premium differentials, (4) the age-premium differentials, (5) the vintage-premium differentials, (6) higher family responsibilities of Indian females and (7) conclusions.

Gendered Distribution of Indian Workers in the United States

For the analysis of gendered distribution of workers by their countries/regions of birth or ethnicity, viz. Indians, Chinese, Asians, foreign-born and natives, the number and percentage shares are examined from Figs. 10.1 and 10.2. The two categories of male and female workers are classified as earlier described, viz. knowledge workers (high-skilled) and service workers (low-skilled). In 2014, the numbers (shares) of Indian knowledge male and female workers in the US labour market were 0.77 million (71%) and 0.44 million (65%), respectively (Fig. 10.1), which implies that Indian males are more active in reaping the higher skill premium in the knowledge-based US labour market. The numbers (shares) of Indian male and female service workers were 0.31 million (29%) and 0.23 million (35%) in the same year. This means that numbers and percentage shares of male and female Indian knowledge workers were higher than their shares and numbers of service workers. Further, the numbers of Indian female knowledge and service workers are lesser than their counterpart males. However, the share of Indian female service workers is slightly higher than their counterpart Indian male service workers.

In comparison to Indian female knowledge and service workers in the United States during 2014, the numbers (shares) of Chinese female knowledge and service workers were higher in numbers at 0.52 million (54%) and 0.45 million (46%), respectively. However, the numbers (shares) of Chinese male knowledge and service workers were 0.53 million (56%) and 0.42 million (44%), respectively. Indian male knowledge workers dominate with their highest number and share in comparison to Chinese male knowledge workers. However, the share of Indian female knowledge workers is slightly higher than their counterpart Chinese females. Thus, the gender distribution of Chinese workers is more balanced than that of Indian

Number of Knowledge and Service Workers in US by Gender and Countries/Region of birth (Millions) in 2014

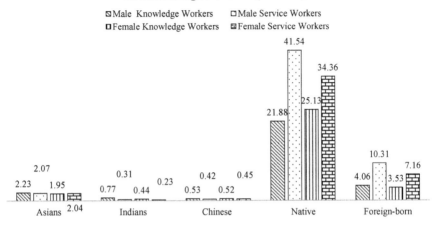

Fig. 10.1 Number of knowledge and service workers in the US by gender and countries/region of birth (Millions) in 2014. *Source* Constructed from data in ACS (2016)

Share of Knowledge and Service Workers in the US by Gender and Countries/region of birth (%) in 2014

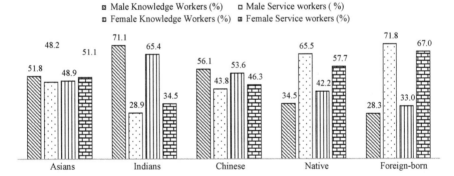

Fig. 10.2 Share of knowledge and service workers in the US by gender and countries/region of birth (%) in 2014. *Source* Constructed from data in ACS (2016)

workers in the United States, in terms of more equal numbers and shares of knowledge and service workers by their gender.

In comparison to Indians, Asians also have a more balanced gender distribution of knowledge and service workers in the US labour market. For example, the numbers and percentage shares of Asian male and female knowledge workers were 2.23 million (52%) and 1.95 million (49%). The respective numbers and shares of Asian male and female service workers were 2.07 million (48%) and 2.04 million (51%). The numbers (percentage shares) of foreign-born male and female

**Percentage-share of Female to Male Knowledge and Service
Workers in US by Countries/Regions of Birth: 2014**

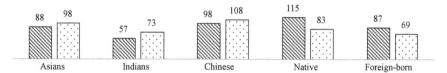

Fig. 10.3 Percentage share of female to male knowledge and service workers in the US by countries/regions of birth: 2014. *Source* Constructed from data in ACS (2016)

knowledge workers were 4.06 million (28%) and 3.53 million (33%) in the United States. Mexico, a neighbouring country, has a higher number and a higher share of male and female service workers. Therefore, the numbers and shares of male and female foreign-born service workers are generally higher than those of knowledge workers which were 10.31 million (72%) and 7.16 million (67%). In comparison to the foreign-born, the numbers and shares of native knowledge male and female workers were higher at 21.88 million (35%) and 25.13 million (42%), respectively, and those of native service male and female workers were 41.54 million (65%) and 34.36 million (58%). Thus, the shares of Chinese (54%), Asians (49%), foreign-born (33%) and native (42%) female knowledge workers are more equal to their counterpart males and service workers than the Indian females (65%). A clear perspective of gender distribution can be assessed by examining the percentage share of female to male knowledge and service workers by the countries/regions of birth (Fig. 10.3). The percentage share of Indian female to male knowledge workers was the lowest at 57% in the US labour market, during 2014, when compared to the shares of Chinese (98%), Asians (88%), foreign-born (87%) and natives (115%). Even the percentage share of Indian female to male service workers was also the lowest at 73%, (though 69% of foreign-born) in comparison to the shares of Chinese (108%), Asians (98%) and natives (83%) (Fig. 10.4).

The share of total female Indian workers when compared to that of their counterparts in the United States was lowest at 38% in comparison to those of the Chinese (51%), Asians (48%), foreign-born (43%) and natives (48%) in 2014. Thus, the participation of Indian female workers in the United States' labour market is the lowest as compared to that of the Chinese, Asians, foreign-born and also natives. It is very important to specifically examine the reasons for this very low participation of female Indian workers.

Number of Employed Population by Gender and Country/Region
of Birth (Million) and Share of Females: 2014

◨ Civilian employed population 16 years and over (Total)

□ Male civilian employed population 16 years and over

⊞ Female civilian employed population 16 years and over

⊞ % of Females in Civilian Employed Population

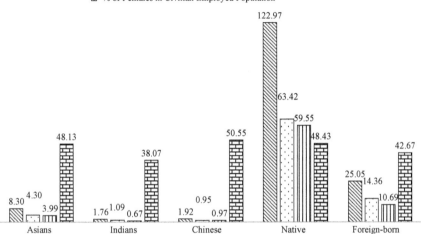

Fig. 10.4 Number of employed population by gender and country/region of birth (Million) and share of females: 2014. *Source* Constructed from data in ACS (2016)

The Wage-Premium Differential

As explained earlier, the lower workforce participation of Indian females especially in the knowledge workers categories in the United States has negatively affected their per capita income, median and mean earnings. The higher skill premium in terms of higher wages is generally attached to the high-skilled workers or the knowledge workers. But the lower female workforce participation of Indian women workers especially in the segment of knowledge workers reduced their share of female to male incomes or earnings.

Table 10.1 shows that the percentage shares of Indian female to male mean earnings were the lowest at 72% in 2014, when compared to those of the Chinese (82%), Asians (77%), foreign-born (80%) and natives (72%). The share of median earnings of the Indian female to the male worker was also the lowest at 74% when compared to those of the Chinese (84%), Asians (79%), foreign-born (87%) and natives (79%). The reasons for the lowest share of wages of Indian females when compared to those of their male counterparts in the United States, even in the case of a higher human capital for females, are family responsibilities, viz. looking after the children and the other family members, which result in and lead to their lower participation in the labour market. The take-home income of the Indian workers would be lower because of their other private expenses like private health insurance. On the one side, the percentage share of private health insurance taken by Indians was highest at 81%, in comparison to the Chinese (70%), Asians (71%), foreign-born (53%) and natives (68%). This could be because of their being increasingly temporary migrants who are not entitled to full government-funded insurance. On the other side, the share of public/government-funded insurance to Indians was the lowest at 15%, when compared to that of the Chinese at 25%, then the Asians (24%), foreign-born (27%) and natives (34%).

The Age-Premium Differential

The median age of Indians in the United States was the lowest at 33.4 years in 2014 and that of Chinese, Asians, foreign-born and natives were 38.2, 36.5, 43.5 and 35.9 years, respectively. The total population of Indians in the United States was 3.44 million and that of Chinese, Asians, foreign-borns and natives was 3.83 million, 16.35 million, 41.41 million and 269.08 million, respectively. Of the total population, the share of children (under the age of 5 years) among Indians was the highest at 8% and that of Chinese was at 4.4%. However, the respective shares of Asians, foreign-born and natives were 5.5, 0.6 and 7.1%. This implies that Indian females as a whole were looking after a larger number of children than the females of other nationalities, viz. Chinese, Asians, foreign-borns and the natives. The percentage share of Indian females in the Indian total population in the United States was the lowest at 48%, which signifies a lower female to male ratio as compared to those of other nationalities. The population of Indians in the younger age group of 18–34 years was 1.04 million, which is almost equal to the population of Chinese in the same age group, which was 1.08 million. This implies that Indians younger population has been increasing in the United States in recent times because in the older age group of 35–64 years, the population of Indians in the United States was significantly lower at 1.34 million than that of Chinese at 1.68 million. The percentage shares of Indian males and females in the younger age group of 18–34 years were 50.4 and 49.6%, respectively; the corresponding gender shares of younger Chinese were 48.9 and 51.1%. However, the shares of Indian males and females in the older age group of 35–64 years were 53 and 47%, respectively, and the respective shares of the Chinese were 45.1 and 54.9%. The corresponding shares of natives in the younger age group were 50.6 and 49.4% and the shares of older age group were 49.1 and 51.1%. This implies that the age premium was lower for the Indian younger females than their counterpart males. The share of Indian younger females is lowest as compared to their counterpart female Chinese, Asians and higher than that of all foreign-born, and more or less equal to the natives (Table 10.2).

Table 10.1 Per capita income, mean and median earnings of workers by countries/regions of birth and gender in 2014

Type/Category	Asians	Indians	Chinese	Native	Foreign-born
Individuals	16,686,960	3,491,052	3,941,615	276,465,262	42,391,794
Per capita income (dollars)	33,355	44,098	35,235	28,557	31,049
With earnings for full-time, year-round workers					
Male	3,315,761	884,965	710,474	48,516,822	11,081,849
	20	25	18	18	26
Female	2,605,220	444,303	626,032	37,428,109	6,750,832
	16	13	16	14	16
Mean earnings (dollars) for full-time, year-round workers					
Male	80,072	105,004	84,774	68,812	58,147
Female	61,281	75,337	69,705	49,601	46,792
	77	72	82	72	80
Median earnings (dollars) full-time, year-round workers					
Male	60,425	85,913	62,499	50,734	37,544
Female	47,766	63,483	52,598	40,052	32,774
	79	74	84	79	87
Health insurance coverage					
Civilian non-institutionalised population	16,601,876	3,485,049	3,927,354	271,862,459	42,027,963
With private health insurance	71.20%	81.10%	70.40%	68.40%	53.00%
With public coverage	24.00%	15.30%	24.70%	34.20%	26.70%

Source Constructed from data in ACS (2016)

Table 10.2 Total population, median age and shares of child and spouses in total population by the country/region of birth in 2014

Relationship/Age/Share	Asians	Indians	Chinese	Native	Foreign-born
Total population	16,686,960	3,491,052	3,941,615	276,465,262	42,391,794
Median age (years)	36.5	33.4	38.2	35.9	43.5
Male	47.4%	51.6%	46.7%	49.3%	48.7%
Female	52.6%	48.4%	53.3%	50.7%	51.3%
Under 5 years	5.5%	8.0%	4.4%	7.1%	0.6%
5–17 years	15.0%	15.9%	13.5%	18.6%	5.3%
18–24 years	9.9%	7.8%	11.8%	10.3%	7.4%
18–34 years	4,486,441	1,040,802	1,084,585	64,007,410	10,869,698
Male	48.6%	50.4%	48.9%	50.6%	52.0%
Female	51.4%	49.6%	51.1%	49.4%	48.0%
35–64 years	6,912,762	1,342,894	1,657,628	101,265,712	22,921,920
Male	46.2%	53.0%	45.1%	49.1%	48.9%
Female	53.8%	47.0%	54.9%	50.9%	51.1%

Source Constructed from data in ACS (2016)

The Vintage-Premium Differential

With the attainment of educational credentials through higher education degrees, Indians have a higher embodied human capital which is defined as 'vintage premium' for the employers of destination countries, like the United States. Table 10.3 shows the level of human capital of population aged 25 years and above in terms of bachelor's degrees or higher, by the countries/regions of birth and gender in the United States. Total populations aged 25 years and above of Indians and Chinese in the United States during 2014 were 2.38 million and 2.77 million, respectively. The percentage shares of Indian and Chinese males with bachelor degree and above were 73% and 56%, respectively. However, the female shares with the same degrees from both countries in the United States were 68% and 51%, respectively.

Therefore, the percentage share of Indian females with higher education degrees is lower by 5% points as compared to their counterpart Indian males. The numbers and shares of Indian females with higher education degrees are greater than those of their Chinese counterparts. The percentage shares of male Asian, foreign-born and native population with bachelor degrees were 54, 29 and 30%, respectively, and those of their counterpart females were 49, 28 and 31% in the same year. This implies that the share of Indian females with higher education degrees is greater than their counterpart other females (Chinese, Asians, foreign-born and natives) in the United States.

Higher Family Responsibilities of Indian Females in the United States

The higher shares of Indian female population with higher embodied human capital did not assure any greater participation by them in the high-skilled segment of the labour market, as compared to their other counterpart females. The reasons for the lower level of participation of Indian females in the developed destination countries, viz. US, are the family responsibilities, like the care and education of their children, the care of their spouses and of the aged parents of their spouse, which are

Table 10.3 Total population aged 25 years and above and shares of population with bachelor degrees and above by gender and countries/regions of birth in the US: 2014

Population and education	Asians	Indians	Chinese	Native	Foreign-born
Population 25 years and over	11,603,727	2,382,971	2,768,031	176,980,069	36,745,555
Bachelor's degree or higher	51.5%	72.5%	53.4%	30.4%	28.5%
Male, bachelor's degree or higher	54.1%	76.5%	55.8%	30.1%	29.1%
Female, bachelor's degree or higher	49.3%	68.3%	51.3%	30.7%	28.0%

Source Constructed from data in ACS (2016)

Table 10.4 Higher family responsibilities of Indian females: children education and married life

	Asians	Indians	Chinese	Native	Foreign-born
1. Children's education					
Population 3 years and over enrolled in school	4,634,342	958,444	1,142,575	76,448,527	5,615,187
Nursery school, preschool	5.3%	8.8%	4.4%	6.3%	1.5%
Kindergarten	4.3%	6.0%	3.2%	5.4%	1.6%
2. Marital status					
Population 15 years and over	13,832,619	2,759,217	3,360,566	217,082,783	40,687,887
Now married, except separated	57.7%	69.2%	56.6%	45.7%	58.4%
Male 15 years and over	6,468,463	1,430,324	1,559,992	105,852,784	19,812,139
Now married, except separated	58.0%	68.5%	57.5%	47.4%	60.6%
Female 15 years and over	7,364,156	1,328,893	1,800,574	111,229,999	20,875,748
Now married, except separated	57.5%	69.9%	55.7%	44.1%	56.4%

Source Constructed from data in ACS (2016)

the main features of the culture of the country of origin/birth. For a comparative analysis of the gendered role of Indian females in the family, two features are examined (Table 10.4): (i) percentage share of children in school going population in nursery and kindergarten (KG) and (ii) marital status of males and females. The percentage shares of children going to nursery and KG of Indians in US schools were highest at 9 and 6%, respectively, in 2014. However, these shares of Chinese were 4 and 3%, respectively, and those of Asians were 5 and 4%.

The percentage shares of foreign-born were 1.5 and 1.6%, respectively, and the corresponding shares of natives were 6 and 5%. Thus, the highest shares of Indian children going to nursery and KG classes adversely affect the entry of Indian females in the US labour market despite their having higher embodied human capital. The second reason for restricting the entry of Indian females is the higher share of married female population in the United States that was highest at 70% in the female age group of 15 years and above.

The share of Chinese female married population in the same age group was 56% and those of Asian, foreign-born and native females were 58, 56 and 44%. The percentages of married males of Indian, Chinese, Asian, foreign-born and native population were 69, 57.5, 58, 58.4 and 46%, respectively. In comparison to their counterpart male population in the United States, the highest share of married Indian male was there. Thus, the highest share of married Indian females has adversely affected their participation and growth in their professional career.

Conclusions

In the global labour market, and specifically with reference to the United States, the migration of Indian professionals has increased significantly during the era of globalisation, to improve their living and working conditions. Both male and female 'younger, educated and high-skilled' Indian workers transmit higher premia to their US employers in terms of 'age-premium, wage-premium and vintage-premium'. However, Indian male high-skilled workers are winners over Indian female high-skilled workers as the former have a higher share of income/earnings. The gender imbalance among Indian workers in terms of the lower participation of Indian females in the high-skilled segment of the US labour market reduces their percentage share of earnings to the lowest level in comparison to the other female counterpart from different country/regions. One of the main reasons for a lower workforce participation of Indian female high-skilled and educated workers in the United States has been their attention to their family responsibilities, viz. children's education and care of spouses and aged parents, which reduces the Indian females' participation in the labour market, and is often reflected in their concentration in part-time jobs rather than full-time. Thus, the gender inequality is not only an important issue in the country of origin, like India, but also in the country of destination, like the United States. This aspect, therefore, identifies the need to establish a comprehensive linkage between gender, migration and development in the context of the UN's Sustainable Development Goals (SDGs) agenda, 2016–2030. The challenge lies in the fact that the issue of migration itself has not been accorded the status of a specific goal among the 17 SDGs, but is spread, as a result, very thinly unfortunately, across a number of the 169 targets. To weave gendered migration into the goal gender equality under SDG-5 could be an effective method to focus on the delicate and sensitive issue of migration (specifically) in the global agenda for development.

References

ACS. 2016. *American Community Survey*. Washington, DC: American Community Survey, US Census Bureau.

Berman, E., J. Bound, and Z. Griliches. 1994. Changes in the Demand for the Skilled Labour Within US Manufacturing: Evidence from the Annual Survey of Manufactures. *The Quarterly Journal of Economics* 109 (2 May): 367–397.

Inderfurth, Karl F., and Persis Khambadda. 2012. India's Economy: The Other Half. *Center for Strategic and International Studies (CSIS)* 2 (2).

Khadria, Binod. 1999. *The Migration of Knowledge Workers-Second-Generation Effects of India's Brain Drain*. New Delhi: Sage Publications India Private Limited.

Khadria, Binod. 2000. Gender-Based Positive Discrimination: Is There a Case? In *Women, Power and the Academy: From Rhetoric to Reality*, ed. Mary-Louise Kearney. New York: UNESCO Publishing/Berghahn Books.

Khadria, Binod. 2009. Adversary Analysis and the Quest for Global Development: Optimising the Dynamic Conflict of Interest in Transnational Migration. *Social Analysis* 53 (3): 106–122.

Khadria, Binod. 2010. The Future of International Migration to OECD Countries Regional Note South Asia. *OECD Journal* 1–22.

Khadria, Binod. 2016. Gender-Based Immigration Visa? On Rationality of a Legislative Innovation. In *India Migration Report 2015: Gender and Migration (Chapter 1)*, ed. I. Rajan. Routledge.

Khadria, B., and N. Thakur. 2016, Forthcoming. Age, Wage and Vintage: Empirical Validation of the Impact of Skill-Biased Technological Change on the Migration of Indian Knowledge Workers to the US. In *International Migration*, Special Issue ed. Wei Li, and B. Khadria.

Krugman, P.R. 2000. Technology, Trade and Factor Prices. *Journal of International Economics* 50: 51–71.

Piketty, T. 2014. *Capital in the Twenty-First Century*. London: The Belknap Press of Harvard University Press.

Rhodes, Francesca. 2016. *IMF on Gender and Income Inequality: From Research to Implementation*. London. http://www.brettonwoodsproject.org/wp-content/uploads/2016/02/At-Issue-gender-Feb16-final-BW.pdf.

Stiglitz, J. 2012. *The Price of Inequality*. New Delhi: Allen Lane.

Thakur, N. 2016. Globalisation of India's Human Capital: Interlinkages Between Education, Migration and Productivity. Ph.D. diss., Jawaharlal Nehru University, New Delhi.

UN. 2015. *Addis Ababa Action Agenda of the Third International Conference on Financing for Development*. New York: United Nations.

WEF. (World Economic Forum). 2015. *The Global Gender Gap Report*, 10th Anniversary ed., Geneva, Switzerland.

Chapter 11
Unemployed Female Skilled Migrants from India in the Netherlands: The Entrepreneurial Self Under Structural Dependency

Kathinka Sinha-Kerkhoff and Kate Kirk

Introduction

Unlike other studies on Indian knowledge migration to the Netherlands (Cf. Bal 2012; Obradović 2013; Kõu et al. 2015), this chapter concerns the wives of so-called high-skilled migrants. These women come to the country as spouses of principal labour migrants via family reunification schemes (Kofman and Raghuram 2005, 151). They are alternatively known as 'ex-pat wives', 'trailing spouses', 'linked movers' or 'family relocation managers' (Cf. Wiesbrock and Hercog 2012, 9). Though their visas include working permits, these Indian women do not generally engage in any paid employment. This chapter concerns itself with their 'entrepreneurial selves', their non-unitary subjectivity and their mental well-being.

Understanding 'neo-liberalism' as more than a set of free market principles, Christina Scharff (2014) argues that the term among other dynamics extends to the organisation of subjectivity. She further argues that under neo-liberalism, individual citizens are construed as entrepreneurs of themselves and their lives. Neo-liberal subjects are thus entrepreneurial subjects continually working to better themselves. In the context of 'high-skilled' migration, it is this neo-liberal 'entrepreneurial self' that is sought after by governments and companies. Governments in both India and the Netherlands hold high expectations of skilled human capital mobility. Within the 'neo-liberal development model' employed by both governments, high-skilled migrants are seen as 'potential leverage for development' (Tejada et al. 2014, 4). In this discourse, the male transnational migrant is centralised and considered an agent

K. Sinha-Kerkhoff
VU University, Amsterdam, The Netherlands
e-mail: ksk@iisg.nl

K. Kirk (✉)
Faculty of Governance and Global Affairs, Institute of Security and Global Affairs,
Tuffmarkt 99, 2522 DP Den Haag, The Netherlands
e-mail: k.m.kirk@fgga.leidenuniv.nl

© Springer Nature Singapore Pte Ltd. 2018   133
A. Pande (ed.), *Women in the Indian Diaspora*,
https://doi.org/10.1007/978-981-10-5951-3_11

of innovation to technology transfer, information flows and capital flows. Being embedded in more than one place at the same time, this migrant is thought to 'promote creativity and novelty, key concepts for value-adding professionalism' (Seele 2008, 98). If women are studied at all, it is mostly as professionals employed in well paid (high-skilled) or in unskilled jobs and/or very badly paid or even unpaid slave-like professions (Cf. Docquier et al. 2008; Raghuram 2004; Kofman 2012).

Kofman and Raghuram (2005) point to these 'gendered contours' of skilled migration policies. They show the notion of skills is not gender neutral and claim the kinds of work that women do are often defined 'prima facie as less skilled'. Our own research also showed that so-called high-skilled work in the Netherlands requires mobile, flexible workers and therefore mainly attracts single men between 25 and 34 (Bal et al. 2016). Notwithstanding, and perhaps even because of, these gendered notions of skills, neo-liberal (post-) feminist research increasingly positions skilled and gainfully employed women as ideal neo-liberal subjects (Walkerdine and Ringrose 2006). At the same time, Kofman (2012) points out that transnational mobile married men require their spouses to withdraw from the labour market and get re-domesticated. Dutch high-skilled migration policies indeed also attract some single (middle-class) women from India but married Indian women arrive almost invariably as 'dependents' of their 'high-skilled' husbands, mostly employed in the IT sector. Dutch policy makers and companies in the Netherlands, therefore, ignore the possibility that these married Indian women might also possess skills and 'entrepreneurial selves'. Consequently, these women are marginalised in (national) development debates and not much is known regarding their employability, identifications or mental well-being.

Research on such migrant wives in Sweden has shown that the government homogenises these women and positions them as unemployed, excluded, caring and dependent, while the women identify themselves 'with their profession and as active agents' (Horgby 2013, 45). Similarly, we found that our informants, though mostly unemployed, are skilled migrants with 'neo liberal subjectivities' in the sense that, just like employed men and women, they are involved in, 'continuously maximizing, bettering and reinventing the self' (Walkerdine and Ringrose 2006). It is this agency and the formation of non-work-based subjectivities and alternative post-arrival life trajectories of such Indian 'trailing women' in the Netherlands that we analyse below.

Structural Dependency, Collective Biography, Comfort Zones, Anxiety Levels and Agency

We do not aim to investigate whether our informants posses 'the qualities of reinvention and making-over the self', which are according to Walkerdine and Ringrose (2006), the core neo-liberal psychological characteristics for the adaptation to market forces as required by neo-liberalism. We also do not analyse the devaluation of existing skills or 'deskilling processes' (Cf. Kofman 2012, 73). Yet, these processes are important and constitute 'structural barriers' which increase the economic dependency of our informants on their sponsor (i.e. husbands), reduce chances on the labour market, increase 'biographical uncertainty' (Roos 2013, 149) and make 'trailing women' more vulnerable in the economic sense (IOM 2014, 86–90). Ivanescu and Suvarierol (2013, 49) describe the space of structural dependency in which our informants displayed agency. Apart from the dependence of married Indian migrant women on their husbands who act as the 'sponsor', formal and informal barriers are at work preventing women's access to high-skilled and well-paid jobs. Insufficient knowledge of the Dutch language, lack of recognition of foreign qualifications and discrimination by employers are some obstacles they mentioned.

We recognise the subject position of our informants (Cf. Hart 2010) but want to look at 'the entrepreneurial self' beyond the field of paid employment and take structural barriers that prevent our informants' participation in the economic field as a starting point. We study 're-skilling' processes and the 'qualities of reinvention and making-over self' that help unemployment but skilled female migrants from India to come at terms with their new subject position in the Netherlands. In order to uncover the ways in which our informants performed, i.e. displayed agency, even if they were implicit in their own subjection, we use the collective biography as a representational mode that brings together shared experiences of isolation, frustration and dependency but also recovery and agency.

Our 2-year research study (2013–2015)[1] into lived experiences of Indian spouses of high-skilled labour migrants in the Netherlands was part of a broader research project examining Indian high-skilled migration to the Netherlands (De Prie 2014). This chapter features parts of transcripts of 38 semi-structured interviews conducted by two junior researchers and a post-doc. All interviews were conducted in English though not all women were equally fluent and since women without any English language skills were not interviewed this might have fostered a certain sociocultural and class/caste/religious bias in our research sample (Cf. Upadhya 2006). We must therefore keep in mind that our research results only apply to female spouses of Indian knowledge workers, who more or less shared the same sociocultural (and economic) capital and Bourdieu's (1984) *habitus* of socialised norms or tendencies that guide behaviour or thinking.

[1]This research was embedded within a broader research project entitled 'Migration, development, and citizenship: Notions of belonging and civic engagement among Indian (knowledge-) migrants in the Netherlands and return migrants in India' funded by the Netherlands Organization for Scientific Research (NWO), under grant number W 07.04.105. We thank Ellen Bal, Sara de Prie, Ratnakar Tripathy, Sarah Janssen, Giulia Sinatti and Ajay Bailey for their valuable input.

Our informants were mostly unemployed and all arrived on dependent/family unification visas. In fact, these 38 women could be described as (highly) educated (at times tertiary level), skilled, English speaking, transnational married migrants in the Netherlands who live in economic as well as social-cultural comfort zones where uncertainty, scarcity and vulnerability as female migrants in a new socio-cultural and economic environment are minimised. The price for this space is, however, (financial) dependency. Their collective biography does indeed specify different and changing levels of anxiety caused by structural barriers that among others prevent participation in the labour market. However, research has shown that moderate anxiety levels are important motivators for the assumption of agency and possible transformation of the status-quo/*habitus* (Cf. White 2008). In this way, we can observe the workings of an 'entrepreneurial self' amongst our informants who were involved in continuously maximising, bettering and reinventing the self and analyse their stepping out of comfort zones and study different subjectivities, here defined as production of identities in a space of structural dependency.

Manifestations of Non-unitary Subjectivity Among Indian Ex-Pat Women in the Netherlands

Analysis of individual interviews brought to light some similarities. We discovered three manifestations of subjectivity in our 'post-arrival memories' representing distinct lived experiences: (1) Dependency and (2) Liminality and (3) Independence. Not all our 38 women lived these experiences or did so in a linear way. Some women returned to India or moved on to other countries during the period of our research and their memories of their stay in the Netherlands did not always encompass all three forms of subjectivity. There were also genuine cases of 'failed migration' (Gupta et al. 2012). One of our informants had an Indian friend whose,

> Husband was in my university [in India] and who came to Amstelveen as a 'kennismigrant' [in this migration stage this informant had started using this Dutch word meaning 'knowledge worker']. They stayed but just for one year. He could have extended his project for longer as he was a consultant but the problem was that she was not getting any job and that's why they went back... she thought: 'okay we give it a try' [in the Netherlands].

Our interviews also reveal that some had got stuck in one form of subjectivity or skipped one or two others and some started with the last and ended up in the first (dependency). Some experienced different subjectivities in the same temporal space but in dissimilar places. Being produced by memory work that always produces non-unitary identities this was of course expected (E.g.: 'That time I felt like...There I thought...Then I became', etc.). We should, however, regard these three mani-festations of subjectivity as illustrative of possible outcomes of agency (i.e. the entrepreneurial self at work) under structural dependency.

Experiencing Dependency

For many women we interviewed, life had been most testing just after arrival when anxiety levels were high because they could not follow the (Dutch) language:

> Initially I was a bit scared because the language is different… it is not an English speaking country so you know at times you feel I don't know because it's not possible in a month or two months that you pick up the language…

Another woman also felt quite anxious when migrating to the Netherlands which she experienced as 'very different' as now for the first time she had to stay with her husband on a permanent basis:

> You know I had never really stayed with my husband because he was in London so he had stayed very less in Bangalore. I was doing up and down that time but hadn't stayed for long in some place with him and usually in India…

Some women felt their lives had become less fulfilling after arrival in the Netherlands as unemployed dependents of employed high-skilled husbands. One woman told us that she had moved from Frankfurt to a small suburb near Amsterdam and had felt much happier in Germany even though she had stopped working there as well:

> …I worked online; I was in the IT as well. But then for two years I didn't do anything only taking care of kid so I just loved Frankfurt. There were lovely parks with lots of kids and lots of cafes and lots of big stores. It was so much fun so I used to be out the whole day and just come back in the evening, like when my husband calls and says: 'okay I am coming back' so I come back, will have dinner…it was so much fun in Frankfurt.

As trailing wives, women did thus experience feelings of isolation, boredom and even frustration. Another woman told us that when she arrived in the Netherlands:

> It was like what I am doing here… I know nobody and my husband goes to work in the mornings and comes back at night and I have a child … and I really was feeling out of place.

Another had felt 'disoriented' as she knew 'nobody' and had no idea where to get her groceries from. Some felt lonely and many said that the biggest difference between India and the Netherlands was that 'here there are no people on the streets'. One informant complained that she rarely left her residence as, 'it always rains in the Netherlands and you always need to put on your coat if you want to go out'. One woman had searched for jobs but:

> …what I find: in any job they want Dutch; that time because I was not able to keep him [son] anywhere and go [out], so finally I searched for all three four months for things and then I gave up. Once I learn Dutch then only it's possible for me to apply somewhere… otherwise every job I tried I have seen they need Dutch.

Another woman with a small child complained of not having 'time for myself'. Some women reported that they had no friends around and often experienced reduced mobility. They missed India 'very much' and what they missed most was their 'family' there. Some longed to go back to India or to move on to an English speaking country. Reduced mobility resulting from a lack of familiarity with the public transport system; cycling; driving on the right-hand side, or driving at all (because in India they had chauffeurs) contributed to their homesickness and feelings of isolation. Several women were even apprehensive about finding their own way around by foot. These women were confined to the house where they had only their family back in India for company via facetime, whatsapp, skype or phone till their husbands could help them in the evenings or weekends.

One informant claimed that it was not her lack of knowledge of the Dutch language that had prevented her from getting jobs but it had been her Indian–English accent. These experiences often generated feelings of social isolation. One other woman confided in the researcher that she had had a bad experience...' it is not really discrimination but still...not a nice experience... you know every morning as I get in the bus I see the driver greet the Dutch people but then he sees me and he keeps mum...'.

Women also experienced deskilling or devaluation of their skills. One woman who had learnt French for two years during her post-graduation studies in India (as her international business course had prescribed one foreign language) said: 'God knows what I studied because I didn't keep in touch with the language...now it's like French is an alien language... at one point of time I could really speak well'. Another had worked in an international school in India and had been paid a full salary but in the Netherlands she had only been allowed to work on a voluntary basis in an international school.

Stepping Out of Comfort Zones: Liminality

This manifestation of subjectivity could be seen as awareness, among our informants, of new possibilities and the experimenting with alternative life-styles. It is a condition in which they tried out new life trajectories and acquired new skills, but never felt fully 'at home' and continued referring to life in India as the 'real' life. For one woman the very arrival in the Netherlands had opened up possibilities rather than limitations:

> We didn't put much stress on America because a lot of violence and all...and my husband was in Switzerland for quite some time so he really liked to be in Europe. I had been to the US and Asian countries like Korea and all these, so it is a really nice experience I thought really good to stay here.

Non-participation in the labour market made it possible for our women to make frequent travels up and down to India with at times extended stays with parents and/or in-laws. One woman said she had taken 1-year maternity leave and therefore could go to India with her child whenever she wanted and sometimes just went for a week or so. Others went to attend weddings and during Indian festivals. Activities outside the home were also undertaken; some women learned how to use the bicycle or to swim. Others started walking/jogging, went to the gym or started looking after pets. They tried out new food, fashion and drinks. They discovered new skills and abilities, made Indian friends in the Netherlands and were thinking of learning new subjects such as Dutch or resume some hobby they had long abandoned like painting, dancing or singing. Some stated they really liked daily life in the Netherlands. For one Indian couple the Netherlands was considered more preferable than the US because of, as the husband expressed it, 'the kind of people in the Netherlands', and the woman added that, 'it is not very materialistic compared to the US, so I like it the way it is, both of us like the way it is; more family oriented and more simple living and people enjoy simple things in life. We have fallen in love with the life style here'. Other women enjoyed 'safety' and 'cleanliness' in the Netherlands and even the Dutch climate:

> Yes India is very different because you can't walk on the road because of the weather and safety. It also is polluted and the roads are full of traffic. Where I live [note: this woman still uses the present form] you can't just go for long walks in the afternoon as it's very hot and lots of traffic and people don't follow that much of rule and driving is not safe. My father only allows me to drive in our colony where there are boundaries and a gate and a security guard sitting there and only people from the office of my father live there.

Another voiced a similar opinion:

> But yeah, night-time Delhi is a problem…after coming to Gurgaon I had become like, it's like I have always to keep in mind that I have to look for transport, means to take me somewhere. I did not like because I wanted to walk, I wanted to move independently…so this is the place [the Netherlands where this is possible].

Though some had good relations with one or two Dutch neighbours, a Dutch landlady or one or two Dutch colleagues from their husband's office, our informants mixed mostly with other Indians. Several made plans to start working again once they had learned enough Dutch and some indeed had already picked up work that could be done from home. One woman explained her choice:

> Yes, I do freelancing online so I usually do like when he is in school or at night… it is freelancing…like suppose I am going on holiday I will tell them [clients] I can't work…if I worked for a company…they have bad hours like sometimes it's like twelve hours a day sometimes like the work has to be done. So if there is a problem you have to stay and get it done….I don't feel that both of us could work because then who is going to take care of the house….I don't want to go out somewhere because I am being in a position now like if someone calls me and say please come to the school…and I just want to have that flexibility…

Instead of going to India repeatedly, some women rather preferred to spend holidays in European destinations. A woman said she never went back to her parents' place in India during the summers as it was 'too hot' for her then. Moreover, instead of going themselves to India again and again, many of our informants had their parents or in-laws to stay with them in the Netherlands. One woman said that it was, therefore, good she did not have to work:

> It is better so…otherwise too much of hassle so this way is very peaceful…like so many issues which get sorted out because one person stays at home I feel peaceful…like my

parents come and visit me…if am working then I will be out the whole day…everyone will be out the whole day…as such it is difficult for them to come because both of them are working so now my father is retiring but even then my mother is working so they will like to come over together so it's again like one month that's it…so…

Some women really liked going out. Many of those with children spent time at their children's International School doing volunteer work. Others frequented Indian ex-pat organisations or organised gatherings at home or at friends' places. In these 'localities' these women celebrate Indian or Dutch or other festivals together, teach, cook different dishes, experiment with other life-styles and meet other Indian/ex-pat women with different sociocultural backgrounds. Some moved houses in order to be able to live closer to 'other Indians'. Women said that mixing with other Indians in the Netherlands provided them with more knowledge about India than they had had while residing in India. They also started trying out Indian dishes they had never tasted or prepared before. Those Indian ex-pat women who worked as volunteers in an international school enjoyed the 'coffee mornings' and 'parent-teachers meetings' with other ex-pat women, Indian or not, and developed 'broad-mindedness or an 'international mindset'. One women explained her relationship with the school saying:

> …as I came here and got involved with the school, it became so easy for me to get accustomed with the city and the culture. You know because of this school, it helped us a lot. Such a positive vibe there: 'please come and enjoy and do some activity with us'. It was kind of that.

Women also experimented with the Dutch health care system and one woman concluded that compared with the Indian hospitals 'for people like us', the Dutch medical system was 'bad' but agreed that for children 'health care facilities are nicer in the Netherlands'. Another woman compared the Indian school system with that in the Netherlands and believed that education in India was much better for 'people of our type', hinting at shared *habitus* and social-cultural and economic capital. She however deemed that schools 'for small kids' were much better in the Netherlands as 'here they are just playschools and there is not so much pressure of exams'.

In general, women were quite unsure regarding the length of stay in the Netherlands as it all depended on their husband's job, they would say. Yet a majority did not mind staying on a few years more. Generally, they sent their children to International (English medium) schools because as one woman explained, 'I don't know if my husband gets transferred again so it will become difficult for him [son] to pick up English'. Another had put her child in a Dutch medium school but elaborated:

> …we are now thinking maybe shifting him to an international school because language stuff….we still don't know whether we will go back to India or where will we go…always that is the big thing…that is always with us…like we are never settled…you can't just settle down in one place like until and unless my husband decides he wants to work here and he is going to get a job here…you can't settle down because you never know where you are going.

Experiencing Freedoms

Some women believed their move to the Netherlands had been the result of their own free will. Asked about the decision to join her husband as a 'trailing wife' one woman told us:

> Hmm…if I had forced a lot then probably we had stayed in India.. but he was forcing that: 'no I don't love to go without the family because otherwise I will have nothing there; so please come with me and if you don't like the place we can go back always'. So that opportunity is there. So that thing also helped me. Because if someone says: 'no you can't do anything… you can't do…', so that bugs me a lot and then I become very stubborn and rigid…. I have to do that. But if someone gives me an opportunity then I think: 'let's see, let's try. I'm open to everything and I'm fine'.

A woman who had stayed on in the Netherlands for a few years observed there was, 'not much of difference between us and native [*authochtoon*] Dutch people except for the language perhaps'. Moreover, one woman learnt Dutch as: 'I could not follow my son sometimes' and another felt her children should learn the language as, 'otherwise they will never get Dutch friends' and 'never really be accepted here'. One mother said to the interviewer: 'I don't want him to be with only Indians; it's not a good thing for him he needs to mingle around and talk to everybody and make friends so probably that will be a challenge for him'. One other mother only decided that her child should learn Dutch after he had come home from school one day stating: 'Mama they don't understand my jokes'. Moreover, if their husbands had permanent jobs in the Netherlands, their children were often sent to Dutch medium schools instead of to an (more expensive) international school. These women perceived that if children adjusted well, they themselves also found it easier to settle and explore the Netherlands. Others believed that their children had stimulated them to mix with the Dutch and learn the language 'in a proper way'. One woman thought she was unable to return to India as: 'My son would never be able to adjust there anymore. Even now when we are there for holidays he keeps on asking me when we will go back to the Netherlands'.

Some women developed different career paths for themselves, like the woman who had never done any cooking while living in India, but—in the Netherlands—she had started a 'birthday cake business'. Her one-woman enterprise was doing very well and mostly produced tailor-made birthday cakes for Indian clients in and around Amsterdam and in The Hague. Another woman, who had been a professional dancer in India, had started Indian classical dance classes for children in the Netherlands. Some women did beauty treatments for other women at home and others had specialised in cooking a variety of dishes and held cooking classes.

A few unemployed informants undertook all kinds of activities exploring the new sociocultural fields in Dutch society and experimenting with different life-styles. A couple of women went to the movies on a regular basis or visited a museum, participated in [Dutch] discussion evenings and developed good friendships with 'the Dutch'. Feelings of 'belonging' could develop often after a few years in the Netherlands, or due to unexpected life events that made these women stop considering the Netherlands 'a foreign country'. One informant stated that she appreciated the Netherlands for being so 'multi-cultural':

> You mix with so many people when you have to stay in Netherlands… better to mix with other people and get to know their ideas instead of sitting here [at home] and….And uh likewise your children also, when they see you interacting with so many people, they become confident, they become interested in other communities and that's good for them. I would like to set an example.

Women also told us that they had several Indian friends who had married Dutch husbands and really liked such 'mixed marriages'. Though hesitating to give up their Indian passport, they do not mind naturalisation of husbands and children as in that way 'they have more chances in life'. But some women had thought of applying for Dutch citizenship and taking the integration exam, and after that planned to apply for an 'Overseas Indian' status. Importantly, many women mentioned—at least once during the interview—that at times and in some places they had felt like masters of their own path in life and at that particular *momentum* during the interview these women did not perceive themselves as followers but as fully in command: trailing women indeed but following only their own life-scripts. Such women felt that the Netherlands provided them with a type of life trajectory not available to them in India. When asked if she thought the Netherlands had hindered or hampered her development one of our informants said:

> It depends on what development you actually mean because I feel in my case the Netherlands gives me more things to develop because I have more time first of all to develop myself. In India you get…you don't get time to develop yourself. But it depends if you are more into Indian culture and all those things you miss those here and if you want to develop in technology and all that, then also I think India is really good specially in IT and all that. But apart from that as a person if you want to develop I think it [Netherlands] is the better place because people are not that conservative. In India you always feel that there is a difference between a girl or woman and a man…so yes for a personal development I feel the Netherlands is a better place.

What was most appreciated in the Netherlands was a newly experienced 'freedom' and here these women did not refer to economic independence but to a more holistic concept of freedom. For one informant this signified spiritual freedom: She converted to Buddhism while in the Netherlands where, she found: 'I can much more freely practice Buddhism'. However, whenever she went to India, she still had to perform—and did so dutifully—all the Hindu rituals along with her family, in order not to antagonise or displease anyone; but, it did not provide her any inner satisfaction. Another woman stated that she enjoyed living away from India and/or family members:

> …but yes once you are away then you can make your decisions and you can live the life you want, which is nice. So you get to do that when you are away and you are married that's nice I like that much.

Another enjoyed having more personal space after her arrival in the Netherlands:

> Of course there is a very very major difference. Because India is a conservative country and you don't get to move around a lot freely. Cause uh we have to, you know, take care of

everything there; so that my father-in-law doesn't get hurt sentiments or whatever. Here I have no restrictions. I can be myself and I have fun. I don't have to feel guilty about anything. That's the major change.

The fact that in the Netherlands they were alone with their husband and children without interference of family members in India was also appreciated by some women:

…in India it's not always possible because of family…I have to wake-up early help mother-in-law or there are other expectations, obligations…yes they affect your life to some extent because then you are not free to make your decisions free to do things the way you want because you have always to keep in mind oh okay maybe I have to do this, maybe I have to do that if not you might end up offending them or have you made hurting them, so you always…that thought is in your mind. If you are back home then you tend to do things accordingly… Even if you stay separately in India even then…yes certainly holidays probably you don't want to visit them you want to go some other place for vacation or something like that may be then they expect you to come visit family because you got the holiday you should come and visit your family so probably all those. Yes, it could be kind of restriction in your life which is not very nice I think that is something I don't like because if you do certain things it should be because you want to do them not because you have been told to do them… but yes when staying far away like this then there is no problem as such because you have your own life then.

Inquiring about changing identities made another informant respond in the following way:

So I would say yes. There is a lot of identity change. But now when you think about it when I go back to India I have written my own self. I am still myself I don't change a lot now. Because earlier I used to think that I should dress up in a different way just to please men but not anymore. I have changed in that way. And even my parents and everyone back home are, you know. They have made their peace with it. Because they know I have changed. And they don't expect me to follow the rules anymore. So they know that I have changed. Yah it is a liberating feeling.

One woman even managed to break down structural barriers to employment that had kept all others encompassed in our collective biography in a financially dependent position. After many years of having lived in the Netherlands on a 'dependent visa', she and her husband decided to swap their roles. Consequently, the woman accepted a paid Ph.D. position, while conversely, it was her husband who enrolled in an MA course in the Netherlands and took on a dependent visa.

Conclusions

Our ethnographic data shows 'entrepreneurial selves' at work and resultant non-unitary subjectivities of financially dependent Indian women in the Netherlands. The collective biographies of post-arrival memories analysed in this chapter, show that a particular state of domination generates possibilities for resistance and freedom. Our informants' embodied memories of power and knowledge and narrated lived experiences of domination while simultaneously narrating assumption of agency and realisation a new 'freedoms'. Our biography that contains the diverse life stories of 38 Indian wives in the Netherlands thus tells a more complex story than that of 'trailing ex-pat women' who are inactive dependents, victims of unequal gender relations and remain silent movers.

Our biography illustrates the psychosocial cost of 'trailing'. Many of our informants did—at least once during the interview—confess to having experienced great levels of anxiety, and to have gone through phases of anonymity, power-lessness, despair and frustration in relation to, among others, the loss of the mar-ketability of their skills and other factors limiting their capacity to obtain an appropriate job (such as discrimination). Yet, we argue that this phase of 'depen-dency subjectivity' is often a temporary mindset. Post-arrival narratives we anal-ysed often encompassed at least two more subjectivities where women seemed to have (partly) regained a sense of control despite or even perhaps because of the absence of financial independency.

As illustrated in this chapter, while sharing similar economic as well as socio-cultural capital and accompanied life-styles and subjected to similar structural barriers preventing financial independence, these women do not constitute a homogenous category in terms of anxiety levels, coping strategies and accompanied subjectivities. While some do step out of their comfort zones, others who have to face anxiety levels far too high for them to cope with, return to these very spaces which, while providing the much-needed security on the one hand, do signify on the other, a clear structural dependency.

References

Bal, Ellen. 2012. Indian Migration to the Netherlands. In *CARIM–India RRRR 2012/07, Robert Schuman Centre for Advanced Studies*. San Domenico di Fiesole (FI): European University Institute.

Bal, Ellen, Kate Kirk, and Sarah Renee Janssen. 2016. Migrants in Liminal Time and Space: An Exploration of the Experiences of Highly Skilled Indian Bachelors in Amsterdam. *Journal of Ethnic and Migration Studies*: (special issue).

Bourdieu, Pierre. 1984. *Distinction: A Social Critique of the Judgement of Taste*. London: Routledge & Kegan Paul.

De Prie, Sara. 2014. Personal Development in a Transnational Space. Identities and Daily Lives of Indian Expat Wives in the Netherlands. Master Degree thesis, Amsterdam: VU University.

de Hart, Betty. 2010. Inleiding. De Regulering van Partnermigratie: Beleid en Gevolgen. *Migranten Studies* 4: 282–286.

Docquier, Frédéric, B. Lindsay Lowell, and Abdeslam Marfouk. 2008. A Gendered Assessment of Highly Skilled Emigration, World Bank Report. Accessed 22 April 2016. (http://siteresources.worldbank.org/INTINTERNATIONAL/Resources/1572846-1283439445793/7368291-12834 39809851/DLM_PDR.pdf.

Gupta, Ritu, Pratyush Banerjee, and Jighyasu Gaur. 2012. Exploring the Role of the Spouse in Expatriate Failure: A Grounded Theory-based Investigation of Expatriate Spouse Adjustment issues from India. *The International Journal of Human Resource Management* 23 (17): 3559–3577.

Horgby, Anna. 2013. Constructions, indentifications and ambivalence—The encounter between perceived and lived reality of immigrated women. Master Degree thesis, Stockholm:

Stockholms Universiteit. https://www.academia.edu/9032723/Constructions_identifications_and_ambivalence_-_the_encounter_between_perceived_and_lived_reality_of_immigrated_women.

IOM. International Organization for Migration 2014. *Harnessing Knowledge on the Migration of Highly Skilled Women.* Geneva: IOM. https://publications.iom.int/system/files/pdf/iom_oecd_gender.pdf.

Ivanescu, Carolina, and Semin Suvarierol. 2013. *Mapping the Conditions of Stay and the Rationale for Entitlements and Restrictions for Family Migrants in the Netherlands.* IMPACIM Rotterdam: Erasmus University. http://www.compas.ox.ac.uk/media/PR-2013-IMPACIM_Mapping_Netherlands.pdf.

Kofman, Eleonore. 2012. Gender and Skilled Migration in Europe. *Cuadernos de Relaciones Laborales* 30 (1): 63–89.

Kofman, Eleonore, and Parvate Raghuram. 2005. Gender and Skilled Migrants: Into and Beyond the Work Place. *Geoforum* 36: 149–154.

Kõu, Anu, Leo van Wissen, Jouke van Dijk, and Ajay Bailey. 2015. A Life Course Approach to High-skilled Migration: Lived Experiences of Indians in The Netherlands. *Journal of Ethnic and Migrations Studies* 41 (10): 1644–1663.

Obradović, Esther. 2013. *Monitor Kennismigranten. Kwantitatieve Analyse.* Rijswijk: Ministerie van Veiligheid en Justitie (Immigratie-en Naturalisatiedienst) INDIAC. https://ind.nl/Documents/2013%20Monitor%20Kennismigranten,%20Kwantitatieve%20analyse.pdf.

Raghuram, P. 2004. The Difference that Skills Make: Gender, Family Migration Strategies and Regulated Labour Markets. *Journal of Ethnic and Migration Studies* 30 (2): 303–321.

Roos, Hannelore. 2013. In the Rhythm of the Global Market: Female Expatriates and Mobile Careers: A Case Study of Indian ICT Professionals on the Move. *Gender, Work and Organization* 20 (2): 147–157.

Scharff, Christina. 2014. Gender and Neoliberalism: Exploring the Exclusions and Contours of Neoliberal Subjectivities. Theory, Culture & Society (Blog Archive). Accessed 22 April 2016. (http://www.theoryculturesociety.org/christina-scharff-on-gender-and-neoliberalism/).

Seele, Peter. 2008. Miles and More: Highly Skilled Migration, Global Innovation Cultures and the question of Regional Embeddedness in India. In *Indian Diaspora. Trends and Issues,* ed A.K. Sahoo and L.K. Narayan, 97–110. New Delhi: Serials Publication.

Tejada, Gabriella, Uttam Bhattacharya, Binod Khadria, and Christiane Kuptsch (eds.). 2014. *Indian Skilled Migration and Development to Europe and Back.* New Delhi: Springer.

Upadhya, Carol. 2006. The Global Indian Software Labour Force IT Professionals in Europe. Working papers series No. 1: Indo-Dutch Programme on Alternatives in Developments (IDPAD). Accessed 22 April 2016. http://gubbilabs.in/demo/nias/sites/default/files/IDPAD-workingpaper.pdf.

Walkerdine, Valerie, and Jessica Ringrose. 2006. Femininities: Reclassifying Upward Mobility and the Neo-liberal Subject. In *The SAGE Handbook of Gender and Education,* ed Skelton, C., B. Francis, and L. Smulyan, 31–47. Thousand Oaks: Sage. https://www.academia.edu/4066542/Femininities_Reclassifying_Upward_Mobility_and_the_Neo-liberal_Subject_Valerie_Walkerdine_and_Jessica_Ringrose.

White, Alasdair. 2008. From Comfort Zone to Performance Management. In *Understanding Development & Performance.* Belgium, Baisy-Thy: White & MacLean Publishing.

Wiesbrock, Anja, and Metka Hercog. 2012. Making Europe More Attractive to Indian Highly-skilled Migrants? The Blue Card Directive and National Law in Germany and the Netherlands. In *CARIM, Developing a Knowledge Base for Policymaking of India-EU Migration, Maastricht University and Robert Shuman Centre for Advanced Studies.* European University Institute, Migration Policy Centre. http://cadmus.eui.eu/bitstream/handle/1814/23487/CARIM-India-RR-2012-09.pdf?sequence=1&isAllowed=y.

Part IV
Diasporas Across the World

Chapter 12
Curry and Race: Gender, Diaspora and Food in South Africa

Movindri Reddy

On 8 March 2016 Cherry Pillay posted a recipe for Crab Curry to the Facebook page *Grey Street Casbar Recipes* (*Durban*). She got 726 likes, 68 comments, and 18 shares. Comments ranged from 'U making me cry' to 'Looks devine' and 'How much was the kg of crab?' The Facebook page has 95,561 members (on 8 March 2016), four administrators (Eshana Suleman, Leila Ally, Ishaan Blunden and Buddy Govender), and a virtual community that has led to actual gatherings in South Africa, Australia, London and the United States. The site has strict instructions, and if members do not comply, their posts are quickly removed. Rules for posting include the following:

When posting pics of prepared meals/desserts, please include the recipe because this is not a 'what we had for dinner picture site' or 'look how talented I am at icing cakes site'... 'it is tedious for member to have to constantly beg for recipes'... racist and derogatory remarks or comments are not tolerated... Members guilty of that will be removed without warning... no video clips, and blog posts...Our recipe group was started mainly to preserve 'old-school' recipes passed down from generation to generation ...

Two other pages have evolved: *Grey Street Casbar Publications* (10,776 members on 8 March 2016) and *Grey Street Casbar Tips and Remedies* (11,311 members on 8 March 2016). Women who post often start by telling fellow members that they had cooked a dish especially for the 'hubby' or 'kids'. Many of the participants use their cell phones to upload pictures and post recipes. The site is rife with grammatical and spelling errors, colloquial responses (yummy, divine and looks delish), word abbreviations, and emoticons (as used for cell phone messaging). Uploaded photos either show food artistically displayed or in aluminium pots on the stove. The site acts as a virtual community that disregards class and religious

M. Reddy (✉)
Department of Diplomacy and World Affairs, Occidental College, 1600 Campus Road,
Los Angeles, CA 90041, USA
e-mail: meerkat@oxy.edu

© Springer Nature Singapore Pte Ltd. 2018
A. Pande (ed.), *Women in the Indian Diaspora*,
https://doi.org/10.1007/978-981-10-5951-3_12

149

differences; everyone is happy to make positive comments about dishes prepared for the various prayers and ceremonies. This is especially noticeable given the wide economic and geographical distances of its members—Indian women in the diaspora outside South Africa are often affluent, while those who post from within the country are from an array of social classes. The dishes that seem to represent the most 'authentic' South African food get the most attention; these are dishes that are unfettered by Western influences. Some of the most popular recipes are for biryani, mutton and chicken curries (red hot using '*Kashmiri*' *chili/masala* or a combination of other brands), tripe, fish and prawn curries, Durban vegetables (herbs, figs), bunny chow, and *roti*. Here is a recipe for Crab Curry from the Facebook page:

Crab Curry

1 onion
3 teaspoons ginger and garlic
Curry leaves
3 green chilies slit in half
6 tablespoons of liquid tamarind
2 cans of tomato and onion mix
3 tablespoons of hot Kashmiri masala
Garam masala and food colouring powder (1/4) teaspoon
Dhania for garnish

Fry onions chilies and curry leaves together. Add ginger and garlic. Add food colouring and garam masala. This must be done on medium heat. Add masala and then tomato and onion mix. Leave to cook on medium heat until it's cooked properly. Now add the liquid tamarind and cook for another 10 min. Put in da crab and cook until done. And garnish with dhania (Pillay 2016: Facebook, Grey Street Casbar).

Several decades earlier, in 1954, the Women's Cultural Group was created by a small group of elite and mainly Muslim women; its aims as stated by one of its founders, Zuleikha Mayat, was to 'promote cultural activities amongst the community and entertain them with plays, debates, etc. Amongst themselves, the members try to discuss and understand various problems that confront the community and to have an intellectual appreciation of religious culture and art' (Vahed and Waetjen 2010, 60). At the time, they were bucking a patriarchal system in place from indenture and exemplified by this piece written by Manilal Gandhi in 1929:

If mother is to be praised for the greatness of man she is equally to be censured for the degradation of man. Mother is the maker of a man—of a nation… Would that the modern mothers realise their true greatness and retained their lovable femininity and directed it in its right channels, than to seek masculine powers or rather the shadow for the substance (61).

The Women's Cultural Group published *Indian Delights* in 1961, a recipe book now in its thirteenth edition with over 350,000 copies sold nationally and internationally (Vahed and Waetjen 2010, 106). To ensure that they included recipes from all ethnic/religious groups, the women first visited the homes of people that they were introduced to through their networks, they then used a snowball method to gather recipes from Tamils, Telugus, Hindi-speaking peoples from North India, Gujaratis, Christians and Muslims (Memon, Surti, and Konkani). However, they were cognizant of the fact that the recipe book prioritised the meals cooked by Hindu and Muslim upper classes (112). Behind the scenes, black domestic labourers often cooked or helped to prepare the dishes for their Indian employers who recorded and wrote the recipes—in the apartheid context racial and class hierarchies placed middle-class Indian women above working class black African women (115). In the period that these books were published Indians were moving towards a cuisine that had similarities across the various ethnic and religious groups; as one member explains: 'In the past, when you went to people's homes, whether they were Memon or Surti or Konkani, Gujarati Hindu, or even Tamilian, they were very distinct tastes. They used different spices and methods and you could see and taste the difference—even the aroma was different. Nowadays they are all similar' (150). This is a recipe for Crayfish Curry from *Indian Delights*:

Crayfish Curry

500 g crayfish (meat and tails)
3 tblsp oil
2 tsp slivered garlic
1 cup coconut cream
½ cup tomato puree
1 tblsp khus khus (poppy seeds)
1 tsp crushed dhunia
1 tsp crushed jeera
1 bunch curry leaves
1½ tsp red pounded chilli (or powdered)
1 tsp salt

Soak poppy seeds in a tablespoon of water and liquidise. Fry slivered garlic, onion and curry leaves in oil and when the onion begins to change colour, add crayfish, khus khus and spices and cook uncovered over low heat till curry becomes dry. Add tomato and coconut cream, close lid and cook slowly till sauce thickens and crayfish done. Garnish with mint or parsley and serve with rotis or rice (Mayat 1982, 176).

Both these examples reflect moments when women appropriated male dominated public spaces to create a sense of community and to celebrate the distinctiveness of the diaspora through food. Despite the differences in technology, print media and mobilisation, the outcomes share similar characteristics and challenge patriarchy. This article attempts to place Indian women in the space that is defined by patriarchy, transnational capitalism, diaspora connections, and racism. It uses food as a metaphor for the identity and status of Indians in places outside India; specifically for Indians indentured during British colonialism in a period defined by global capitalism and epitomised by the sense of Western cultural superiority and white male entitlement and racism. All women, and particularly women of colour, experienced the system as oppressive, humiliating and demeaning. Relegated to the domestic space, Indian women have tirelessly sustained and reproduced Diaspora communities through cultural innovations and overt and covert political activism.

Food is a central component for imagining culture—it works to resist and affirm notions of home and belonging (Mannur 2009). Food is also associated with desire, and in this case, it reflects the desire for the imagined motherland, a 'collective yearning for an authentic tradition or pure place of origin' (Maira 2002, 194). It simultaneously shows a desire for inclusion and acceptance; diaspora food is strongly influenced by local ingredients and local cuisine. Cooking is largely gendered; women cook, and most rely on their mothers, grandmothers, aunts, cousins, and neighbours for lessons and recipes. Many also rely on cookbooks, which as Appadurai observes, are designed to standardise kitchen practices and culinary lore (1988, 6). But Eagleton makes a keen observation that 'If there is one thing about food, it is that it is never just food—it is endlessly interpretable—materialized emotion' (1998, 204). Food is often used to signify ethnic otherness—diaspora Indians are associated with curry, chutney, and masala. It emphasises connectedness to India, but also displacement and indigenization in places outside India.

Transnational Locality, Settler Colonialism and Indigenized Identities

Membership in a diaspora, their particular position in a racial minority under segregation and apartheid, and their place in patriarchal cultural systems (both white and Indian) circumscribe the location of Indian women in South Africa. All three dimensions have worked to situate them in an oppressive, subservient and largely silent space. Public political resistance is not commonplace while everyday hidden forms of resistance are normative (Scott 1990).

The propositions in this chapter are threefold. First, I propose that South Africa Indians, just like other Diasporas, occupy a space that I call the 'transnational locality'—they are perceived as not belonging to either the state they left behind (India) or the state they have lived in for several generations (Reddy 2014, 2015). This space is objectively and subjectively defined. At the transnational level, diasporas have identities that are associated with like communities dispersed from the same point of origin, and who share similar cultural foundations regarding language, religion, and customs. At the trans-state level, by maintaining (or presuming to maintain) an association with a homeland (as myth or real), they are distinguished as having dual identities. At the level of the nation-state, diaspora identities are localised, indigenized through generations, but nevertheless continue to represent difference, an otherness that contributes towards definitions of nationhood, but which also challenges it. The transnational locality encapsulates their indigenization *and* transnationality; in the case of South African Indians, it emphasises their otherness *and* Africanisation. The place of women in this context reflects their 'Indianness' that is at once considered 'foreign' *and* peculiar to the country. Indian food reflects these paradoxes with identifiable continuities with India, and discontinuities regarding ingredients, tastes, and cultural distinctiveness.

Second, the particular implications of *settler colonial states*, which most appropriately define the various state formations in South Africa had a definitive effect on identity formation among Indians in general and women in particular. Settler colonialism is different to colonialism although both sets of institutions obviously intersect; settlers are 'made by conquest, not just by immigration', (Mamdani 1998), they 'are *founders* of political orders and carry their sovereignty with them' (Veracini 2010, 3). They settle in land appropriated by imperial nations and then proceed to create and establish independent and sovereign homelands for themselves—a sovereignty not associated with a state, but with the capacity and authority to make laws and to control the local economy. The collective identities of settler colonialists were defined by 'permanent residency and sovereign entitlement' (20). Wolfe shows that an important difference between colonialism and settler colonialism was that for the latter, indigenous peoples were dispensable: 'The primary object of settler-colonization is the land itself rather than the surplus value to be derived from mixing native labour with it. Though in practice, Indigenous labour was indispensable to Europeans, settler-colonization is at base a winner-take-all project whose dominant feature is not exploitation but replacement...invasion is a structure not an event' (Wolfe 1999, 163). Others argued for the transnational and global character of settler colonialism, as its particular positioning in terms of Empire, global capitalist networks and race, are different to colonialism and require a separate theoretical frame of analysis (Thelen 1999; Lester 2002; Elkins and Pedersen 2005). Unlike colonial administrators or those representing the metropole in the colonies, settlers dislike imperial interference and prefer to demarcate their territorial integrity by managing the local economy themselves. Different to the colonial phenomenon with its 'construction of inferior otherness' (Osterhammel 1997, 108), settler colonials sought to establish themselves as normative. They are righteous; their claim to land and resources is often associated with a religious quest and higher purpose. While colonials attempt to dominate indigenous peoples to exploit them, settlers aim to dominate them for the purpose of moving them off the land—in South Africa, indigenous peoples became 'foreigners' and Indians were coded as 'temporary residents' and perpetual 'outsiders'. This coding was to become a permanent definition for Indians.

Indentured Indians experienced the implications of colonialism in India and settler colonialism in South Africa. While they were considered citizens in India, they were treated as temporary workers in South Africa. White settlers saw them as labour, subservient and with an inferior culture. Yet they were keenly aware of Indian competition in the local economy once indentured contracts were completed. Indian women experienced further discrimination—in terms of education, upward mobility and other activities in the public arena (like sports and professional opportunities) by white settlers as well as by Indian men. They were nevertheless looked upon to sustain Indian cultural activities and to reproduce relations of power.

Of particular significance here is the *present–absent* quality of settler states—colonial, post-colonial and apartheid (Reddy 1992, 2016). These are states that are intrusive, seeking to use overt and covert violence to control civil society and maintain power. Ethnic, communal and other differences are often employed to exaggerate divisions and undermine united resistance. At the same time, these states are largely absent with respect to the provision of adequate social welfare like health, education, care for the aged and other benefits. In the space left by the absent state, people come to rely extensively on neighbours, family, friends, colleagues, co-workers, comrades, gangs, and ethnic organisations. These are the institutions they turn to for childcare, elderly care, folk medicines, backstreet abortions, mid-wives, spiritual healing, protection, and advice. They also assist them with loans, food and security when needed. Religious and ethnic networks are strengthened under such conditions. Women play a significant role in nurturing these community networks through cultural organisations, religious institutions, and political movements. Food plays an important part in sustaining an Indianness that is dynamic and organic; which also acts as a site of resistance, insularity, and assimilation.

Third, the Indian indentured diaspora, in general, has hybrid/mixed/indigenised identities. Nevertheless, Indians are categorised in terms of ethnicity across the diaspora reflecting in part their own desire to separate themselves from indigenous and local peoples on the basis of 'purity' and historical authenticity derived from the motherland (India). Indigenous or Creole communities, in turn, have sought to delineate themselves as belonging to the land, thereby claiming indigeneity or indigenous status and rights in relation to Indians. Indentured Indians have also been marginalised and seen as 'unauthentic' by the motherland, although this perspective has changed more recently (Varadarajan 2010). In South Africa, Indians have been ethnically classified as 'coolie' (pejoratively), Asiatic (a colonial category that included Indians, Arabs, Malays and Chinese) and Indian (a colonial, apartheid and post-apartheid classification); the rest of South Africa is classified in terms of race: Black African, White, Coloured. This classification *others* them in regarding nationality, they are not African but Indian, they occupy the *transnational locality* neither wholly belonging to South Africa nor India (Reddy 2015). Further, India's cultural boycott of South Africa and the general isolation of the apartheid regime have made South African Indians one of the most indigenized in the diaspora—they *are* Africans who have a mixed/Creolized/hybrid culture that is deeply impacted by race and racism, as well as ethnicity and diaspora connections to India. It is in this context that women have been the bearers of cultural continuity *and* discontinuity. Their roles in maintaining some religious and cultural inheritances from India has contributed towards the Indianness that exists; their roles in supporting upward mobility, assimilation and competitiveness in South Africa has contributed towards the organic character of Indianness. This article will explore these themes as they relate to Indian women in South Africa.

Indenture, Segregation, Apartheid to Post-Apartheid South Africa

Indians constitute 2.5% of the population or 1,362,000, and of this 2.4% or 673,900 are women (Statistics South Africa 2015). Indians are a part of a diaspora indentured during British colonialism, 154,641 entered Natal between 1860 and 1911, this number increased by about 5,500 'passenger' Indians who immigrated to the region (Swanson 1983, 404). After completing their contracts, indentured Indians moved rapidly out of agriculture, by the 1970s the majority was employed in urban-related industries (Freund 1995). Indians were also successful in market gardening and other local industries. Segregation laws were passed to undermine competition from Indians who outperformed whites by providing personalised services, lower prices and longer hours (Vahed 2005, 469). Indenture separated Indians from India spatially and psychologically; they became more entrenched in local affairs—resistance and accommodation became part of permanent settlement and survival. Under the Union government established in 1910 when the four British colonies of Cape Town, Natal, Transvaal and Orange River united as a dominion of the British Empire, racism and segregation became structurally embedded in the sociopolitical system of South Africa. When the National Party came into power in 1948 and began to institute apartheid laws, Indians continued to be treated as 'temporary sojourners in South Africa', to be 'repatriated as soon as possible', this after being in the country for nearly 90 years (Elphick and Davenport 1997, 203). They symbolised 'everything that the Afrikaner Volk (nation) opposed —they were *outlanders* (outsiders), city folk and trading people' (van den Berge 1962, 602). Spatial and physical segregation were the cornerstones of apartheid; cities and towns, capital and trade were for whites, while people of colour provided labour and services when needed. By 1961 the apartheid regime moved to include Indians as a separate ethnic group granting them citizenship with a separate Department of Indian Affairs. Under the reform initiatives of the 1980s, a tricameral parliament was created with a House of Assembly for whites, a House of Representatives for Coloureds and a House of Delegates for Indians with proportional representation of 4:2:1. Black Africans were excluded. This led to a widespread movement to boycott the elections spearheaded by the newly formed United Democratic Front (UDF), an umbrella body that included the Natal Indian Congress and the Transvaal Indian Congress. Nearly, 80% of eligible Indian voters boycotted the elections.

The democratic transition that began in the early 1990s resulted in a neoliberal state that embraced structural adjustment with less government spending, tax cuts for the wealthy, tax incentives for foreign investors, the lifting of exchange controls and the privatisation of government holdings. The state was defined by budget cuts, liberalisation, deregulation, privatisation and tight monetary policies (Kahn 2000). In line with the post-apartheid constitution that is based on substantive equality, the state has also attempted to empower black upward mobility and to increase the ranks of the middle classes with programmes such as Black Economic

Empowerment (BEE). But even these programmes have produced incremental reforms that have reaffirmed exclusion (Klotz 2013). While these efforts succeeded in slightly increasing the middle and wealthy black classes, the gap between the rich and poor has also increased: 45–55% live in poverty (Ballard et al. 2005, 620–621). An Income Dynamic Study found that those with incomes below the poverty line rose from 35% in 1993 to 42% in 1998 (Seekings and Nattrass 2002, 11).

Even though affirmative action policies included Indians and Coloureds, its implementation was mainly for Black Africans. The unemployment rate for Indians in 2014 was 18% as opposed to 8% for Whites, 28% for Coloureds and 43% for Black Africans (Statistics South Africa 2016). The real income of workers has also dropped given the higher prices for rents, services, and goods. Residential evictions have led to the formation of social movements like the Concerned Citizens Forum in the Indian township of Chatsworth, which linked with similar organisations throughout the country. The two-pronged strategy adopted by the post-apartheid system of retaining the racial and ethnic classifications of apartheid and affirmative action mainly for Black Africans, has affected Indians in that as a minority, they have little political leverage, and they continue to be viewed as ethnic outsiders.

Patriarchy and Capitalism

Spivak writes: 'Between patriarchy and imperialism, subject-constitution and object-formation, the figure of the woman disappears, not into a pristine nothingness, but into a violent shuttling which is the displaced figuration of the "third-world" caught between tradition and modernization' (1994, 102). To write about Indian women in South Africa is to recognise their oppression and marginalisation by capitalism, patriarchy, and gender, all within the framework of globalisation and the transnational movement of capital and labour. From colonialism through to post-apartheid South Africa patriarchy persisted and 'performs physical, psychic and discursive violence against women' (Samuelson 2007, 11). Differences related to class, ethnicity (regarding regional points of origin from India) and generation, defies any attempt to talk of Indian women as a coherent category. Particularly, under apartheid, racial segregation also imposed geographically defined class divisions; working class and poor Indians were relocated to two townships in Durban (Chatsworth and Phoenix), while the middle classes lived in smaller racially designated residential areas like Reservoir Hills and Asherville. Chatsworth consists of undulating rows of semi-detached concrete block housing with few common spaces, recreational areas, or community and sporting facilities. Planned for 165,000 people, by 2002 it was estimated that more than 300,000 people lived in the area (Freund 1995, 73; Desai 2002, 15). While the ranks of the poor swelled, the numbers of Indians in tertiary education increased. By 1985 over 17,000 Indians were enrolled in South African universities, and a further 8,201 were registered for correspondence degree courses at the University of South Africa (UNISA), a number three times higher than Coloured, but 40% lower than whites

(Lemon 1990, 136). By 1978 in Natal, 96% of Indians between the ages of 15 and 35 were literate in English, and illiterate in Tamil, Telugu or Hindi (Maasdorp and Pillay 1977, 92). The numbers of women in universities steadily increased as did their movement towards a more creolized and indigenous South African culture—under apartheid Indians went to English schools but learned Afrikaans from the first grade. With access to education by 1973, nearly 40% of all Indian students in high school were girls (Freund 1991, 423). Over generations there were few opportunities to learn any Indian languages and apart from movies, there was little exposure.

Women were first indentured to Mauritius and British Guiana in the 1830s by private importers and by 1842 their indenture was brought under government controls; between 1843 and 1919 a sex ratio was instituted that specified approximately 40 women for every 100 indentured men (Carter 2012, 198). By 1911 of the 152,641 Indians indentured to Natal, 104,619 were men and boys, and 48,022 were women and girls (Beall 1990, 147). Indentured Indians came mainly from Madras and Calcutta. Speaking Tamil and Telugu, 83% were Hindus, 12% were Muslims, and 5% were Christians (Brooks and Webb 1965, 85). 'Passenger Indians' were predominantly Urdu-speaking Muslims from the Bombay area and included Gujarati's and Muslims. Life on the plantations was difficult, women were to receive rations and 5 shillings a month, but in practice most were only paid and given rations when they worked on various discreet tasks (Beall 1990, 153; Meer 1969). Those women who were assigned to the Natal Government Railways (the largest official employer of indentured labour) were assumed to be dependent on men to support them; many found work on small farms or in private homes. Evidence shows that 'both Indian men and their employers regarded women as property, to be bought, sold or given away' (Beall 1990, 155). On the plantations, women were 'treated almost as chattels, and even marriage was regarded with contempt in some quarters' (Swan 1985, 37). Marital relations were challenging, and sexual exploitation by Indian (husbands, sirdars[1]) *and* white (employers, managers) men was not uncommon. Indentured men sometimes bought and sold women 'for a shilling, with the tacit approval of the employers and sirdars and even of the women themselves (Beall 1990, 162). Indian women moved out of indenture into wage labour to form a large working class; between 1951 and 1970 they increased as a percentage of the Indian workforce from 7.3 to 18.6% (Freund 1991, 422).

Indian Women in South Africa Today

Marginalized in contemporary South Africa some Indian women have sought to reinvigorate and reinvent Diaspora ties with India in an effort to reinforce notions of rootedness with India. This is in line with Jung's observation that: 'The protection

---

[1]sirdar: Indian foreman, headman.

of minority rights, the expression of the rights of groups (essential, and essentially political units)…now anchor opposition to the ANC government…' (2000, 225). Nationalist discourses have taken ethnocentric and racial lines. A sector of Indian women, for example, supported the conservative National Party (the apartheid era party that was displaced by the African National Congress), and more are moving away from the dominant versions of Hinduism to a 'more abstract, service-oriented, and humanist version' like the teachings of Satya Sai Baba, the Divine Life Society, or the Ramakrishna Society (Radhakrishnan 2005, 276). Indianness also includes racist stereotypes of Black Africans, and this reinforces the notion that Indians are 'inside outsiders'. By focusing on connections to India (imagined or otherwise), Indian women are at the centre of constructing an Indianness that is dynamic and often influenced by generation and class.

For women who fought relentlessly on the side of the anti-apartheid organisations, being black as opposed to Indian, has more resonance. Muthal Naidoo, a well-known playwright, expresses these nuances well:

> Some Indians have sought to emulate white norms, values and customs at the expense of their inherited culture. Others have acknowledged the strong influence of the West on their socialisation but do not deny their origins. Still others have asserted their rights to be called African, while acknowledging their South African inheritance (1997, 30).

> She herself has rejected the term Indian: '… I have a residual culture that originated in India but that is where my "Indianness" begins and ends… What I try to express in my work is my South African heritage, a mixture of Western, African, and Indian influences' (31).

Conclusion

In Durban where the majority of Indians reside (more than 78% of all Indians live in the province, Central Statistics, 1999, 8), areas like Chatsworth and Phoenix have exhibited a marked shift towards reinventing Indianness regarding the celebration of ceremonies of India. This more definitive identification with India acts to separate them from the Black African majority, but in a country where ethnicity is an intrinsic part of the state, there is an expectation that ethnic groups will celebrate their ethnicity. South Africa advertises itself as a rainbow nation—multicultural with discreet and separate ethnic groups. At another extreme, the wealthy move towards greater westernisation that is more overtly associated with the white elite and with the material and cultural symbols of affluence. Across classes, Indian women have been simultaneously empowered and disempowered. They have more access to Black Economic Empowerment jobs, they often earn more than their husbands and are—increasingly—more educated than men, some have high profile business and professional positions, and others are strong community activists. But the majority experiences some level of erasure by men and by the state. They have sought to fight back through overt resistance and also through other means. The virtual community of the *Grey Street Casbar* and the community formed around the publication of *Indian Delights* by the Women's Cultural Groups are some of the ways in which women have effectively appropriated the discourses of patriarchy and capitalism.

References

Appadurai, Arjun. 1988. How to Make a National Cuisine: Cookbooks in Contemporary India. *Comparative Studies in Society and History* 30 (1): 3–24. doi:10.1017/S0010417500015024.

Ballard, Richard, Adam Habib, Imraan Valodia, and Elke Zuern. 2005. Globalization, Marginalization and Contemporary Social Movements. *African Affairs* 104 (417): 615–634.

Beall, Josephine. 1990. Women under indentured labor in colonial Natal, 1860–1911. In *Women and Gender in Southern Africa to 1945*, ed. Cheryl Walker, 146–167. Cape Town: David Philip.

Brooks, Edgar H., and Colin de B. Webb. 1965. *A History of Natal*. Pietermaritzburg: University of Natal Press.

Carter, Marina. 2012. Women & Indenture. In *Experiences of Indian Labour Migrants*. United Kingdom: Pink Pigeon Press.

Central Statistics. 1999. Living in KwaZulu-Natal. Selected Findings of the 1995 October Household Survey. Accessed September 16, 2016. http://www.statssa.gov.za/publications/LivingInKZN/LivingInKZN.pdf.

den Berghe, Van, and L. Pierre. 1962. Apartheid, Fascism, and the Golden Age. *Chairs d'Études Africaines* 2 (6): 598–608.

Desai, Ashwin. 2002. *We are the Poors: Community Struggles in Post-Apartheid South Africa*. New York: Monthly Review Press.

Eagleton, Terry. 1998. Edible écriture. In *Consuming Passions: Food in the Age of Anxiety*, ed. Sian Griffiths and Jennifer Wallace, 203–208. Manchester: Manchester University Press.

Elkins, Caroline, and Susan Pedersen (eds.). 2005. *Settler Colonialism in the Twentieth Century*. London and New York: Routledge.

Elphick, R., and R. Davenport (eds.). 1997. *Christianity in South Africa: A Political, Social and Cultural History*. Cape Town: David Philip.

Freund, Bill. 1991. Indian Women and the Changing Character of the Working Class Indian Households in Natal 1860–1990. *Journal of Southern African Studies* 17 (3): 414–429.

Freund, Bill. 1995. *Insiders and Outsiders: The Indian Working Class of Durban, 1910–1990*. Portsmouth: Heinemann Publishers.

Jung, Courtney. 2000. *Then I was Black: South African Political Identities in Transition*. New Haven: Yale University Press.

Kahn, Brian. 2000. Debates over IMF reform in South Africa. Studies on International Financial Architecture. Accessed September 4, 2016. http://library.fes.de/fulltext/iez/00793.htm.

Klotz, Audie. 2013. *Migration and National Identity in South Africa, 1860–2010*. Cambridge: Cambridge University Press.

Lemon, Anthony. 1990. The Political Position of Indians in South Africa. In *South Asians Overseas: Migration and Ethnicity*, ed. Colin Clarke, Ceri Peach, and Steven Vertovec. Cambridge: Cambridge University Press.

Lester, Alan. 2002. British Settler Discourse and the Circuits of Empire. *History Workshop Journal* 54 (1): 24–48. doi:10.1093/hwj/54.1.24.

Maasdorp, Gavin, and Nesen Pillay. 1977. *Urban Relocation and Racial Segregation: The Case of Indian South Africans*. Durban: Department of Economics, University of Natal.

Maira, Sunaina. 2002. *Desis in the House: Indian American Youth Culture in New York City*. Philadelphia: Temple University Press.

Mamdani, Mahmood. 1998. *When Does a Settler Become a Native? Reflections on the Colonial Roots of Citizenship in Equatorial and South Africa*. Inaugural Lecture, University of Cape Town, New Series no. 208, May 13.

Mannur, Anita. 2009. *Culinary Fictions: Food in South Asian Diaspora Culture*. Philadelphia: Temple University Press.

Mayat, Zuleikha. 1982. *Indian Delights*. Durban: Women's Cultural Group.

Meer, Fatima. 1969. *Portrait of Indian South Africans*. Durban: Aron House.

Naidoo, Muthal. 1997. The Search for Cultural Identity: A Personal View of South African "Indian" Theatre. *Theatre Journal* 49 (1): L 29–39.

Osterhammel, Jürgen. 1997. *Colonialism. A Theoretical Overview* (1995). Translated by Shelly Frisch. Princeton, NJ: Markus Weiner.

Radhakrishnan, Smitha. 2005. 'Time to Show Our True Colors': The Gendered Politics of "Indianness" in Post-Apartheid South Africa. *Gender and Society* 19 (2): 262–281.

Reddy, Movindri. 1992. *Conflicts of Consciousness: The State, Inkatha, and Ethnic Violence in South Africa*. Ph.D. diss.: University of Cambridge.

Reddy, Movindri. 2014. Transnational Locality: Diasporas and indentured South Asians. *Diaspora Studies* 8 (1): 1–17.

Reddy, Movindri. 2015. *Social Movements and the Indian Diaspora*. London and New York: Routledge.

Reddy Movindri. 2016. Theories of Revolution and Southern Africa: South Africa and Zimbabwe. Paper presented at the Western Political Science Association, March 23–26, San Diego.

Samuelson, Meg. 2007. *Remembering the Nation, Dismembering Women?: Stories of the South African Transition*. Durban: University of KwaZulu Natal Press.

Scott, James C. 1990. *Domination and the Arts of Resistance: Hidden Transcripts*. New Haven, CT: Yale University Press.

Seekings, Jeremy, and Nicoli Nattrass. 2002. Class, Distribution and Redistribution in Post-Apartheid South Africa. *In Transformation: Critical Perspectives in Southern Africa* 50 (1): 1–30.

Spivak, Gayatri Chakravorty. 1994. Can the Subaltern Speak? In *Colonial Discourses and Post-Colonial Theory*, ed. Patrick Williams and Laura Chrisman. New York: Columbia University Press.

Statistics South Africa. 2015. *Mid-year Population Estimates: 2015*. Accessed July 4, 2016. https://www.statssa.gov.za/publications/P0302/P03022015.pdf.

Statistics South Africa. 2016. Employment, unemployment, skills and economic growth. An exploration of household survey evidence on skills and development and unemployment between 1994 and 2014. Accessed September 4. http://www.statssa.gov.za/presentation/Stats%20SA%20presentation%20on%20skills%20and%20unemployment_16%20September.pdf.

Swan, Maureen. 1985. *Gandhi: The South African Experience*. Johannesburg: Raven Press.

Swanson, Maynard. W. 1983. The Asiatic Menace': Creating Segregation in Durban, 1870–1900. *The International Journal of African Historical Studies* 16 (3): 401–421.

Thelen, David. 1999. The Nation and Beyond: Transnational Perspectives on United States History. *The Journal of American History* 86 (3): 965–975.

Vahed, Goolam. 2005. Passengers, Partnerships, and Promissory Notes: Gujarati Traders in Colonial Natal, 1870–1920. *The International Journal of African Historical Studies* 38 (3): 449–479.

Vahed, Goolam, and Thembisa Waetjen. 2010. Gender, Modernity & Indian Delights. In *The Women's Cultural Group of Durban, 1954–2010*. South Africa: HSRC Press.

Varadarajan, Latha. 2010. *The Domestic Abroad*. Diaspora in International Relations. New York: Oxford University Press.

Veracini, Lorenzo. 2010. *Settler Colonialism*. A Theoretical Overview: Palgrave Macmillan.

Wolfe, Patrick. 1999. Settler Colonialism and the Transformation of Anthropology. In *The Politics and Poetics of an Ethnographic Event*. London and New York: Cassell.

Chapter 13
Diversities, Continuities and Discontinuities of Tradition in the Contemporary Sikh Diaspora: Gender and Social Dimensions

Shinder S. Thandi

Introduction

The 2 million strong diaspora of Punjabi Sikhs, now predominantly settled in rich countries of the West, began to emerge during the British colonial period, and grew further and consolidated during the 70 year postcolonial period. As a diaspora, far from being homogeneous, it exhibits the diversity and heterogeneity prevailing in Punjab even today. Thus, factors such as periods of migration and settlement; economic and political status; class, caste, gender and religious traditions define the heterogeneity within the Sikh Punjabi diaspora. In fact, it may be more accurate to state that there are many Sikh diasporas with their own specificities in terms of formations, subjectivities and sensibilities. This heterogeneity and diversity generates inter-generational and intra-generational challenges, family break-ups due to tradition-bound patriarchal practices and impassioned discourses on the meaning of home, belonging, gender relations, religious and cultural identities. Needless to say, there are emergent tensions over the nature of tradition to be transmitted, interpreted and reinvented, leading to considerable diversity in the lived experience and practices of diasporan Sikhs.

This paper explores several such issues and tensions, which have risen to the fore in recent years, especially those evident in community discourses: the changing role of Sikh women within the household, within the community and workplace domains, the impact of education, integration and social mobility, challenges posed by inter- and intra-generational tensions and the increased incidence of domestic violence and abuse in transnational marriages. After this introduction, the paper is divided into four further sections. The second provides an overview of the context and salient features in the formation of the Sikh diaspora. The third discusses settlement patterns, evolution in family life, continuities and discontinuities in

S.S. Thandi (✉)
Department of Global Studies, University of California, Santa Barbara, CA, USA
e-mail: thandi@global.ucsb.edu

© Springer Nature Singapore Pte Ltd. 2018
A. Pande (ed.), *Women in the Indian Diaspora*,
https://doi.org/10.1007/978-981-10-5951-3_13

tradition and emergent diversities and challenges. The fourth section analyses prevailing views on gender-focused discourses in largely diaspora contexts and the fifth and final section pulls together the main arguments of the paper.

Making of the Sikh Diaspora

Punjabis have historically demonstrated considerable mobility as they sojourned or settled away from their homes, taking advantage of the new opportunity structures which became available to them during different historical periods. Even before the arrival of the British, often viewed as the period ushering in modernity and overseas migration, Sikh Punjabis were already scattered over a very wide geographical area, in fact, wherever trading opportunities or historical religious sites and pilgrimages took them. Nevertheless, the modern period of migration, especially in terms of scale and scope, whether internal or external, is conveniently dated to the arrival of the British.

Currently, Punjabi migrants—historically predominantly Sikhs and in this paper the terms Sikhs and Punjabis are synonymous unless other Punjabis are specifically identified —are estimated at around 2 million, that is, around eight per cent of the total Indian Diaspora currently estimated at 25 million. They are geographically dispersed in over 75 countries in southeast and eastern Asia, Australasia, Africa, Europe and North America. This geographical spread started around the middle of the nineteenth century and reflected both, the changing socio-economic conditions in Punjab—the subdivision of already small family landholdings, rising farmer debts, frequent famines together with regular incidences of plagues and epidemics —motivating Sikhs and other Punjabis to move out of Punjab, and the changing structure of employment opportunities abroad. Sikh migration was largely voluntary, economic, adventure seeking and opportunistic, and begins during the final quarter of the nineteenth century. It reflected the growing strategic importance of Punjab within the context of an expanding British Empire and its associated demanding requirements. Punjab's critical role resulted in substantial public investments in its physical infrastructure and agriculture, especially through establishment of the Canal Colonies to boost agricultural production and exports and in the increased army and police recruitment from Punjab to provide security to the expanding empire (Tan 2005; Mazumdar 2003). By the beginning of the twentieth century Sikh and Punjabi Hindus together comprised 26%, while the Jat Sikhs, a particularly favoured 'martial race' and caste group, alone comprised 15% of the total recruitment to the army (Omissi 1998, 20).

The majority of the earliest migrants from Punjab who went to Burma, Malaysia, Hong Kong, Fiji, Australia and Canada were Jat Sikhs from the rural areas of Punjab and most of them went abroad either through military postings, police service or in some other security-related operations (Thandi 2009). The first quarter of the twentieth century saw further expansion of this migration to East African countries of Uganda, Tanzania and Kenya with many initially recruited to build railroads and others subsequently taking advantage of the new trade, professional and commercial opportunities which British rule was creating. The East African connection broadened the socio-economic background of Punjabi migrants, especially for the *Ramgharia* community which was better positioned to supply the kind of skilled labour required in this earlier phase of migration to East Africa. Having been exposed to wider horizons through the imperial connection, the number of Sikh passenger migrants seeking opportunities or adventure abroad expanded rapidly, especially to the Pacific coast of North America, and to Australia and New Zealand. However, unlike earlier 'managed' migrations associated with Empire duties, much of this independent migration was confined largely to the central (*Doaba*) districts of Punjab and was not necessarily associated with the 'martial races' army recruitment policy (Tan 2005; Omissi 1998).

In the 1920s a series of restrictive immigration policies, especially in North America and Australasia limited the further expansion of Sikh migration. However, as favourable conditions re-emerged in the postcolonial period, the *Doaba* re-established itself as the dominant subregion for sending migrants abroad. Thus, the mass movements of the 1950s and 1960s to UK and from the mid-1960s to USA and Canada, to the Gulf States in the 1980s and the more recent movements during the 1990s to newer locations such as Greece, Italy and Spain in southern Europe, mainly have their roots in the central *Doaba* districts (Thandi 2012). With growing awareness of the relative success of overseas *Doaba* Sikhs, overseas migration from the *Malwa* and *Majha* districts also increased over time. It is important to underscore that new employment opportunities in the post-independent decades opened up horizons for different types of Punjabi migrants. For instance, from the late 1970s, the Gulf States became an important migration destination for various Punjabi Dalit and artisan groups as well as other previously under-represented sections of Punjabi society.

In summarising the historical migration experience, there are four important features to note. First, over time, almost *all* districts of Punjab developed a dynamic migration culture, although *Doaba* migrants still constitute the largest category amongst the Sikh diaspora. Second, Punjabis of all socio-economic backgrounds and castes and sub-castes are represented abroad. In fact the 'Little Punjabs' that are transplanted abroad emulate the socio-religious and political landscape of the homeland of Punjab. Thus, just as we have different types of religious traditions and sectarian groupings within or at the margins of Sikhism represented abroad—for example, *Udassis*, *Nirankaris*, *Nanaksarias* and various *Sants*—there are also different categories of Punjabi Hindu and Dalit groups visible as well. This diversity is clearly demonstrated in caste, religious and political organisations, mobilisations and expressions within the Punjabi diaspora. Third, irrespective of the historical period or length of settlement abroad, Sikhs in all diaspora locations—albeit in varying degrees —maintain circular, multiple and multi-layered transnational linkages with their ancestral homeland of Punjab. Fourth, an important dimension largely ignored or glossed over in Punjabi migration narratives, is that the gender of pioneer communities was almost exclusively male. How do we explain this gender bias? There are two inter-related explanations. First, this gender bias is not atypical because it is also commonly observed in most migration histories. Young male migrants often saw themselves as sojourners rather than settlers, hoping to make a quick '*paisa*' and then returning. A second important factor may have been the strict immigration rules, apparent in most instances, which did not permit pioneer migrants to bring their wives and children. Although it is difficult to generalise this aspect for *all* earlier migrants, certainly the migrations of pioneer Sikhs to the Pacific coasts of Canada and USA and to the UK were predominantly those of males. Thus, even by the end of the second decade of the twentieth century, after some 45 years of migration history, the number of Sikh female migrants in both Canada and USA was probably no more than a dozen in each country. This dimension of Sikh migration becomes abundantly clear when one glances at photographs of pioneer migrants, which dramatically show, with one or two exceptions, female migrants as simply missing or 'invisible'. Of course many of these pioneer migrants did return to their families in Punjab, some were able to reunite with their families, whilst some married local women, as was the experience among some in California (Leonard 1992).

Although it is difficult to be conclusive, especially given limited ethnographic research, the widespread absence of women and a settled family life in the new environments did have implications for the social and cultural dynamics among early Sikh communities: the functioning of all-male households and multiple occupancy; restricted inter-group and gender relations and limited participation in and integration with the host society. It is also worth emphasising here that most early migrants departed from a largely homogeneous ethnic and cultural setting (Punjab and Punjabiyat) to arrive in multi-ethnic, multicultural, multireligious and often hostile environments, each with their individual nuances and complexities. For example, it was for the first time that Sikhs were interacting and competing with 'strangers' far away from their homeland, whether these were Malays, Kenyans, Chinese, Japanese or Maoris, etc.

Settling and Making Family Life Abroad

As already intimated above, the development of a normal family life abroad was distorted by immigration rules and to some extent by the geographical distance from Punjab. Family reunions were less costly and legally easier in the Southeast Asian region than in the UK, in Australasia or the Pacific coast of North America. In any case, by the end of the second decade of the twentieth century, USA and the white settler countries of Canada, Australia and New Zealand—the latter two decreeing 'White Only' policies—had passed legislation to restrict or ban 'all' Indian migration and this of course disproportionately affected Punjabi Sikhs. However, fragmentary evidence suggests Sikh migration still continued in some clandestine ways, thereby allowing the communities to grow. However, British borders still remained open but migration during this period was limited to students belonging to the wealthy elite, to members of royalty and to adventurous groups who, due to their ingenuity, managed to land in port cities. A good example of this being members of the *Bhatra* community in the UK, who after landing in port cities made their living by 'peddling' small household goods from house to house.

The situation begins to change somewhat by the time of Indian independence. In the UK, the economic devastation caused by WW2 lead to an increase in demand for unskilled labour—which many young Punjabis willingly supplied from the early 1950s—and they also reunited with their families a decade or so later. Following the Immigration Acts in USA and Canada in 1965 and 1967 respectively, starts the process of mass migration there and subsequently leading to family reunions. Thus for the majority of overseas Punjabis, settled family life really started from the mid-1960s to early 1970s or even later in some cases. Thereafter, with the natural growth in population, fresh migration and family reunions there emerged a sizable diaspora-born second or third generations and communities began to flourish in all spheres of life—in employment and self-employment and business, in education and cultural industries. With increased access to quality suburban housing in de-sirable neighbourhoods, they began enjoying a relatively comfortable lifestyle, albeit at different levels depending on length of settlement and income.

Growing Socio-economic Differentiation

As we would expect within any diaspora community, diasporic experiences can follow very different trajectories—some taking a very successful path and others taking one less so. Thus Sikhs who migrated in the early postcolonial phase, especially if they happened to be educated economic migrants, were able to con-solidate income security and family life fairly quickly, and to achieve upward social mobility: their children, whether arriving as child-migrants or diaspora-born, became university-educated graduates, were able to access employment in well-paid professions, afford more desirable suburban housing and become more integrated with their hostland communities without losing the essence of their own cultural and religious identity. On the other hand, those Sikh families that migrated later, particularly where the majority of them were unskilled, uneducated and hailed largely from villages, struggled to make a living and continue to be marginalised in many places even today. Undoubtedly some second or third generation diaspora-born Sikhs were able to 'break-out' by using education as a strategic vehicle and move up the economic ladder but they remain a minority, especially in countries with more recent settlement like Italy and Spain. Thus we can conclude, at the risk of some generalisation, that though all Sikhs have experienced an increase in absolute standards of living, socio-economic diversities within Sikh communities have also increased over time. Length of settlement, level of education and access to well-paid jobs remain crucial factors in facilitating and perpetuating socio-economic diversities among the Sikh diaspora today.

Family Life and Gender Relations

Traditional Punjabi family life and gender dynamics, still evident in contemporary Punjab villages, have been transplanted into the first-generation overseas migrant households. The strong patriarchal family structure meant that there was a clear division regarding household chores with many women staying at home as homemakers and nurturers of tradition, and men assuming the role of 'bread-winners'. Son preference, a strong patriarchal practice still relevant in the diaspora today, implied that the male child had priority over choices whether relating to lifestyle or education. In fact, given that girls were perceived as *begana dhan* or *prayi amanat* (someone else's wealth) and 'socialized' as such, many parents did not desire or expect their daughters to study beyond the mandated school years. Parents fulfilled their obligation by marrying off their daughters as soon as was practical, always in fear of the daughter bringing dishonour (*behzti*) or harming the honour (*izzat*) of the family. Amrit Wilson, one of the earliest champions of Sikh women's rights in Britain, writing in 1978 stated '...*izzat* can...be translated as honour, self-respect and sometimes plain male ego. It is a quality basic to the emotional life of a Punjabi. It is essentially male but it is women's lives and actions which affect it most. A woman can have *izzat* but it is not her own—it is her brother's or father's. Her *izzat* is a reflection of the male pride of the family as a whole' (Wilson 1978). Izzat figures heavily in gendered discourses around inter-caste and inter-racial marriages, sexual orientation and as recent concerns in Britain strongly suggest, sexual grooming of young Sikh girls by largely Muslim men as well as allegations of 'forced conversions' to Islam (BBC 2013; Sian 2015).

As most marriages were usually arranged, an important aspiration of parents was to find a suitable groom or bride for their child through their kinship network within their country of residence, or, especially if immigration rules allowed, to import one from Punjab. Generally, boys tended to have more leverage over decisions about whom to marry compared with girls. Thus there was a constant inflow of newly wed spouses, the relative proportion of brides or grooms dependent on immigration rules, and these practices reinforced traditional patriarchal norms, values and behaviours within many families. It is noteworthy that Sikhism, as a modern, egalitarian and progressive religion, places great importance on equality—both in terms of caste and gender—and yet Punjabis in general and Sikhs in particular have not been able to fully escape the powerful hold of patriarchy over gender and social relations. Part of the reason may be, although Nanak did reject gender discrimination in matters of spiritual and religious practices, he did not question patriarchal relations as they operated within the ambit of a household (Grewal 1993).

Over time, these earlier traditional attitudes did weaken and were transformed as the values of modernity began to sink into Sikh migrant consciousness. For example, more and more women were able to participate in the labour market and there was a change in attitudes towards equal treatment of boys and girls, and a greater sharing of household chores and responsibilities. Even in matters of marriage, children were now beginning to have greater freedom and choice over selecting a partner, giving rise to the growing phenomenon of 'assisted', 'negotiated' and 'love' marriages. In many families the notion of 'extended family living' gave way to a tolerance for nuclear families, especially as diaspora-born children rejected 'communal living' which they perceived as impinging on their individual freedom and private space. Embracing modernity also raised other aspirations: a strong desire for a university education as an avenue to the professions, living in more desirable and less ethnically segregated suburban neighbourhoods, developing a middle class lifestyle and moving away from a position where a holiday usually implied a regular trip to the ancestral village in Punjab.

However, as we have witnessed in many Sikh diaspora locations, as among different Indian Diaspora communities, the grip of patriarchal power structures is not easily dislodged and can, in fact, persist from generation to generation until a new generation begins to question the structures more critically and directly (Nayar 2004). The recent popularity of *bhangra* music and Punjabi films, which overwhelmingly celebrate different attributes of Sikh masculinities, further perpetuates patriarchal practices. Diaspora literature, for example Shauna Singh Baldwin's *English Lessons and Other Stories* (1999) also highlights notions of religio-cultural masculinity dominant in Sikh families (Chanda and Ford 2010). The challenges these present often manifest themselves in intra- and inter-generational tensions, encounters that can, at least superficially, be identified as conflicts between tradition and modernity and religious versus cultural identities, leading to much heartache for the families involved.

One issue which has received considerable attention in the UK, especially in the context of South Asian Muslim women, but which also affects Sikh Punjabi women is that of 'forced marriages' of diaspora-born children, especially girls who are still in their mid-teens. Despite several years of diaspora settlement and living, there are still many parents who want their daughters to be wedded according to traditional arranged marriage rules. While this does partly reflect their desire to uphold tradition, it also gives them the much sought-after control over the selection of prospective in-laws, an aspect important for extending kinship relations. According to British government statistics, anything from 8,000 to 10,000 British girls (of South Asian descent) are being 'forced' into a marriage each year. A seminar organised in Jalandhar in December 2015 in collaboration with the British High Commission on the 'Prevention of Forced Marriages to British Nationals' reported that the practice was still rampant in Punjab with over 1,200 potential cases a year despite forced marriages being outlawed in the UK a year earlier (Tribune 2015).

Where a daughter does not agree to an arranged marriage there may be consequences for her, which may involve threats, physical abuse, emotional and psychological violence designed to make the daughter feel as if she is betraying the family and bringing it dishonour and shame. It is not surprising that under such pressure, many girls run away from home. One well-known example is that of Jasvinder Sanghera, who in light of her own and sister's experiences has become a champion against forced marriages and other honour-based violence in the UK. Sanghera's family, especially her mother, despite being a devout Sikh with lengthy residency in Britain, tried to force her into an arranged marriage in India as she had previously done for her two elder sisters. Sanghera's objections led to her being withdrawn from school and imprisoned in her bedroom, whilst arrangements for her marriage continued. With flights booked and family members ready to leave, Sanghera managed to escape from home to stay with her boyfriend. Not surprisingly, she was 'disowned' by the family for bringing shame. Reflecting on her experiences, she says, 'My family said I could come home if I did what they said and went through with the marriage—or from that day forward I was dead in their eyes. This is one of the reasons I feel so strongly about criminalising forced marriage; I was the victim but I was made to feel as if I'd done something wrong' (Express and Star 2015).

Several years later one of her married sisters, unable to escape an abusive marriage, committed suicide. This was the final straw which gave Sanghera a strong desire to set up a charity named *Karma Nirvana*, to offer support and campaign actively against forced marriages. Over the years, she has not only penned books on her own experiences and those of other women (*Shame* and *Daughters of Shame*), she has also worked with various councils and government agencies to raise awareness, and helped in setting up a specialist Forced Marriage Unit administered jointly by the Home and Foreign Office. She was also instrumental in the drafting of new legislation in 2014—Anti-social Behaviour, Crime and Policing Act—which declared forced marriages unlawful and a criminal offence. Unfortunately, although this legislation may act as a deterrent, it is unlikely to stop forced marriages altogether as parents may use more ingenious methods to make them happen.

Finally, a more extreme form of violence—'honour killings'—are not unknown within the Sikh community, whether in Punjab or in the diaspora. There have been several cases, where the killing was either undertaken by family members or arranged as a contract killing in Punjab. An example of the latter type occurred in Coventry where a mother of two, Surjit Athwal, was allegedly murdered through a contract killing arranged by her husband and mother-in-law after having been taken to Punjab under some pretext or the other in 1998. She had gone through an arranged marriage when only 16-years old, but appeared unhappy in her marriage and was keen to get a divorce. In a landmark case at the Old Bailey in 2007, both son and mother were convicted and jailed for life for an outsourced honour killing. Another case from Canada, still waiting for closure in Indian courts since 2000, was the honour killing of 25-year-old Jaswinder Sidhu (Jassi), who was apparently murdered by members of her own family whilst on holiday in India because she fell in love with a young rickshaw driver from a lowly background. The most recent twist in this case was where a Canadian court disallowed the extradition of the main accused, Jassi's mother and her brother, because, as their lawyer rather bizarrely but successfully argued, they would not get a fair trial in India and because of India's poor human rights record (Tribune 2016). It seems international treaties and laws, when applied to NRI issues, leave a lot to be desired given their ambiguities and complexities when put to test and this allows such transnational abuses to continue unabated.

In the following Section, I focus on some further dimensions of the challenges facing Sikh migrant communities especially as they relate to migrant women's experiences and the emerging diversities in these experiences.

Dominant Narratives on Sikh Diaspora Women's Experiences

Applying a broad-brush approach when examining Punjabi diaspora women's experiences, two dominant narratives can be identified. On the one hand, we have a well-established and extensively researched narrative on diaspora women as victims of patriarchal norms. In this narrative women are represented as being caught in a variety of unequal familial and social, economic and political situations, which make them lead subjugated lives. These experiences usually start at the family household level and inevitably involve the operation of rigid patriarchal and gendered power relations. These negative experiences can range from sexual violence, alcoholic or drug abuse resulting in intimate partner violence. The inevitable consequences of these forms of violence are usually broken families and wrecked marriages, where women disproportionately bear the burden as well as consequences. Extensive research in both the UK and North America has documented these experiences and according to one source as many as 20 organisations were operating in the Bay Area in California alone, to offer refuge, rehabilitation, security and mediation to South Asian victims of domestic and other forms of abuse (Nankani 2000; Rehal and Maguire 2014). Whilst migrant women of all backgrounds and classes can get caught up in these forms of violence, recently migrated women, coming as long married and separated wives or as new brides, tend to be disproportionately affected, given their greater degree of marginality and vulnerability associated with being in a foreign land with limited family or community support networks. During the past decade, two popular Bollywood films—*Provoked* (2006) and *Heaven on Earth* (2008) have also used domestic or spousal violence within the Sikh community as their backdrop. Based on the true experiences of Chand Dhillon (from Brampton, Ontario, Canada) and Kiranjit Ahluwalia (from London, UK) both films explore the issues around traditional versus Western values, how cultural and religious factors may legitimise domestic violence, different forms of abuse and difficulties in obtaining legal remedies and justice. I discuss further some of the challenges emerging out of the recent discourse associated with increase in abuse in transnational marriages below.

Outside the household domain, South Asian women, including Sikh women, are said to suffer from an educational disadvantage which limits their chances of obtaining educational qualifications and training, blocking their access to better paid jobs. Relatively new migrant women, due to language, cultural and educational barriers, are inevitably forced to work in the low-paid, poorly regulated and semi-informal sectors, often for owners who may themselves belong to the South

Asian community. Some of these female-dominated sectors include clothing, gar-
ment and hosiery, beauty business and food preparation and packaging. It is not
surprising therefore, that in some of these cases there is evidence of resistance in the
form of labour strikes and other forms of direct action. A good, recent example of
this is the strike by largely Punjabi women at Gate Gourmet in West London in
2005. Gate Gourmet supplied airline meals to British Airways at Heathrow and in
order to cut costs decided to sack unionised labour in favour of new and younger
non-unionised workers so that wages and working conditions could be lowered.
Although many of the employees managed to get some redundancy compensation
or were re-hired on inferior terms and conditions than before, a group of about 56
chose to fight redundancies for some considerable time but with mixed results.
Interestingly, the prolonged dispute demonstrated how Asian workers and community institutions such as *Gurdwaras* can unite and work together for common
aims (Muir 2005). This strike, including some earlier ones which largely involved
South Asian women workers, such as Grunwick, also shattered the stereotype of
Asian women as timid, docile and domesticated (Puwar and Raghuram 2003;
Anitha and Pearson 2013).

In the political domain and in community affairs, women participation and
representation remains limited due both to patriarchal pressures and lack of integration into local society. Most of the cultural, religious and political organisations
such as the Indian Workers Associations, political parties of various shades and
religious organisations remain dominated by men with little female involvement,
especially at leadership levels. In the sports domain, Sikh women participation is
even more conspicuous by its absence. In the wider society, opportunities to participate in local, regional and national elections are often discouraged and thus
representation remains limited, with few notable exceptions. In many instances the
only opportunity to participate outside the home or work environment is a visit to
the local *Gurdwara,* where a sense of community belonging can prevail, albeit
temporarily. In fact, in many locations, women form strong self-support networks
and meet regularly under protection offered by the sacred space of a *Gurdwara.*
All-women *diwans* and *kirtan* sessions and even female management of *Gurdwaras*
have become popular in recent years (Purewal 2009).

Transnational Marriages and Discourses of Abuse

Transnational marriages within the Sikh community have a long history and the
vast majority of them have been successful, creating balanced and resilient
family-based communities abroad. More often than not, it was the 'new brides'
migrating into diaspora locations who played an important role as nurturers,
homemakers and critical bearers of the tradition. In many cases the new brides also
arranged marriages of their sisters, cousins and friends who also migrated to the
same locality, creating strong self-support systems among them. However as
underlying contexts began to change they created a situation where the incidence

and popularity of transnational marriages began to increase. The main reasons for this included stricter immigration controls in every advanced country, which halted primary migration especially of single male migrants, and the deteriorating economic and political situation in Punjab, generating an even greater desire to migrate. Given the gendered nature of immigration rules, an important strategy for migration abroad was through arranging the marriage of their female children abroad (Mooney 2006). Thus, the active seeking of '*vilayati munday*' (foreign-based boys) acted to further re-enforce the nexus between marriage and migration. This new context opened up possibilities of hurriedly arranged marriages, relaxed checking of antecedents and compatibilities, increasing the probability of mismatches and the potential for abuse. The incidence of transnational marriages continued to increase over the 1990s and beyond. Evidence suggests that women ended up becoming the main 'victims' in this changed situation. Below I discuss some of the main forms of 'bride abuse' as identified by academics, journalists, feminists, women's groups and other activists. These include increased abuse arising from 'arrangement' of transnational marriages and subsequent marital experiences, which have led to increased abuse and violence within married life and in many cases leading even to the extreme action of suicide by the abused.

An important form of gender abuse, which received considerable media interest, was the NRI marriage scam where many Punjabi brides, whom the NRI Punjabi males married whilst on a holiday visit to Punjab, were left behind abused. In some such cases, the Punjabi NRI sent the relevant immigration papers enabling his new wife to join him in his country of residence but troubles for the new bride started soon after. In many other cases, the Punjabi NRI promised to send legal papers sponsoring her after marriage but no such papers arrived as he basically 'deserted' her, forcing her to return to her maternal home. Many of these marriages ended in failure because the groom or groom's family demanded extra dowry, had misrepresented his income or occupation or because of the groom's lack of interest in the marriage, sometimes due to his already married status or sexual orientation. But several hundred females and their parents were 'duped', largely by Canadian-based Punjabi NRIs, leading to an outcry by the media and some politicians. Although the issue is more complex than the simplified way it is being presented here, it became clear that women were the main victims, either because of abusive actions by the husband or her in-laws or because the bride's own parents had ulterior motives in arranging a marriage where their daughter's happiness was the last thing on their mind (Thandi 2013; Fortney 2005).

The above are examples of transnational marriages which terminated quite quickly, sometimes within a few months or years of the marriage, although the legal struggle to recover dowry, obtain custody of children if any or of other assets may have continued for some time afterwards. The focus on this aspect alone, however, masks a set of other issues which recently migrated wives or newly-wed female migrants face in many diaspora locations. Evidence provided by women's groups such as the Southall Black Sisters in the UK, reports by governments and other voluntary associations suggests that there is a significant incidence of domestic violence and abuse in such marriages. Patriarchal attitudes and cultural sensitivity, couched around concepts such as 'honour' (*izzat*) and 'shame' (*sharam* or *behzti*), means that honour-based women abuse and violence remains a taboo subject within the community and remains 'hidden'. Abused women themselves remain trapped, helpless and voiceless in exposing abuse and continue to put up with it until a tipping point is reached. It took an internal report of a London train company, trying to understand cause of delays on trains arriving into Paddington Station in West London, to fully expose the extent of the problem in some localities in the UK.

The report revealed that 80 out of the 240 rail suicides (that is, one-third) nationally in 2005 were on the track lines into Paddington, West London. These lines run through the towns of Slough and Southall, both having a large Sikh settlement. The Southall rail station, in particular, became a focal point in raising awareness about domestic violence and suicides among Sikh women. Subsequent investigations suggested that suicides by Sikh women were a regular occurrence and connected these to high levels of domestic abuse and violence prevalent among Southall's large Sikh community. This issue raised national awareness in 2005 when a 27-year-old Navjeet Sidhu, jumped in front of a Heathrow Express train at Southall, firmly clutching her 5-year-old daughter and 2-year-old son. All three were killed instantly and to make matters worse, some 6 months later, her mother, Satwant Kaur, also killed herself at the same station. Although there appeared to be no suggestion that Navjeet Sidhu was abused, at the inquest, however, it was revealed that 'she felt she had failed in her duties as a Sikh woman to be a good mother and home-maker' (Owen and Wadeson 2007). There have been several suicides since, with the Southall station earning the dreaded label, the 'Suicide Station', among the locals and forcing the rail authorities to provide more security fencing around the station.

Although no detailed case studies on causes of Sikh women suicides exist, there is some evidence to suggest that many of the causes are related to harassment and violence associated with demands for more dowry, the tolerance of abuse and violence by parents of the boy due to persistence of patriarchal norms, mismatches and incompatibilities in educational backgrounds where girls may have much higher educational qualifications, unfulfilled expectations from marriage and lack of understanding and support whether within the household or the community. As suicides rates for South Asian women (and men) in the UK are almost three times higher than the national average there is clearly a deep-seated cultural problem which requires more thorough research.

Counter Narrative: Women's Agency and Empowerment

The counter narrative to the above discussion, although still a minority discourse but with a significant potential for further development, emphasises a positive migration and diasporic experience, enabling women empowerment and giving them agency. Empowerment and agency are generally understood as giving women command over resources, allowing them a high degree of freedom to pursue opportunities available and having real power to make strategic life choices, enabling them to act as agents of their own well-being. This empowerment and agency also has the potential to be transformative, leading to wider societal change which equalises gender power relations. Has this been achieved, is it real and what evidence is there?

We tend to witness greater progress in women empowerment and agency largely in countries that have enacted, implemented and rigorously enforced equal opportunities legislation to cover all forms of discrimination, especially as it related to gender. Another important factor impinging on empowerment is access to higher education which has the potential to open many windows. In many Sikh diaspora locations, there is evidence to suggest that, at both school and at university, female Sikh students have outperformed their male counterpoints. The cumulative effect of this has been to enable Sikh women to enter better paid and higher status occupations enlarging their opportunities and choices, including marital options. The structural shift in the economies of many advanced countries has created more service sector jobs which have disproportionately favoured females, again giving them greater earning power and choices.

Another important development in many Sikh diaspora locations, especially among diaspora-born second- or third-generation Sikh women, has been the increase in the number of Sikh female entrepreneurs who have started their own businesses, are successful academics or entered traditionally male-dominated professions such as law, medicine and dentistry, pharmacy and accounting and finance. This development, taken in all its forms, has produced a category of highly successful Sikh professional women who are thriving in their chosen careers, hold positions of high responsibility and control huge budgets and resources. We also witness their success in the creative industries, with an increasing number of high profile actors, writers, fashion designers, film producers, journalists, TV and radio presenters, theatre and musical artistes, etc. Albeit still numerically small but growing fast, these Sikh women are countering stereotypes, redefining gender roles, renegotiating family relationships and acting as great role advocates and role models for the next generation of Sikh women as well as men. Parminder Bhachu is one of a few academics, who has consistently emphasised the agency of Sikh diaspora women in her writings (Bhachu 1991, 2003, 2015) whilst Gurinder Chadha's films such as *Bend it Like Beckham* (2002) and *Bride and Prejudice* (2004) have provided a positive representation of Punjabi Sikh women (Oliete 2010). However, generally speaking, Sikh diaspora scholarship has largely failed to adequately capture this aspect of women's diasporic experiences.

Some Tentative Conclusions

This paper has argued that 150 years of Sikh migration has created an overseas community, which is geographically spread and densely connected both within the diaspora and with their ancestral and spiritual homeland of Punjab. Migration experiences have enabled them to emerge as a prosperous, dynamic and progressive transnational community able to fully celebrate its religious and cultural heritage. This is clearly illustrated in the recently elected Canadian Prime Minister Justin Trudeau's decision to induct four Sikhs into his Cabinet, three men and one woman. Furthermore, the same Prime Minister's recent apology to Sikhs for the racist treatment meted out to them by Canada during the *Komagata Maru* affair illustrates the leverage Sikhs are able to exercise over the government. However, different periods of settlement, under different contexts, means that the community is not as homogeneous as often assumed by some Diaspora Studies scholars. The community exhibits all forms of diversities: in terms of class, gender and caste, economic and employment status, length of settlement, participation and integration into local societies. Whilst religion, ethnicity and culture bind the community together, there are significant fissures regarding continuities in or rejection of patriarchal norms and degrees of embracement of modernity. As I have hopefully demonstrated, even decades of living abroad does not necessarily produce a major impact on weakening patriarchal value systems. This causes intergenerational and intra-generational tensions, which are played out in different domains: style of living, marriage arrangements, educational choices and participation in the wider civil society which still disproportionality disadvantages women. Gender inequalities, with its extreme features associated with varied forms of domestic or honour-based violence, represent the dark underbelly of migration experience. These tensions are also not equally shared as some sections of the community, especially the educated, professional and long settled members, have been able to transcend patriarchal legacies to a large extent, moving closer to the high ideals set by the Sikh Gurus. In such cases, there is evidence to suggest gender and social relations within the household and at community level have become more egalitarian. However among the more unskilled, uneducated and recently migrated households, the patriarchal village mind-set has merely got transplanted into a diaspora setting. Segregated living, constant reference to 'idealized' or 'imagined' life back home despite rapid social changes there (Sandhu 2009), peer and community pressures based around norms of *izzat* and shame means the 'Punjabi Bubble' (Nayar 2004) continues to hold sway. We can see this operating among those living in dense and relatively segregated localities such as Vancouver and Surrey (in Canada), Yuba City (in USA) and Southall and Midlands cities such as Coventry, Birmingham, Wolverhampton, Dudley and Walsall in the UK. It is here where the tensions are most acute and sometimes boil over, also affecting other minority ethnic communities. Whether upward social mobility, a longer settlement period and assimilation makes these communities move away from a *'pendu'* mind-set, only time will tell. As we well know, just as transnationalism and transnational practices have the power to be a modernising and homogenising force, they also have the power to re-enforce, re-galvanise and revitalise traditions.

References

Anitha, S., and R. Pearson. 2013. *Striking Women*. Accessed March 15, 2016. https://www.striking-women.org.
BBC (British Broadcasting Corp.) 2013. *Inside Out*. A 30-minute documentary broadcast on 2 September. https://www.youtube.com/watch?v=4QmhckXBh5Q.
Bhachu, Parminder. 1991. Culture, Ethnicity and Class among Punjabi Sikh Women in 1990s Britain. *New Community* 17 (3): 401–412.
Bhachu, Parminder. 2003. *Dangerous Designs: Asian Women Fashion the Diaspora Economies*. London: Routledge.
Bhachu, Parminder. 2015. The Invisibility of Diasporic Capital and Multiply Migrant Creativity. In *Mutuality: Anthropology's Changing Terms of Engagement*, ed. Roger Sanjek, 81–98. Philadelphia: University of Pennsylvania Press.
Chanda, Geetanjali Singh, and Staci Ford. 2010. Sikh Masculinity, Religion and Diaspora in Shauna Singh Baldwin's English Lessons and Other Stories. *Men and Masculinities* 12 (4).
Express and Star. 2015. Revealed: Full Extent of West Midlands' Forced Marriage Shame. June 15.
Fortney, Valerie. 2005. Abandoned Wives: Canada's Shame and India's Sorrow. *The Calgary Herald* October 16–20.
Grewal, J.S. 1993. *Guru Nanak and Patriarchy*. Shimla: Indian Institute of Advanced Studies.
Leonard, Karen. 1992. *Making Ethnic Choices: California's Punjabi Mexican Americans*. Temple University Press.
Mazumdar, Rajit K. 2003. *The Indian Army and the Making of Punjab*. Permanent Black.
Mooney, Nicola. 2006. Aspirations. Reunification and Gender Transformation in Jat Sikh Marriages from India to Canada. *Global Networks* 6 (4): 389–403.
Muir, Hugh. 2005. Tee and Gee Zindabad (That's long live T & G in Hindi). *The Guardian*. August 15.
Nankani, Sandhya, ed. 2000. *Breaking the Silence: Domestic Violence in the South Asian-American Community: An Anthology*. Xlibris Corporation.
Nayar, Kamala E. 2004. *The Sikh Diaspora in Vancouver: Three Generations Amid Tradition, Modernity and Multiculturalism*. Toronto: University of Toronto Press.
Oliete, Elena. 2010. Brides Against Prejudices: New Representations of Race and Gender Relationships in Gurinder Chadha's Transnational Film 'Bride and Prejudice'. *The International Journal of Interdisciplinary Social Sciences* 5 (5): 1833–1882.
Omissi, David. 1998. *The Sepoy and the Raj: The Indian Army 1860–1940*. Palgrave Macmillan.
Owen, Glen, and Oliver Wadeson. 2007. 'Abused' Asian Women Behind Soaring Toll of Railway Suicides. *The Daily Mail*. September 22. http://www.dailymail.co.uk/news/article-483315/Abused-Asian-women-soaring-toll-railway-suicides.html#ixzz3XUqqH8Tu.
Purewal, Navtej. 2009. Gender, Seva and Social Institutions: A Case Study of the Bebe Nanaki Gurdwara and Charitable Trust, Birmingham, UK. In *Sikh Diaspora Philanthropy in Punjab: Global Giving for Local Good*, ed. Verne A. Dusenbery and Darshan S. Tatla. New Delhi: Oxford University Press.
Puwar, Nirmal, and Parvati Raghuram (eds.). 2003. *South Asian Women in the Diaspora*. Oxford: Berg Publishers.
Rehal, Manjit, and Sylvia Maguire. 2014. *The Price of Honour*. Report by CRASAC, Coventry. February.

Sandhu, Amarinder. 2009. *Jat Sikh Women Social Transformation: Changing Status and Life Style*. Chandigarh: Unistar.

Sian, Katy P. 2015. *Unsettling Sikh and Muslim Conflict: Mistaken Identities, Forced Conversions and Post-Colonial Formations*. Lexington Books.

Tan, Tai Yong. 2005. *The Garrison State: The Military, Government and Society in Colonial Punjab 1849–1947*. Delhi: Sage Publications Pvt. Ltd.

Thandi, Shinder S. 2009. Discourses on Cultural Adaptation, Transmission, and Identities within the Sikh Diasporas: Some Comparative Perspectives. In *Sikhs in Southeast Asia: Negotiating an Identity*, ed. A.B. Shamsul and Arunajeet Kaur, 78–102. Singapore: ISEAS.

Thandi, Shinder S. 2012. Migration and Comparative Experience of Sikhs in Europe: Reflections on Issues of Cultural Transmission and Identity 30 Years on. In *Sikhs Across Borders: Transnational Practices of European Sikhs* ed. Knut A. Jacobsen and Kristina Myrvold. London: Bloomsbury.

Thandi, Shinder S. 2013. Shady Character, Hidden Design, and Masked Faces: Reflections on Vilayati Sikh Marriages and Discourses of Abuse. In *Sikh Diaspora: Theory, Agency and Experience* ed. Michael Hawley. Leiden: Brill.

Tribune. 2015. *State Reports Highest Level of 'Forced Marriage' Cases of UK Nationals*. December 9.

Tribune. 2016. *Jassi Murder Case: Canadian Court Stops Accused's Extradition to India*. February 27.

Wilson, Amrit. 1978. *Finding a Voice: Asian Women in Britain*. Virago.

Chapter 14
Anglo-Indian Women: A Narrative of Matriarchy in a Global Diaspora

Ann Lobo

A Historical Introduction—Indian Independence: 1947

Astrologers had chosen 15th August 1947 as the most propitious day for India to gain Independence. Just before midnight, Nehru addressed the legislative assembly:

> Long years ago we made a tryst with destiny, and now the time comes when we shall redeem our pledge. At the stroke of the midnight hour, when the world sleeps, India will awake to life and freedom. (Lawrence 1997, 632)

India's liberation signalled the end of privilege job-status for Anglo-Indian men. Anglo-Indians had actively co-operated with the British. How could the Anglo-Indians promote a sense of national identity in the knowledge that the great majority of them submitted to the British? The Indians were filled with happiness at national self-determination (Lawrence 1997, 645). The Anglo-Indians became desperately insecure. Many families experienced hardship, due to the exclusion of Anglo-Indian men from the labour market. Men were facing competition from Indian men, who were becoming qualified in artisanal, technical and clerical skills (Caplan 2010, 82–83).

The Anglo-Indian world of secure jobs-for-life in the Indian railways, police, excise and customs had radically changed. Hindi would become the national language, and English, the mother tongue of the Anglo-Indians might disappear. Indians started to compete with the Anglo-Indians for their jobs. As one Anglo-Indian woman respondent wrote, 'the very stuff of our lives had vanished'. The community was suddenly faced with a postcolonial identification crisis. Another wrote, 'The first morning I woke up in England, I heard voices speaking

A. Lobo (✉)
University of Reading, Reading, UK
e-mail: AnnSelkirk@aol.com

© Springer Nature Singapore Pte Ltd. 2018
A. Pande (ed.), *Women in the Indian Diaspora*,
https://doi.org/10.1007/978-981-10-5951-3_14

English on the street'. Their economic and cultural marginalisation had ended when the British Raj collapsed. The community had to urgently rewrite and negotiate their identity politics. There were social, economic and political reasons for migrating to the United Kingdom. Diaspora? The word did not enter their vocabulary. They were merely going home to the United Kingdom.

They had an advantage. Anglo-Indians had all been educated at Anglo-Indian English medium schools and had taken the Senior Cambridge examinations at 16+. Very few were bilingual in an Indian language. They took French or Latin as a Second Language in school. A number of women respondents observed that the men rarely bothered to ask their mothers and grandmothers about migrating. After all, the women were not the breadwinners in the family. They did not provide their families with homes in railway colonies. Anglo-Indian women worked as nurses, teachers, telephone operators and stenographers (Caplan 2010, 182–83). They also served in the Women's Auxiliary Corps (India) (Veldhuizen 2010, 93). They were selected as air hostesses (Mitchell 2010, 41).

This modern diaspora of an ethnic minority group was voluntary. They were not being expelled or fleeing persecution from the Indians. They were not starving, exiled or deported from India. Their insecurity was based on the insecurity of the job market in the railways, police, excise and customs. They were positive that they could exchange their jobs in India for similar employment in the U.K. They were not looking for benefits. They were not refugees or asylum seekers. They were British subjects returning home. They paid up their full subscription to the Anglo-Indian Association; and applied successfully for Indian passports. They resigned their jobs, threw their farewell parties, and spent part of their provident fund on buying tickets and a few warm clothes. They boarded ships sailing for the U.K.

Migration of the Anglo-Indian Community: 1950

It is a bleak post-monsoon afternoon, and I am standing on Ballard Pier in Bombay, feverishly clutching my father's hand. I am watching relatives and friends climb the gangway to a ship waiting to take them to the U.K. I follow the Anglo-Indian families into their cabins on a lower deck for last-minute hugs and goodbyes. There is a row of stone jars filled with pickles and chutneys, sealed with wooden caps and wax neatly tucked in the corners of most of their cabins. I listen to the soft crying, and whispers of 'We'll meet again.' I knew that was wishful thinking. My father had no intention of leaving India. He was perplexed at what he described as 'panicky migration'. The ship sails. I sob quietly. Our family is ruptured apart (Radhakrishnan 1996, 175–76). I started asking myself questions about why my world was collapsing. I could spell politics, but I could not understand politics.

Meeting Lord Mountbatten, Singapore: 1975

Lord Mountbatten was the last Viceroy of India. His decision to end the Raj in seventy-three days and to stick unswervingly to his timetable brought him criticism. In 1975, Lord Mountbatten was the President of the United World Colleges and I met him in Singapore on the campus of the United World College of South-East Asia. I was a member of the teaching faculty. He spoke of Indian Independence. I asked him his opinion about the migration of the Anglo-Indians to Australia, Canada, United Kingdom and the United States of America. He was aware of the migration of the community to the U.K. However, he was surprised at the scale at which the community left India. I listened attentively. Who was I to condemn Mountbatten? He was not the architect of India like Curzon or Irwin. He had come to demolish the British Raj. His work demanded a different outlook and method. It resulted in the diaspora of the Anglo-Indians.

After receiving a British passport many of them opted to migrate to two other countries in the Commonwealth, Australia and Canada. Anglo-Indians also migrated to the U.S.A. The diaspora community have established strong relationships with other Anglo-Indian communities. International Reunions started in 1989 in England. These reunions have been held every 3 years. Australia has hosted four reunions, India and Canada two each and New Zealand one reunion (Deefholts 2015, 140).

Were there any groups of Anglo-Indians who 'stayed put'? In 1990, I met two groups who did not migrate after 1947.

Doctoral Research: 1990

In the monsoon of 1990, I did my field research in India for my doctorate (Lobo 1994). I interviewed face-to-face six hundred and thirty Anglo-Indians in Bangalore, Faridabad, Calcutta, Cochin, Coonoor, Devlali, Madras, Mumbai, Mysore, New Delhi and Shillong. It was in Cochin and Shillong that I met Anglo-Indian women, whose families 'stayed put' as they described it. None of the Anglo-Indian families in Cochin and Shillong had migrated to the U.K. after 1947.

The State of Meghalaya: Schedule Tribe Anglo-Indians Living in the Capital City of Shillong

Diversity and eclecticism mark a unique community of Anglo-Indians residing in Shillong. These Anglo-Indians are the descendants of Khasi tribal women and British colonialists. The Khasi tribal women belong to the Palaungs, a tribe inhabiting one of Burma's Shan states to the northeast of Mandalay. They speak

Khasi, which is one of the Mon-Khmer families of languages, and is the only surviving one in India. They cultivate paan leaves, and grow oranges and potatoes (Barooah 1970, 248). The mineral rich and tea-growing areas of the North-East Frontier attracted the British who worked for the East India Company in the late eighteenth century. The British arrived in the small Khasi hamlet of Shillong in 1833. By 1874, the political penetration of the Khasi Hills by civil servants and army officers was complete.

Missionaries arrived in Shillong: Welsh Calvinists, Scottish Presbyterians, English Anglicans and English Roman Catholics. They built their churches, schools and hospitals. These missionaries became the catalysts of hidden and slow-burning processes of change among the tribal groups. Christianity grew in regions furthest removed from the reach of Brahmanical Hinduism. The Khasi tribe is located outside the Hindu caste system. The Khasi non-heiresses converted to Christianity when they married British colonialists. They crashed through the taboos surrounding their society and changed their lives. Christian schools, hospitals and churches would fit in quite well with their plan as they clung to their matrilineal 'iing' or clan. This altered their status of marginalised 'losers' to inclusive 'winners'. They included their Anglo-Saxon surnames when naming children. These British surnames are still used by the community. The three names established Christianity, paternity and the Khasi iing. Although the British man resided in a house that he purchased, he lived within his wife's matrilineal clan (Elwin 1959, 3). These Khasi women converted to Christianity. By the laws of succession the youngest daughter inherits the whole of her parents' property.

There is a sign on a road leading to the capital city of Meghalaya, Shillong, 'Equitable distribution of self-acquired property rights'. The society of the Khasi Scheduled Tribe continues to be completely matriarchal.

I interviewed face-to-face forty-three Khasi Anglo-Indians. There were thirty-five Khasi Anglo-Indian women, who explained that they registered as Anglo-Indians when they studied at Anglo-Indian schools. After completing their secondary schooling, they adopted the tribal name to apply to University. They revert back to their Tribal status, because the Indian Government offers positive discrimination in favour of jobs and Higher Education to members of the Scheduled Tribes. A number of Khasi Anglo-Indian women have studied at the North-Eastern Hill University.

The youngest daughter inherits her parent's property. Her home is also home to all members of her 'iing' or clan. The word 'homeless' does not exist in the Khasi language. If the youngest sister does not have a daughter, she will designate another woman in her family as the next heiress. Her elder sisters and brothers are landless, and must branch out and form their own 'iing' or clan group. By the third generation, the non-heiress has created another 'iing' (Lobo 2012, 203).

The State of Kerala: Other Backward Classes Anglo-Indians Living in the Capital City of Cochin

A lust for pepper and souls drove the great Portuguese adventurer Albuquerque to build his fort at Cochin in 1504 (Hall 1996, 215). Governor Albuquerque had a vision of building cities on Indian soil. The prime obstacle, however, was a complete lack of Christian families, because no women were allowed to travel in the fleets leaving Lisbon for the Indies. He made a decision that would leave its stamp on the Portuguese empire. He would populate his conquests with the Catholic progeny of Portuguese men married to Indian women (221–22). Albuquerque constructed an urban social framework and through the large number of marriages between Indian women and Portuguese men, a large work force grew to support the growing economy of Cochin (Otto 2015, 102–03). By 1514 a list clearly shows that Nair women converted to Roman Catholicism married Portuguese men (Padua 2005, 32–35). Nair women belonged to a dignified martial nobility caste of matriarchal tradition. The women took their husbands surnames. These women belonging to a matriarchal society owned property in their own right. They created a new domestic culture, which involved sexual, socio-economic and political exchange between the Indians and their colonial masters (Appadurai and Breckenridge 1989, i–iv).

Historically, Nairs lived in large family units called Theravadas that housed descendants of one common female ancestor. The Nairs operated a matrilineal joint family structure, and in anthropological literature on matrilineality the Nairs have achieved an unparalleled eminence (Fuller 1975, 1976). Only the women lived in the main house; men lived in separate rooms and on some occasions, lived in a separate house nearby. In 1990 I met the women in their homes. They had Portuguese surnames. Orchards surrounding their homes were abundant with coconut, plantain, jackfruit and mango trees. Some of the women had access to market gardens. None of the women knew any Anglo-Indian family, who had migrated to the United Kingdom after 1947.

Conclusion

I met both these matriarchal groups by sheer coincidence. I was researching Anglo-Indian schools in India. Matriachalism and its family structure were not on my mind. First, a Khasi/Anglo-Indian man writing to me with a Tribal first name and surname and an Anglo-Saxon surname as the middle name invited me to visit Shillong. I was intrigued. I made a detour and travelled to Shillong. Second, a Nair/Portuguese Anglo-Indian woman offered me her comfortable home to live in. Stephen Padua, the leader of the Anglo-Indian community in Cochin who had organised my itinerary in Kerala had contacted her. She introduced me to her family and friends.

These two groups of matriarchal women are multilingual. The Anglo-Indian women in Shillong speak English, Hindi and Khasi. The Anglo-Indian women in Cochin speak English, Hindi and Malayalam. Both groups of women own property. Both groups of women had access to higher education. From a linguistic point of view the Greek word arche can mean beginning as well as domination or rule. Therefore, matriarchy can be translated as the mothers from the beginning. Reclaiming this term for women means to understand that cultures that have been created by women are humane, based on needs, is peaceful and non-violent (Goettner-Abendroth 2009).

In 1947, the two groups living in their clan groups had no reason to leave India for the United Kingdom. Their societies had no patriarchal bias, which characterised the Anglo-Indian community in the rest of India. In other words, they had created a socio-cultural format that represented a new paradigm. These two groups have undergone firstly, the societal problems of missionisation; that is conversion to Roman Catholicism in the Nair/Portuguese marriages and Anglicanism in the Khasi/British marriages. Secondly political problems associated with colonisation, that is, the mixed–race status of their families. There is an absence of scientific rigour. This needs to be opened up to debate stereotypical sexist and racist attitudes towards women. The Khasi/Anglo-Indian/Scheduled Tribe women in Shillong and the Nair/Portuguese/Anglo-Indian/Other Backward Classes women in Cochin recognise the need to tilt themselves within a political framework in order to survive. Both these societies with their own rules stayed put and did not migrate. Why? There are four reasons for not migrating after 1947.

(i)   They were matriarchal and had control over their lives;
(ii)   They owned property in their own right;
(iii) They had all entered institutions of higher education;
(iv)   They were multilingual knowing English and two Indian languages.

The Research: Spring 2016

I selected empirical research, because it carefully assesses objective reality, by calculating and judging it against subjective belief (Cohen and Holliday 1982, 199). In this type of research, the researcher can turn to experience for validation. My decision to use empirical research was taken, because it offered me an opportunity to use experience also for validation. Empirical research allowed me the freedom to be subjective after carefully assessing, calculating and judging evidence in an objective way. I made use of two Case Studies I had conducted in 1990 in India. Combining the survey mode with the two Case Studies offered me the most efficient mode for designing the field research.

The Sample Frame

The target population was widely dispersed. The selection of the sample was made via four books of the CTR publications, New Jersey, USA (Deefholts and Staub 2004; Deefholts and Deefholts 2010; Lumb 2012; Cassity and Almeida 2015).

I wrote to all the women and men writers. I asked the men to forward the e-mail questionnaire to Anglo-Indian women whom they knew. A few men and women forwarded to me a further list of e-mail addresses. I wrote a total of ninety-two e-mail questionnaires to Anglo-Indian women living in Australia, Canada, Europe, New Zealand and the United States of America.

The Time Scale Constraint

The e-mail questionnaires were written towards the end of January 2016. The deadline for receiving the completed questionnaires was twenty-ninth February 2016. I received fifty-five completed questionnaires from all the countries.

Structure of the Questionnaire

1. Place of Birth; first name and surname; age; nationality; country of residence; job/profession; educational qualifications.
2. In your experience what did you find most difficult to cope with during the process and settlement in a new country?
3. Name one important aspect of Anglo-Indian cultural life that you value most in your life.
4. Please offer one suggestion on how you could transmit to the next generation in your family the social history of the Anglo-Indian community.
5. Your personal comment.

Analysis

Question one offered me vital information about names, surnames, age, residence/nationality, work, and educational qualifications.

Question two had details of the struggle women faced to create a new space and identity in the new country. In self-identification all the women described themselves as Anglo-Indian and used their nationality as their new identity. None of the women described themselves as South Asian American/Canadian/European/. The majority referred back to India and invoked a frame of reference alien to their current cultural landscape. However, since the local is inextricably intertwined with India a conceptual framework emerged of Anglo-Indian women who created a metaphorical 'border' within their own families.

Question three centred on family, friendships and cuisine. Many of the answers were detailed and described a cultural trauma of emotional anguish due to displacement. The answers spun out silk-like webs between families and descriptions of everyday lived spaces in their new homelands. Societal influences played a vital role in their competitive inclinations. They needed to become self-sufficient in order to survive in their new homelands. The women found their needs, desires and interests fulfilled in organising family functions and offering Anglo-Indian cuisine (Lobo 2015, 62).

Question four centred on education. There were observations about the lack of higher education among their grandmothers and mothers in India. Comments on Anglo-Indian social history had a useful and positive side. The future belongs to 'those who are ready to take in a bit of the other, as well as being what they themselves are' (Hall 1997, 299).

Question five offered diasporic Anglo-Indian women the opportunity to write about themselves. They recognised that home meant more than a physical home space, but also home as their nation. In their everyday lived spaces they prized the fact that they had educated themselves and either contributed to or purchased property for themselves.

These women were writing their own histories, very different from those of their mothers and grandmothers. Instead of fixating on biological sex differences, these women focussed more on the cultural and societal influences of their new homelands. They were gradually stripping away the cultural influences of a patriarchal society. The new homeland and nationality helped them to reclaim their liberty, by enabling them to equalise their position in the community.

The women realised that the old perpetuation of colonial racial and group segregation of the railway colonies had ceased. Many Anglo-Indian women had married Anglo-Indians they met in their new homeland, but a number of their children had married non-Anglo-Indians. Some of their children had voiced a disinterest in the 'Indianess' of their heritage. The diasporic Anglo-Indian woman had created new bridges, formed new alliances by becoming educated, property owners. They have created their own '...conditional citizenship' (Joseph 1999, 2).

Conclusion

In their diaspora, Anglo-Indian women are game-changers. Arriving in their new homelands, they left behind, the historical/cinematic/media stereotype of an Anglo-Indian woman as women of easy virtue (Williams 2010, 210). Diaspora and Anglo-Indian gender has implied an analytical category that has foundations in a modern matriarchal gender-egalitarian society. There was not one Anglo-Indian woman who observed that her power relations with her husband or partner made her feel superior to him. The diasporic Anglo-Indian women have helped to create a society and culture that has the foundations of a modern matriarchal gender-egalitarian society. In their families, they have no hierarchies or domination of one gender by the other (Goettner-Abendroth 2009).

References

Appadurai, Arjun, and C. Breckenridge. 1989. On Moving Targets. *Public Culture* 2.1: i–iv.
Barooah, N.K. 1970. David Scott in North-East India 1802–1831: A Study in British Paternalism. Originally published in David Scott, *Report on the Garrow Country*. (New Delhi: Munshiram Manoharlal, 1816).
Caplan, Lionel. 2010. Anglo-Indian Women in the Economy. In *Women of Anglo-India: Tales and Memoirs*, ed. Margaret Deefholts and Susan Deefholts. New Jersey, USA: CTR Inc. Publishing.
Cassity, Kathleen, and Rochelle Almeida (eds.). 2015. *Curtain Call: Anglo-Indian Reflections*. New Jersey, USA: CTR Inc. Publishing.
Cohen, L., and M. Holliday. 1982. *Statistics for Social Scientists: An Introductory Text with Computer Programs in BASIC*. London: Harper and Row.
Deefholts, Margaret. 2015. Dancing in a Bubble: International Anglo-Indian Reunions. In *Curtain Call: Anglo-Indian Reflections*, ed. Kathleen Cassity and Rochelle Almeida. New Jersey, USA: CTR Inc. Publishing.
Deefholts, Margaret, and Susan Deefholts (eds.). 2010. *Women of Anglo-India: Tales and Memoirs*. New Jersey, USA: CTR Inc., Publishing.
Deefholts, Margaret, and Sylvia W. Staub (eds.). 2004. *Voices on the Verandah*. New Jersey, USA: CTR Inc., Publishing.
Elwin, V. 1959. *India's Northeast Frontier in the Nineteenth Century*. Oxford: Oxford University Press.
Fuller, Christopher. 1975. The Internal Structure of the Nayar Caste. *Journal of Anthropological Research* 31 (4): 283–312. [JSTOR 3629883].
Fuller, Christopher. 1976. *The Nayars Today*. Cambridge University Press.
Goettner-Abendroth, Heide (ed.). 2009. *Societies of Peace. Matriarchies Past, Present and Future*. Toronto: Inanna Publications and Educations Inc.
Hall, Richard. 1996. *Empires of the Monsoon: A History of the Indian Ocean and Its Invaders*. London: HarperCollins.
Hall, Stuart. 1997. Subjects in History: Making Diasporic Identities. In *The House that Race Built*, ed. Wahneema Lubiano, 299. New York: Pantheon Books.
James, Lawrence. 1997. *Raj: The Making and Unmaking of British India*. London: Little Brown and Company.
Joseph, May. 1999. *Nomadic Identities: The Performance of Citizenship*. Minneapolis: University of Minnesota Press.
Lobo, Maeve. 2015. Heirlooms from the Kitchen. In *Curtain Call: Anglo-Indian Reflections*, ed. Kathleen Cassity and Rochelle Almeida. New Jersey: USA CTR Publishing.
Lobo, Antoinette. 1994. *A Comparative Study of Educational Disadvantage in India within the Anglo-Indian Community: A Historical and Contemporary Analysis*. Unpublished Doctoral thesis, University of London, Institute of Education.
Lobo, Antoinette. 2012. Matrilineal Anglo-Indians. In *More Voices on the Verandah: An Anglo-Indian Anthology*, ed. Lionel Lumb. New Jersey, USA: CTR Inc. Publishing.

Lumb, Lionel (ed.). 2012. *More Voices on the Verandah: An Anglo-Indian Anthology*. New Jersey, USA: CTR Inc., Publishing.

Mitchell, Joyce. 2010. Angels with Wings: Air-India's First Anglo-Indian Air Hostesses. In *Women of Anglo-India: Tales and Memoirs*, ed. Margaret Deefholts and Susan Deefholts. New Jersey, USA: CTR Inc. Publishing.

Otto, Brent. 2015. Cochin: An Historic Centre in the Anglo-Indian Story. In *Curtain Call: Anglo-Indian Reflections*, ed. Kathleen Cassity and Rochelle Almeida. New Jersey, USA: CTR Publishing.

Padua, Stephen. 2005. *Threads of Continuity: History of the Anglo-Indian Community in Kerala*. Cochin.

Radhakrishnan, R. 1996. *Diasporic Mediations: Between Home and Locations*. Minneapolis: University of Minnesota Press.

Veldhuizen, Deborah Van. 2010. Serving in the Women's Auxiliary Corps (India). In *Women of Anglo-India: Tales and Memoirs*, ed. Margaret Deefholts and Susan Deefholts. New Jersey, USA: CTR Inc. Publishing.

Williams, Blair. 2010. An Anglo-Indian Male's Perspective. In *Women of Anglo-India: Tales and Memoirs*, ed. Margaret Deefholts and Susan Deefholts. New Jersey, USA: CTR Inc. Publishing.

Chapter 15
Lived Experiences of Sikh Women in Canada: Past and Present

Amrit Kaur Basra

The present article seeks to analyse the processes of migration, settlement and integration in Canadian society from the perspective of Sikh women. For this purpose, the nature of the existing historiography on Canada with a focus on women's studies, and the evolution of Canadian society across time and space have been explored to situate the experiences of Sikh women. The methodology used in the chapter is located in the interdisciplinary approach of feminist historians that has enriched the history of women in Canada. An attempt has been made to use written and oral records to show the changes in the role and identity of Sikh women who have become an integral part of Canada. Initially, the experiences of Sikh women were determined by space acquired by men in the Canadian society. The family as a unit and the place of women within that family acted as a major determinant. From families, links with wider society were then set up. The inter-generation experiences in contemporary society point to the variegated and often contested experiences of the younger generation. The chapter in the end focuses on the theoretical formulations connected with forgoing analysis to explore the relationship between gender and identity, individual and family, community and society and between different generations of settled Sikh women. In the process role of patriarchy, agency, power structure in either enabling or restricting the experiences of women in diasporic society of Canada is explored.

A.K. Basra (✉)
Delhi College of Arts and Commerce, University of Delhi, Netaji Nagar,
New Delhi 110021, India
e-mail: amritdcac@gmail.com

© Springer Nature Singapore Pte Ltd. 2018
A. Pande (ed.), *Women in the Indian Diaspora*,
https://doi.org/10.1007/978-981-10-5951-3_15

187

Introduction

It is a historical fact that Canada has been settled by immigrant communities. The process has been shaped as much by the geography of Canada as by the historical changes shaped by immigrant communities. The influx of South Asians—mainly Sikhs—to Canada was the part of free migration. Initially, they faced racial discrimination and struggled for their rightful place in the host country. The coming of Sikh women to Canada was part of family migration and their initial experiences were permeated by the struggle of male migrants. Gradually, changes in official immigration policies and the historical legacy of early settlers hastened the process of integration of Sikhs in the society, polity and culture of Canada. At the historiographical level, though the history and the role of early Sikh immigrants, mainly males, have been widely codified, the legacy of women and their role have been marginalised.

The chapter uses oral, pictorial and written records to highlight the experiences of Sikh women. Initially, the very identity and existence of women revolved within domestic spaces only. The role of Gurudwaras and kinship ties both within Canada and back home determined the mobility of women. At one level, there is still a continuum as matrimonial alliances and inter-familial relations are entwined with it yet at other level, generations born and raised in Canada have established wider networks of relations. The emergence of contestation within domestic spaces and the questioning of cultural norms are part of ongoing changes. The chapter in the end analyses theoretical formulations/concepts within feminist scholarships to map the experiences of Sikh women.

The Historiography of Canada

When Jacques Cartier came to the Lawrence valley in 1534, the land was inhabited by various indigenous groups. His explorations paved the way for the establishment of a 'New France'. Alongside, British merchants, explorers and missionaries were active in the western parts of Canada. The Treaty of Paris signed in 1763 marked the end of French colonial rule and the beginning of British supremacy in Canada (Basra 2007, 33–46). The process of settlement by the British and the French was also marked by the codification of information about land, the resources and the people. The basis of writing Canada's history can be traced back in this process. By the late nineteenth century, the basis of professional history writings had been laid. The role of Professor M. Wrong who published the first volume of the *Annual Review of Historical Publications on Canada* and starting of the *Canadian Historical Review* was significant in this regard (Berger 1987, 8–18).

Among the emergent themes in Canadian historiography, change can be gleaned over the period of time. The role of the British and the French as the 'Founding Fathers' (Berger 1987), the role of historical geography and economic resources— two themes which still engage the attention of historians (Krueger 1982, 11–78), the issues of the 'French survival', the domination of Ontario, and the 'subordination of the West', have engaged the attention of historians and political scientists (Morton 1967, 44–49). Alongside, the focus on national leaders like Sir John Macdonald (Creighton 1967, 50–62) has been followed by researches on regions, local leaders and regional political parties (Schultz 1990, 1–27).

Once neglected in historical scholarship, research on the role of native Indians has come to occupy centre stage. The role of the Hurons in establishing trade links with the French (Basra 2002, 142), and further, helping them gain a foothold in the Lawrence valley has been highlighted by Trigger (1985). There are several works on the social history of Canada. The nature of hierarchical society by the turn of the nineteenth century (Potter 1965) and the changing profile of Canadian society has been explored. The role of multiculturalism is also a point of analysis in several works (Raj and Mc Andrew 2009).

The early history of migrants from South Asia and Sikhs, in particular, has been mapped over the period of time. The Government of Canada has also codified the events related to the Komagata Maru.[1] Hugh Johnston's seminal work on the Komagata Maru can be analysed in the context of the narrative of Baba Gurdit Singh (Johnston 1979; Singh 1921) who had chartered the ship Komagata Maru. The experiential aspects of early Sikh migrants who built another *Paldi* in Western Canada (Verma 2002), the changing profile of Sikhs, and their role in Canadian polity and society (Judge 1994) all throw light on the history of Canada. However, most of these works have been male centric and the identity of women have been subsumed in the meta narration. It was only with the emergence of feminist writings that the visibility of women in the pages of history and their agency in the making of Canadian history has come to the forefront.

The emergence of gender perspective in writing Canadian history is connected with starting of organised women's movements. Initially, the initiative was taken by anglophone Canadian women and alongside 'distinct' franco-phone Canadian women movement could be seen. The second phase of the feminist movement in the 1960s saw the coming together of women leaders. There was a demand for equal rights for women in public spaces. Issues like education, health and wages came to engage the attention of organisations working for women. Feminism emerged both as an ideology and a movement (Burt et al. 1991).

Feminist writings, while highlighting the role of women across time and space in Canada, also demanded justice and equity for women (Basra 2015, 70–86). The varied experiences of women also brought out themes of 'women hood'. In this regard, mention can be made of a book edited by Veronica Strong-Boag and others wherein the plural voices of women have been mapped in several works. It has been underlined that the history of Canada cannot be mapped if 50% of women are excluded from it (Strong-Boag et al. 1991).

---

[1]There are several sites from which details about South Asians including Sikhs can be studied. Statistics Canada is one such site. In 2004 Ali Kazimi made a documentary on the Komagata Maru called *Continuous Journey*. See, www.statcan.gc.ca, https://www.nfb.ca/film/continuous_journey/.

Several works have highlighted the role of ethnicity, class, religion, politics and spaces in shaping the lives of women and their responses. These writings have challenged the preexisting generalisations about Canadian history. In the process, in historical narrations and analysis, the role of gender has come to the forefront.

The role of native Indians as the 'first nation' in the making of Canadian history and the contribution of native women in society, the economy and polity of Canada have been highlighted by Sylvia Van Kirk in her analysis of the activities of the Hudson Bay Company and the North West Company in western Canada. She has highlighted the role of women like Thanadelthur in negotiating trading transactions between the Europeans and the tribes of the Ojibwa, the Crees and the Chipewyan. In the words of Sylvia Van Kirk, such women acted as 'women in between' males of ethnic groups. They also took care of the physical comforts of Europeans. Many native women married Europeans. However, over the passage of time European women started coming to British Columbia and as a result, many married native women with their children were abandoned by their European husbands (Van Kirk 1980).

The role of French women over the period of time and their responses at the levels of families, religions and political ideologies have been underlined in several works. During the period of 'New France', French women remained occupied with domestic responsibilities. Marie Rollet, wife of Louis Hébert, a farmer, was the first European woman to settle in New France (Dumont and Jean 1987, 17). Such women endorsed patriarchal domination and responded to the contours of French nationalism (Trofimenkoff 1982). While French women supported the cause of French nationalism and saw themselves as nurturing mothers, in the second phase of the feminist movement, they also demanded rights in public spaces. Leaders like Marie Gérin-Lajoie, Thérèse Casgrain, Lise Payette and Jeanne Sauvé stood up for the rights of French women (Prentice et al. 1988). There are records to show that many English women came to settle in Upper Canada in the nineteenth century. They shared the then dominant ideology of the British Empire and preferred to remain within their community. They looked down upon native Indians.

Writings on the female face of immigration have underlined that the twentieth century was marked by the 'feminisation of migration' (Boyd and Grieco 2003). Single women also migrated to different countries in search of jobs and security. In the case of Canada, the migration of Irish women since the 1860s can be seen as part of the process referred to above. Most of them became domestic servants and within their familial domains faced abuse, exploitation and deprivation. However over the period of time, they started organising themselves at an ethnic level and ensured that those who followed the early immigrants from Ireland were not to face exploitation (Barber 1991).

Within the above-mentioned writings whenever an attempt is made to study the experiences of Sikh women—who had also entered Canada in the second decade of the twentieth century as part of family migration—then several difficulties are encountered. There are still no substantial works that map the experiences of

Canadian women across ethnicities. No doubt, there are several works on Sikhs but by and large the focus has remained on men. There are only very few works on Sikh women. The issues of social inclusion, 'domestic violence', 'identity', and 'relationship with religion' have all been explored. Most of them reflect on contemporary Canada (George and Chaze 2015, 94–104; Judge 1994, 99–117).

There is a need to recover female voices from sources written by males. From the contemporary visual and written records, autobiographies, literacy works, an attempt can be made. In this connection, the autobiography of Tara Singh Bains written in association with Hugh Johnston is very significant (Bains and Johnston 1979). The Sikh community at its level had also mapped its past. The writing of 'Canadian Sikhan da Itihas' is significant in several ways. Written in Punjabi by Sohan Singh Sangha Sakrulvi, it has original material in form of photographs, newspapers writings and political documents. Through it, the early phase of Sikh migration and the process of settlement from a gender perspective can be gleaned. Alongside, the Khalsa Samachar,[2] published from Amritsar, also contained details about them. The relationship between Canada and Britain and the place of India and its residents was explored to underline the fact that as a part of the British Empire, Sikhs were being denied their rightful place in Canada.

The use of oral sources in constructing feminist historians has been underlined in several works. For the present work, the life journeys of several Sikh women have been mapped and used.[3]

The Making of Canadian Society

Canadian society evolved over time and space. In the expanse of geographical space stretching from coast to coast, native Indians resided and were part of the socio-economic milieu in which natural resources were not over exploited (Bumstead 1992, 10–50). The 'Age of Discovery' in fifteenth-century Europe initiated the process of colonisation. The lead taken by Spain was very soon taken over by France and England with Jacques Cartier starting the process from the eastern side of Canada (Basra 2002).

When Cartier arrived in the Lawrence valley, it was inhabited by various indigenous communities. Prominent among them were the Hurons, the Iroquois, the Haida, the Nootka and the Algonkians. The 'New France', which came under the domination

---

[2]*The Khalsa Samachar* was started by Bhai Vir Singh, the saint poet of Punjab in 1899. The paper was published in *Gurumukhi* from Amritsar. It was devoted to spread the tenets of Sikh religion, the Sikh way of life, the spread of *Gurumukhi* and played the main role in the construction of the Sikh identity. It focused on the lives of Sikh migrants in Canada and espoused their cause.

[3]The oral narrations have been collected through random sampling. The narrations from family members are also based on observations.

of Britain in 1763, had a substantial population of French. Thereafter along with the British, Jews, Lowlanders and Americans came to settle in Upper Canada. While indigenous people were deprived of their rights, society was also becoming more differentiated. With the formation of the Confederation on 1 July 1867, the process of nation building also commenced. The national policy of Macdonald envisaged the settlement of Canada West, by forging links between the East and the West with the construction of the Canadian Pacific Railways. The construction of CPR was in fact linked with the integration of various regions and British Columbia was integrated with rest of Canada on this very promise.

For economic growth and political unity, there was need to evolve an immigration policy encouraging the settlement of immigrants in the West. The government of Macdonald sought the help of Britain in this regard but the out flow to America could not be stopped. With the help of private companies mainly the CPR, the immigration policy was implemented. The situation changed when the Liberals assumed office under Laurier in 1896. Clifford Sifton who was the first minister in charge of immigration insisted upon attracting large numbers of peasants from Central and Eastern Europe. However, for the construction of CPR, cheap labour was needed, and so, for this purpose, Chinese labourers were welcomed. Alongside, an agreement was signed with Japan in 1907, which allowed the entry of the Japanese (Johnston 1979).

The process of colonisation of India by Britain started in the second half of the eighteenth century. The process that began from Bengal in 1757 ended with the annexation of the Punjab in 1849. While the British were sending indentured labour to its colonies from many parts of India, the situation in the case of British Punjab was different. From Punjab, Sikhs went to Canada as free immigrants. The Royal Proclamation of Queen Victoria had declared that Indians would not be discriminated on the basis of caste, creed, colour, race or religion within British dominions, but in reality, the rulers used divisive policies to strengthen their rule. The support of Sikhs who constituted a large proportion of the British army was valued (Grewal 1998, 138–140).

By the 1880s, Sikh villagers were travelling great distances in search of employment. The employment in the British army gave them an opportunity to travel and work in East Africa and the Far East. In Hong Kong, Singapore and Malaya, Sikhs were employed as policemen, watchmen and caretakers. In Malaya, they worked as dairymen, car drivers and mine labour. A few also left for Austria (Judge 1994). In 1891, the Canadian Pacific Railways (or CPR) introduced a transpacific passenger service from Hong Kong to Vancouver and on 1 April 1904, a vanguard of four Sikhs reached British Columbia on a CPR Liner. From the outset, they faced a hostile and racially charged environment, as the locals disdained the presence of people from eastern countries. The situation had become volatile by 1907.

Lived Experiences of Sikh Women

The lived experiences of early Sikh migrants from a gender perspective need to be located in the political and social milieu of Canada in general and British Columbia in particular where Sikhs had come to work initially. It was also linked with the Imperialist policies of Britain pertaining to India and the relationship with Canada. The role of immigration policies played a decisive part in shaping the lives of early immigrants. It can be said that from 1904 to 1914, Sikhs had to fight for their just place in Canadian society. Their consciousness emanated from their understanding of the politics of Canada, Britain and their subordinate position in Punjab. There was a struggle to gain a foothold and then settle in Canada. The entry of Sikh women as part of family migration was entwined with this very process. In this way, the struggle of Sikhs as a community shaped the identity and consciousness of Sikh women.

We do have contemporary resources in the form of newspapers, petitions, records of Khalsa Dewan society in Vancouver outlining the struggle waged by Sikh men, and the voices of women need to be rescued and reconstructed from these very sources. In Punjab, *Khalsa Samachar* also gave extensive coverage to the lives of early migrants and has been used in the present work. There are also works like that of Sohan Singh Sangha Sakrulvi incorporating contemporary visual and written records throwing light on the lives of early women migrants.

Initial reports about Sikhs in local newspapers focused on and appreciated their physical features and their ability to work hard. Gradually they changed as it was feared that white labour would face competition from them and might not find work. At a political level, pressure was exerted to restrict the entry of immigrants. Racial prejudices came to dominate political ideology. Newspapers in Vancouver and Victoria described South Asians, as they were identified as, to be 'undesirable, degraded, sick, hungry and a menace to women and children'. A columnist wrote:

> Their habits of life are unsatisfactory. They do not bring their wives with them, and will not make homes and rear families. They are totally unfitted for a white man's country …. For the Sikh in his home, we have every respect; for the Sikh in Canada there is no proper place, and it is a great unkindness to a well-meaning people to bring them here. (Ward and White 2002, 83–84)

Initially, the government in Canada took the decision that Punjabis, being British citizens, could not be expelled. However, by 1907, the situation had changed. The economy of British Columbia had tumbled, leading to widespread unemployment among white labourers. Four hundred Indian mill workers were driven out of Bellingham, Washington across the Canadian border. There were riots against Chinese and Japanese workers in Vancouver.

To restrict immigration, an act was passed in 1908 which introduced the regulation of continuous journey. It stipulated that immigrants could come by continuous passage from India. It was also regulated that immigrants coming to Canada must possess $200. Outwardly, there was no ban on bringing wives, children and dependents by Sikhs settled in Canada but provisions clearly stated that in such a situation, the head was supposed to possess sufficient funds for their maintenance. It was clear that the act was meant to ban the entry of Sikhs in Canada, and further, those who were already settled would also face problems in bringing their families to Canada. Moreover, there was no facility of continuous passage from India to Canada. The early struggle of Sikhs was directed against this policy (Johnston 1979).

It was evident that it was not easy for married women and their children to join their husbands in Canada. Yet steps were taken and when entry was denied, then not only was there extensive reporting in newspapers, but court cases were also fought. Help was sought for both in Punjab and in Canada at the community level and the intervention of Britain was also sought. It was underlined that while the Japanese were allowed entry due to a political treaty with Britain, the same facility was denied to Punjabis. It was stressed that as Sikhs were part of the British Empire and with Canada also part of it, so Sikhs deserved their rights. The hardworking nature of Sikhs and Punjabis was underlined and it was pointed out that the community had invested more than Rs. 1 Crore in properties and would permanently settle in Canada. It was urged that the wives and children of those who had settled in Canada should be allowed to join them. The restrictions were seen as contrary to the civilised norms of Britain. In 1912, a Sikh delegation came to India and met Lord Hardinge (Khalsa Samachar 1912–1913). The Government at Ottawa was also approached but there was little change in official policy. It was clear that those Sikh women who had decided to join their husbands in Canada were willing to face the challenges entailed in the very process of migration from the home country to that of the settlement. It was the men who fought the struggle on their behalf.

Hira Singh who had settled in Vancouver for 4 years returned to Punjab to bring his wife and daughter to his place of work and habitation. He returned to Vancouver on 21 July 1911 on the steamship Monteagle. He was allowed to disembark as he was a resident of Vancouver but his wife and children were ordered to be deported. He furnished a bond of 1000 dollars and subsequently, his wife and daughter were also allowed to disembark subject to the outcome of a hearing pending in the court and the granting of habeas corpus. Eventually, both were allowed to stay as an act of grace (Khalsa Samachar 1913).

Bhag Singh and Balwant Singh also brought their families to live in Canada. However, permission was denied to them. Both applied to the Minister of the Interior and furnished cash bond of $600 pending the hearing in the court. The litigation lasted for 3 months and eventually the families were allowed to stay on in Canada as an act of grace. Hakim Singh came to Vancouver as a tourist but decided to stay back. When he decided to bring his family, he also had to fight a case (Sakrulvi 1999, 187–189).

H.H. Stevens, member of the Indian emigrants department lost no opportunity to speak against them. At a meeting on 30 September 1913 in Vancouver, he condemned the Indian demand for allowing children and wives to stay in Canada. For him 'their religion and intelligence are rubbish' (Sakrulvi 1999, 190). The situation became volatile when in 1914, Komagata Maru, the ship with 376 Sikh passengers arrived in Vancouver. The immigration authorities did not allow the passengers to disembark. It remained stranded for 3 months and had to return to India (Singh 1921). Thereafter, the entry of Sikhs to Canada came to almost naught. By 1914, their numerical strength was 4500 but gradually the situation changed. From pictorial representation and scanty evidences, it is evident that few women who entered Canada remained part of their domestic spaces. Outside, their lives revolved around the Gurudwara and the celebration of religious ceremonies. The early immigrants like Duman Singh who had come in 1906 and Pratap Singh Johan who came in the 1920s, with their families could send their children to schools and colleges. Children were raised and many went to school and college.

India became independent on 15 August 1947 and the Canadian government also changed its immigrant's policy by fixing a quota for India. The definite change in the 1960s and the demographic pattern in Canada show that more than 15% of the population in Canada had come from outside. There have been multiple changes under the policy of multiculturalism and various ethnic groups in Canada have become a part of Canadian society.

The changes in Canada and the experiences in the lives of Sikhs there can be gleaned from the autobiographical account of Tara Singh Bains. His life journey, written by Hugh Johnston, is called *The Four Quarters of the Night: The Life-Journey of an Emigrant Sikh*. It offers an insight into the complexities of a minority community and the processes of settlement in the host country by an immigrant from this community. It can be read at several levels. Outwardly, it is the life journey of Tara Singh Bains who was born in Sarhad Khurd, lost his mother at the age of four, faced atrocities by his father and went out to earn his living in Canada. During his life journey, he was provided sustenance, motivation and guidance by Sikhism. Over a period of time, he came to live a harmonious life and was at ease both in Canada and Punjab. However, a closer look shows that the narration provided by Bains provides an insight into the lives of immigrants from a gender perspective. Here the voices, mostly of his wife (as his equal partner) but also of his sister—married and settled in Canada—come into the limelight. Karam Kaur, his wife, is spoken about in his narration, yet it is evident that she was treated with dignity and was accorded equality in both familial and outside spaces. This made the life journey of the couple easy and comfortable.

The first description of Karam Kaur is heartwarming:

> She was such a nice person and the affection that was so abundant in my mind had an outlet at last and I had a measure of it, for life, to live for. (Bains and Johnston 1995, 13–14)

As far as Bain's sister was concerned, she had been married when he was not even 4, in his younger days, and so he had no recollection of her. However later, when she came to know about his financial situation, she sponsored him and that is how he came to Canada in 1953. In this way within family migration, his sister took an independent decision to invite him to settle in Canada. From the outset within familial space, he was pressurised to discard his identity of a baptised Sikh. For his sister and nephews, it was essential for upward mobility and for easy assimilation with the host society but he refused. In his words as said to his nephews:

> Look here fellows, faith is faith. I do not feel inferior being an Indian or being a Sikh, and I
> never thought it would be my own people who would hate my hair. No white man has done
> that to me so far. (Bains and Johnston 1995, 58)

The first time he went to Canada alone, and when he was asked to return by his wife, he came back. He looked after his wife and children. The second phase of immigration in 1966 saw the settlement of his family including his wife, children and younger brother in Canada. He encouraged and endorsed the decision of his daughter to obtain a university education. However, both husband and wife decided to finally settle in Punjab. They felt financially secure, when they became eligible to get security and pension from the Canadian government. In this way, the lived experiences of the two passed through physical spaces which transcended two countries, incidentally, in two separate continents.

The emotional and social network also revolved around kinship ties and man–woman relationship within the family. In this process, the relocation from the mother country to the host country, the passages from entry to settlement, all play an important role. Above all, both have been part of a global scenario where the home is experienced both in the motherland and in the adopted country. This process is continuing with changes seen at the level of education and status. The difficulties faced by the early immigrants are not there anymore. It is easy to settle down within domesticity. When Renu took the decision to migrate to Canada in 2000s with her family, the decision rested on her desire to live closer to her aunts who had migrated to Toronto in the 1980s. She is more than happy with her decision. However, in the process she also discarded many of her responsibilities towards her in-laws. The aged couple is living all alone in New Delhi (Renu, Oral History Transcript, January–December, 2000). It can be said that the decision made by Renu is based on the concept of the nuclear family where looking after in-laws is secondary.

Presently women constitute more than 50% of Canada's population. Sikhs were the early immigrants from India and second and third generation born in Canada is also there. It is this generation having access to education, jobs and culture of host country that is having difficulties in negotiating their lives at the level of family, community and society. They want to be part of 'what can be identified as Canadian cultural milieu'. They are conscious of their gender identity and aspire for equity within familial domain. Several surveys have been conducted that show that young women deciding to marry outside their community face hostility. It has been underlined by many that while the Sikh religion accorded women equality, but it was not practiced by men (Nayar 2010). In fact, the women are experiencing violence in multiple forms. However, there is resentment and resistance to this resulting in intervention by the state in the lives of women. Existing researches show that nearly 50% of women in Canada have faced violence in one or another form. Married Sikh women have been victims of violence at the individual and at the community level. It is constitutive of physical abuse, intimidation within families, restriction on meeting family members, sexual abuses, and restriction in going to Gurudwaras. The available data shows that abused women have found it difficult to get remedial measures. The response of family and community has remained negative. When women take decision to leave homes, then they face many difficulties. The help extended by volunteer organisations play an important role in addressing the problems of affected women (Mutta and Kaur 2003).

The experiences of second-generation Sikh women are multilayered. There are issues connected with domestic violence. It is connected with institutional and cultural norms (George and Chaze 2015, 96).

The entire process can be mapped through the life journey of Harvinder Kaur. She was born in New Delhi in 1961 and could not complete education beyond high school. When her father died in 1982, her married sister fixed her marriage with a truck driver living in Montreal. The marriage was arranged through village level ties as the families of the groom and of the in-laws of her sister lived in same village. Harvinder went to live in Montreal and also did odd jobs to supplement the income of her family. She was blessed with two children. In her middle age, she was inflicted with several life threatening diseases. The medical support by the state is helping her to survive. Worst followed when her husband refused to take care of her. Her eldest daughter did not take any interest in studies, fell in love and was married at the age of 18 (Harvinder Kaur. Oral History Transcripts, 2000–2001. New Delhi). Harvinder Kaur has learnt to live with her difficulties. She has maintained links with her family in New Delhi. The latter also have helped her in sustaining at emotional level.[4]

The above narration by focusing on lived experiences of Sikh women has shown that domesticity plays an important role in shaping the responses of women within familial and communal spaces. In this regard, relation with Punjab and kinship ties remains important. A recent survey conducted by author[5] shows that many Sikh Canadian families are returning to Punjab and in the process, the educational aspirations of the daughters of the families are also taken care of. In this respect, Sikh women are part of global spaces.

---

[4]It is a historical fact that the maximum migration from Punjab has been from the *Doaba* region. From my family, relatives have gone to Canada since 1960s. Harvinder Kaur is my first cousin from my father's side. Her life journey has been culled from her observations and self-reflections on her life.

[5]The survey is based on the collection of data of Sikh Canadians who have taken admission in various courses in the University of Delhi from 2014–2016. The data so collected shows that the diasporic Indian community is returning from developed countries for the education of their children in India. There is a desire to study in the University of Delhi under the facilities provided by the University. In some cases, it was observed that the entire family has decided to come back.

Theorising Women's Experiences

The theorising of the above-mentioned narration brings out the fundamental issue of the sources required to construct their experiences. It remains a fact that for the early phases, documentation, if any, was fragmentary. The multiple sources like pictures, diaries, reports in newspapers, official documents even when they carry male-centric biases can still be deconstructed to rescue the voices of the women involved. The issue of interpretation is also linked with it. Here, the insight provided by feminist writings and researches is useful. The intersectionality of women at class, caste, religious, community and geographical levels within immigration theories becomes crucial in studying the experiences of Sikh women in Canada.

While the agency of women in shaping their lives cannot be denied but focus on their agency needs to be contextualised within a broader frame work. The foregoing narration clearly shows how married women as part of the family immigration processes were subjected to political decisions having a bearing on their settlement in Canada. In the initial phase, patriarchy worked at several levels. While Sikhs asserted their rights to bring their families on account of being part of British Empire, the same was denied by the Governments in Canada, India and Britain. The power relationship between dominant and subordinate groups came to the forefront. Under these circumstances, women who could join their husbands lived within familial spaces. Within the patriarchal set-ups, they participated in community-based activities. The Gurudwaras shaped their activities in public spaces. No one entered the job sector and within domesticity, women fulfilled their responsibilities as wives and mothers. Thus, they could see their space and were in a position to negotiate their place. The issues of survival and sustenance played a crucial role in the lives of first generation. Over the period of time as the process of integration was strengthened and generations born and raised in Canada were exposed to inter-cultural influences then their role as independent makers of their destinies also surfaced. It led to the emergence of contestation within familial and communal spaces. The voices resenting matrimonial alliances at the behest of males within families, refusal to accept exploitation and violence within domesticity and seeking help from governmental agencies are part of this contestation. Yet by and large, research used for paper shows that family continues to play an important role in constructing consciousness of Sikh women. Moreover, cultural norms also play a dynamic role and are being constructed and reformulated. The ethnographical studies at the level of 'specifies' and 'general' also become crucial. One can conclude by positing that theoretical formulations for analysing experiential dimensions of Sikh women need to be put within broad context of what can be called 'Start, Process and settlement'. While the formal denotes the land of origin and connected ties, second denotes the process of adopting land of settlement. The last is connected with living realities in country of adoption. In many ways, all three are interconnected. In this, the role of patriarchy in shaping domesticity becomes crucial. The space of Sikh women is shaped by patriarchal norms in which they also play an important role.

References

Bains, Tara Singh, and Hugh J.M. Johnston. 1995. *The Four Quarters of the Night: The Life-Journey of an Emigrant Sikh.* McGill-Queen's University Press-MQUP.

Barber, Marilyn. 1991. *Immigrant Domestic Servants in Canada.* Ottawa: Canadian Historical Association.

Basra, Amrit Kaur. 2002. Voyage of Jacques Cartier: Narration, History and Historiography of Canada. In *Discovering French Canada*, ed. K.R.G. Nair, and R. Borges, 136–145. New Delhi: Allied Publishers.

Basra, Amrit Kaur. 2007. British Colonialism: India and Canada. In *New Horizons of Globalization*: *India and Canada*, ed. Gyan P. Agrawal, 33–46. New Delhi: Deep and Deep Publications.

Basra, Amrit Kaur. 2015. Gender, History and Historiography in India and Canada: Some Reflections. In *Gender and Diversity: India, Canada and Beyond*, ed. Malashri Lal, Chandra Mohan, Enakshi K. Sharma, Devika Khanna Narula, and Amrit Kaur Basra. New Delhi: Rawat Publications. http://rawatbooks.com/book_more_detail.aspx?id=1369.

Berger, Carl. 1987. *The Writing of Canadian History: Aspects of English Canadian Historical Writing Since 1990.* Toronto: Oxford University Press.

Boyd, Monica, and Elizabeth Grieco. 2003. *Women and Migration: Incorporating Gender into International Migration Theory.* March 1, 2003. Migration Information Source. www.migrationpolicy.org.

Bumstead, J.M. 1992. *The People of Canada: A Pre-Confederation History.* Canada: Oxford University Press.

Burt, Sandra, Lorraine Code, and Lindsay Dorney (eds.). 1991. *Changing Patterns: Women in Canada.* Toronto: McClelland and Steward.

Creighton, D.G. 1967. Sir John Macdonald and Canadian Historians. In *Approaches to Canadian History*, ed. Ramsay Cook, Craig Brown, and Carl Berger, 100–115. Toronto: University of Toronto Press.

Dumont, Micheline, Michele Jean, Marie Lavigne, and Jennifer Stoddart. 1987. *Quebec Women: A History*, Trans. by Roger Gannon, and Rosaline Gill. Toronto: The Women's Press.

George, Usha, and Ferzana Chaze. 2015. Punjabis/Sikhs in Canada. In *Migration, Mobility and Multiple Affiliations*, ed. S. Irudaya Rajan, V.J. Varghese, and Aswini Kumar Nanda, 94–104. New Delhi: Cambridge Press.

Grewal, J.S. 1998. *The Sikhs of the Punjab. The New Cambridge History of India.* New Delhi: Cambridge University Press.

Johnston, Hugh. 1979. *The Voyage of the Komagata Maru: The Sikh Challenge to Canada's Colour Bar.* New Delhi: Oxford University Press.

Judge, Paramjit S. 1994. *Punjabis in Canada: A Study of Formation of an Ethic Community.* New Delhi: Chanakya Creative Books.

Khalsa Samachar. Canada, 29 June, 1911, p. 6; Sikh te Canada, 14, November, 1912, p. 2; Canada Niwasi Khalsa Ji da Sankhep itihas, 28 December, 1912, p. 6; Canada te Diwan, 5 June, 1913, p. 3; Canada wich Sikhs, 12 June, 1913, p. 2; Canada wich Hindustaniya di durdasha, 17 July, 1913, p. 4; Canadian Hindi bhrawan layi jalsa, 11 August, 1913, p. 2; Canada wich Hindustani, 14 August, 1913, p. 2; Canadian bhrawan layi Gurmata, September, 18, 1913, p. 2; Canada wich Hindustani Vir, September, 25, 1913, p. 3, 7; Canadaniwasi Hindustaniya layi Shimla wich Jalsa, p. 5; Shri Hazur Panjab Laat de Canada de Sikh, 2 October, 1913, p. 2; Canada niwasi Hindi Vir, 16 October, 1913, p. 2.

Kirk, Sylvia Van. 1980. *Many Tender Ties: Women in Fur-Trade Society: 1670–1870.* Winnipeg: Watson and Dwyer Publishing.

Krueger, Ralph R. 1982. A Geographical Perspective: The Setting of the Settlement. In *Understanding Canada: A Multidisciplinary Introduction to Canadian Studies*, ed. William Metcalfe, 11–78. New York: New York University Press.

Morton, W.L. 1967. Clio in Canada: The Interpretation of Canadian History. In *Approaches to Canadian History*, ed. Cook, Craig Brown Carl Berger, 42–49. Toronto: University of Toronto Press.

Mutta, Baldev, and Amandeep Kaur. 2003. *Women Abuse: Sad State of Affairs in the Sikh Community in Canada*. http://www.angelfire.com.

Nayar, Kamala Elizabeth. 2010. Sikh Women in Vancouver: An Analysis of Their Psychosocial Issues. In *Sikhism and Women: History, Text and Experiences*, ed. Doris R. Jakubsh, 252–275. New Delhi: Oxford University Press.

Potter, John. 1965. *Vertical Mosaic: An Analysis of Social Class and Power in Canada*. Toronto: University of Toronto Press.

Prentice, Alison, Paula Bourne, Gail Cuthbert Brandt, Beth Light, Wendy Mitchinson, and Naomi Black. 1988. *Canadian Women: A History*. Toronto: Harcourt Brace Jovanovich.

Raj, Christopher, and Marie Mc Andrew. 2009. *Multiculturalism: Public Policy and Problems Areas in Canada and India*. New Delhi: Manak Publications Pvt. Ltd.

Records at Foreign Students Registry, University of Delhi, 2016.

Sakrulvi, Sohan Singh Sanga. 1999. *Canadian Sikhan da Itihas: 1800–2000, Part-1*. Vancouver: Khalsa Dewan Society.

Schultz, Harold J. 1990. *Writing About Canada: A Handbook for Modern Canadian History*. Scarborough: Prentice Hall Canada.

Singh, Baba Gurdit. (1921). 2007. *Julmi Katha*, ed. Darshan Singh Tatla (Reprint). Chandigarh: Unistar Books Ltd.

Strong-Boag, Veronica, Mona Gleason, and Adele Perry. 1991. *Rethinking Canada: The Promise of Women's History*. Toronto: Copp Clark Pitman.

Trigger, G.T. Bruce. 1985. *Natives and Newcomers: Canada's "Heroic Age" Reconsidered*. Montreal: McGill-Queen's University Press.

Trofimenkoff, Susan Mann. 1982. *The Dream of a Nation: A Social and Intellectual History of Quebec*. Toronto: Gage Publishing Limited.

Verma, Archana. 2002. *The Making of Little Punjab in Canada: Patterns of Immigration*. New Delhi: Sage.

Ward, W., and Peter White. 2002. *Canada Forever: Popular Attitudes and Policy towards Orientals in British Columbia*. Montreal, Ontario: McGill-Queen's University Press.